DISCOVERING CHINESE NATIONALISM IN CHINA
Modernization, Identity, and International Relations

The revival of Chinese nationalism in the 1990s requires a reassessment of China's place in world politics. Yongnian Zheng explores the complicated nature of this revived nationalism in China and presents the reader with a very different picture to that portrayed in Western readings on Chinese nationalism. He argues that China's new nationalism is a reaction to changes in the country's international circumstances and can be regarded as a "voice" over the existing unjustified international order. Zheng shows that the present Chinese leadership is pursuing strategies not to isolate China, but to integrate it into the international community. Based on the author's extensive research in China, the book provides a set of provocative arguments against prevailing Western attitudes to and perceptions of China's nationalism.

YONGNIAN ZHENG is a Research Fellow in the East Asian Institute of the National University of Singapore. He is the author of *The Revival of China's Nationalism* and *Central–Local Relations in China*. Yongnian Zheng has published widely in *Political Science Quarterly*, *Asian Survey* and *Asian Affairs*, and is currently a columnist on China's political affairs for *Hong Kong Economic Journal*.

D1456320

CAMBRIDGE ASIA–PACIFIC STUDIES

Cambridge Asia-Pacific Studies aims to provide a focus and forum for scholarly work on the Asia-Pacific region as a whole, and its component sub-regions, namely Northeast Asia, Southeast Asia and the Pacific Islands. The series is produced in association with the Research School of Pacific and Asian Studies at the Australian National University and the Australian Institute of International Affairs.

Editor: John Ravenhill

Editorial Board: James Cotton, Donald Denoon, Mark Elvin, David Goodman, Stephen Henningham, Hal Hill, David Lim, Ron May, Anthony Milner, Tessa Morris-Suzuki.

*To my mother, Chu Fengxiang,
and to the memory of my father,
Zheng Tangtu (1911–1997)*

DISCOVERING CHINESE NATIONALISM IN CHINA

Modernization, Identity, and International Relations

YONGNIAN ZHENG

National University of Singapore

CAMBRIDGE
UNIVERSITY PRESS

PUBLISHED BY THE PRESS SYNDICATE OF THE UNIVERSITY OF CAMBRIDGE
The Pitt Building, Trumpington Street, Cambridge, United Kingdom

CAMBRIDGE UNIVERSITY PRESS
The Edinburgh Building, Cambridge CB2 2RU, UK http://www.cup.cam.ac.uk
40 West 20th Street, New York, NY 10011–4211, USA http://www.cup.org
10 Stamford Road, Oakleigh, Melbourne 3166, Australia

First published 1999

Printed in Hong Kong by Colorcraft Ltd

Typeset in New Baskerville 10/12 pt

A catalogue record for this book is available from the British Library

Library of Congress Cataloguing in Publication data

Zheng, Yong-Nian, 1962–
Discovering Chinese nationalism in China: modernization, identity, and international
relations / Yongnian Zheng.
p. cm. – (Cambridge Asia-Pacific studies)
Includes bibliographical references and index.
ISBN 0-521-64180-2 (alk. paper). – ISBN 0-521-64590-5 (pbk. : alk. paper)
1. Nationalism – China. 2. China – Foreign relations – 1976–
I. Title. II. Series.
DS779.215.Z43 1999
320.54'0951–dc21   98-44813

National Library of Australia Cataloguing in Publication data

Zheng, Yong-Nian.
Discovering Chinese nationalism in China : modernization, identity, and international
relations.
Bibliography.
Includes index.
ISBN 0 521 64180 2.
ISBN 0 521 64590 5 (pbk).
1. Nationalism – China. 2. China – Politics and government – 1976– . 3. China – Foreign
relations – 1976– . I. Title. (Series : Cambridge Asia-Pacific studies).

320.540951

ISBN 0 521 64180 2 hardback
ISBN 0 521 64590 5 paperback

Contents

Preface

I first thought of writing a book about China's new nationalism when I was pursuing a doctoral degree at Princeton University. In 1992, during a visit to south China, senior leader Deng Xiaoping made an important speech on how the country would continue to achieve high economic growth if it learned from capitalism. Deng did not expect this speech to trigger a long wave of rapid economic development. It did and China became stronger economically. Many Chinese citizens felt a strong sense of national pride, and many social and political groups became nationalistic over various issues. Outside analysts began to consider the implications of the rise of China on the world system. Historically, the rise of a great power has been disruptive to the existing international system. As a result, the international community had sound reasons to worry about China's rise and its intention. Nevertheless, many Chinese did not understand why outsiders were so obsessive about China's rise since it was still poor compared to the advanced West.

In understanding the impact of China's rise on the world system, it is important to take domestic factors into account. After discussing my initial idea with Atul Kohli, Professor of Politics at Princeton University, I realized how important the rise and fall of the State is for developing countries like China. I gained enough courage to write a book on this topic.

Defining Nationalism

During my reviewing of literature on nationalism, I found that a serious problem for the student of the subject is the ambiguity in the meaning of the term "nationalism". The literature dealing with the concept of nationalism is enormous, but no single definition can cover all aspects of nationalism. This is typical of the study of Chinese nationalism, which, as Wang Gungwu (1996b) pointed out, is a many-layered and multi-faceted phenomenon. Without doubt, it is difficult, if not impossible, to highlight all aspects of Chinese nationalism in a single study like this one. For the sake of making it manageable, I will focus on nationalism as a nation–state identity and its impact on Chinese perceptions of China's position in the nation–state system.

Nationalism is about the "nation", a term which is not easy to define or explain. In interpreting nationalism, many scholars have attempted to avoid using the word. According to Charles Tilly (1975: 6), nation is "one of the most puzzling and tendentious items in the political lexicon". He prefers the term "state". Yet, nation and state are apparently not identical. As Arthur Waldron (1985: 417) argued, the "'nation' captures something that 'state' misses: a feeling, a passion, a legitimating power that the word 'nationalism' possesses to an unequalled degree". This is because, as James Kellas (1991: 2) pointed out, nations have objective characteristics such as language, a religion, or common descent on the one hand, and subjective characteristics, essentially a people's awareness of its nationality and affection for it on the other.

While the definitions of nationalism around the concept of nation–state vary, its main content is not unclear. Nationalism contains two important elements of the nation–state; that is, as an institution and as an identity. First, nationalism is eventually expressed by institutions. It becomes important only after it is organized. Individuals may have nationalistic ideas or feelings, but these ideas and feelings do not matter, especially in the context of international relations. In modern society, especially in the nation–state system, the most important institution is the State. As Crawford Young pointed out (1976: 72), "nationalism can be successfully expressed only through the modern state". Second, nationalism is about loyalty or identity. Different types of identities exist such as race, ethnicity, culture, language, religion and so forth. But national identity should not be confused with these identities. National identity is associated with the uniqueness of the particular nation–state. C. Young (1976: 71) asserted that "nationalism is an ideological formulation of identity. By stipulating the nation as a terminal community, to whom ultimate loyalty is owned, it invests the nation with transcendent moral sanction and authority. It is a profoundly political theory; implicit within it is active obligation to the national community and not merely passive acceptance of subject status". In its extreme form, national identity is "the supreme loyalty for people who are prepared to die for their nation" (Kellas 1991: 3).

Nation–state and national identity are two related aspects of nationalism. F. H. Hinsley argued that nationalism can be understood as:

[t]he state of mind in which the political loyalty is felt to be owed to the nation. It does not assume that, when nationalism comes to exist where it has not existed before, it does so because men have discovered a political loyalty which they previously lacked. On the contrary, it implies that men have then transferred to the nation the political loyalty which they previously gave to some other structure – that what has changed is not the quality of this loyalty but the object on which it is shown or the vehicle through which it is expressed (1973: 19).

Indeed, the formation of national identity can be attributed to the rise and growth of modern states. The modern state in effect often becomes a creator of national identity. According to Hinsley:

The rise of the state is the key to the movement of the political loyalty into the national stage. The clan, the tribe, the collection of tribes, even the city state, are political communities in which the composition of society has not yet become so mixed as to produce the administrative principle of rule that goes with the state, and in which this principle has not been imposed by a state from outside (1973: 28).

Further, there is an international dimension of nationalism. Nationalism here is about people's perceptions of China's position in the nation–state system. In other words, it is about China's sovereignty, independence and its proper relations with other nation–states. The importance of nationalism for the nation–state system or international society is without doubt, because, as James Mayall (1991: 2) pointed out, nationalism means that "the world is (or should be) divided into nations and that the nation is the only proper basis for a sovereign state and the ultimate source of government authority". According to Mayall, the principle of sovereignty has significant meaning for the nation–state. First, sovereign authorities must recognize one another as sovereign in order to secure a legal settlement of the inter-state problems. Second, sovereign authorities must recognize each other as a monopoly of jurisdiction within the State. Any agreement between them will have to be either self-policing, or it will have to rely on policing by the separate parties themselves. Third, the principle of sovereignty is the transcending of territory from being just somewhere people hunt, farm or go to the factory to the ultimate object of political life. Finally, the principle of sovereignty is the requirement of non-interference in the domestic affairs of other states. Otherwise, sovereign authorities would be most unlikely to enter into agreements (Mayall 1991: 19–20). The State, as the representative of the nation, links nation and society to the international system. In the modern world, various domestic blocks of nationalism such as culture, race, and language play an important part in the international system only through the nation–state.

About This Book

The book is organized into seven chapters. After reviewing the realist and liberal approaches to Chinese nationalism, Chapter 1 attempts to develop what I call "a Chinese understanding of Chinese nationalism". This chapter focuses on discussing why the "strong state complex" came to become the major theme of Chinese nationalism throughout modern China.

Chapter 2 discusses the most important aspect of "China's problems"; that is, the crisis of state power and its impact on China's new nationalism. Deng's reform promoted economic growth, but the impact of economic reform went far beyond economic arenas. Statism became the major theme of the new nationalism. This chapter examines different aspects of the crisis of state power, and discusses the responses of the new nationalists to the crisis in the context of statism.

Chapter 3 discusses the anti-westernization movement by the "New Left". The new nationalism is a response to the decline of national identity. The proponents of the "New Left" attributed the crisis of national identity to westernization-oriented modernization in post-Mao China, and argued that in order to establish a new national identity, a local theory of Chinese modernization has to be developed. The "New Left" made great efforts to criticize various themes of so-called westernization while attempting to develop a theory that emphasizes the "Chineseness" or local experience of China's post-Mao development.

Chapter 4 discusses the civilizational facet of the new nationalism. A major theme of the new nationalism was to revive China's traditional values. While in the 1980s Chinese tradition became a target for criticism, the 1990s saw a movement towards anti-West sentiment. This chapter examines how Chinese intellectuals used the differences between the West and China to construct a Chinese tradition-centered nationalism.

Chapters 5 and 6 discuss how Chinese officials have responded to changes in China's internal and external environments. Many in the West argued that the Chinese leadership has appealed to nationalism to strengthen its political legitimacy; that this new nationalism could become a threat to international peace and security. The two chapters attempt to provide a different picture based on a detailed examination of China's perceptions of its national interests and the way the Chinese leadership handles the rise of nationalism. Chapter 5 discusses how the Chinese leadership constructs patriotism as official nationalism and how the contradiction between official nationalism and popular nationalism led the government to organize a campaign against various "anti-China" theories in order to constrain popular nationalism. Chapter 6 examines the impact of changing Chinese perceptions of national interest on

China's international relations, as exemplified by recent changes in China's policies towards the United States, the way that the government handled the Diaoyutai dispute (see page 131) with Japan in 1996, and the rise of multilateralism towards South-east Asian countries. The two chapters show the complicated nature of the new nationalism for international relations.

The concluding chapter summarizes major findings of the study and sheds light on why "voice" rather than "exit" and 'loyalty", using Albert Hirschman's analogy, tends to be China's international strategy. A "voice strategy" means that the leadership is willing to integrate China into the international system, which needs to be modified in order to accord with China's national interests. It shows how the Chinese perceive such a strategy to be in accordance with China's national interests and regard it as the way for China to be a strong nation–state. Chapter 7 also examines how the rise of liberalism and globalism in China constrains the new nationalism and discusses the implications of Chinese globalism for world politics.

Acknowledgments

I have received special guidance from a number of scholars. I am grateful to Wang Gungwu, who read my manuscript twice and provided me with useful criticism and steady encouragement, as well as his own knowledge of Chinese nationalism; to Peter Katzenstein, who contributed significantly to my view of nationalism from a perspective of world politics; and to Benjamin Schwartz, who encouraged me to examine China's new nationalism from an historical point of view.

For useful critiques, comments, and advice, I thank Paul A. Cohen, Eric Heginbotham, Yasheng Huang, Xiaoyuan Liu, Ido Oren, Robert Ross, Etel Solingen, Guoguang Wu, Ashutosh Varshney, Xiaodong Wang, and John Wong. I am also grateful to the two anonymous referees from Cambridge University Press for their constructive comments, which were very helpful in sharpening my view in linking China's new nationalism to international politics. For general assistance, I think Huang Shanqi, Qiu Zeqi, Ezra Vogel, James L. Watson, and Wong Chee Kong.

John Ravenhill, editor of the Cambridge Asia–Pacific Studies Series, encouraged me to submit the manuscript to this series. I also want to acknowledge the helpful editorial support provided by Cambridge University Press, especially by Phillipa McGuinness, who worked with this manuscript from the initial review process to the beginning of its production, and Paul Watt and Edward Caruso who made great efforts in editing the manuscript. I would also like to thank Russell Brooks for preparing the index.

Finally, I want to acknowledge the considerable institutional support that has made this project possible. For research funding, I wish to thank the Social Science Research Council/MacArthur Fellowship Program in International Peace and Security. My thanks also go to the Fairbank Center for East Asian Research of Harvard University and the East Asian Institute of the National University of Singapore. The Fairbank Center, under the directorship of Ezra Vogel, provided me (and many other China scholars) with an intellectual environment, and the East Asian Institute, under the directorship of Wang Gungwu, provided me with a conducive academic location in one of the most commercialized cities of the world. I am enormously grateful to the library staff in the East Asian Institute for all their assistance.

Abbreviations of Cited Chinese Newspapers and Journals

Newspapers

BJQNB	*Beijing Qingnian Bao (Beijing Youth Newspaper)*
CD	*Zhongguo Ribao (China Daily)*
JJSB	*Jingji Shibao (Economic Times)*
LHB	*Lianhe Bao (United Daily News, Taiwan)*
LHZB	*Lianhe Zaobao (Singapore)*
MP	*Ming Pao (Hong Kong)*
RMRB	*Renmin Ribao (People's Daily)*
WHB	*Wenhui Bao (Hong Kong)*
XB	*Xin Bao (Hong Kong Economic Journal, Hong Kong)*
ZGGFB	*Zhongguo Guofang Bao (China National Defence)*

Journals

BR	*Beijing Review*
CM	*Cheng Ming (Forum, Hong Kong)*
DDYK	*Dangdai Yuekan (Current Affairs Monthly)*
DDZGYJ	*Dangdai Zhongguo Yanjiu (Modern China Studies)*
DF	*Dong Fang (The Orient)*
DS	*Dushu (Reading Monthly)*
DWJMYJ	*Duiwai Jingmao Yanjiu (Studies of Foreign Trade and Economy)*
ESYSJ	*Ershiyi shiji (The Twenty First Century, Hong Kong)*
GJWTLT	*Guoji Wenti Luntan (International Review)*
GJWTYJ	*Guoji Wenti Yanjiu (Studies of International Affairs)*

JJYJ	*Jingji Yanjiu (Economic Research)*
JSND	*Jiushi Niandai (The 1990s)*
LW	*Liaowang (Outlook)*
QS	*Qiushi (Seeking Truth)*
SJJJZZ	*Shijie Jingji Yu Zhengzhi (World Economy and Politics)*
TPYXB	*Taipingyang Xuebao (The Pacific Journal)*
XDGJGX	*Xiandai Guoji Guanxi (Contemporary International Relations)*
XGSHKXXB	*Xiangang Shehui Kexue Xuebao (Hong Kong Journal of Social Sciences, Hong Kong)*
XHYB	*Xinhua Yuebao (China News Agency Monthly)*
XSYJDT	*Xueshu Yanjiu Dongtai (Trends in Academic Research)*
YZZK	*Yazhou Zhoukan (Asia Weekly)*
ZGDLYJ	*Zhongguo Dalu Yanjiu (Mainland China Studies)*
ZGGQGL	*Zhongguo Guoqing Guoli (China National Condition and National Power)*
ZGSBZK	*Zhongguo Shibao Zhoukan (China Times Weekly)*
ZGSHKXJK	*Zhongguo Shehui Kexue Jikan (Chinese Social Sciences Quarterly, Hong Kong)*
ZGSP	*Zhongguo Shuping (China Book Review, Hong Kong)*
ZLGL	*Zhanlue Yu Guanli (Strategy and Management)*
ZSFZ	*Zhishi Fenzi (Intellectuals)*

CHAPTER 1

Discovering Chinese Nationalism in China

One of the most important events in international relations in the late 20th century is the rise of nationalism in the People's Republic of China. This new nationalism coincides with China's rapid economic growth, an increase in military budget, military modernization, growing anti-West sentiment, and assertiveness in its foreign behavior. What does this new nationalism mean for international relations? How should it be coped with? Internationally, Chinese nationalism has been compared to the rise of German nationalism under the National Socialists and that of expansionist Japan under the military nationalists. For example, Samuel Huntington (1995) believes that unless China becomes democratic and/or coopted into the world establishment, it will become dangerous, like Germany when it became more powerful in the 1930s. James Kurth (1996) also believes that in the first half of the 21st century, China will pose both a strong military and economic threat to the United States, and to international security and economic order. The rapid rise after 1976 of Chinese economic power and the recent modernization of Chinese military power together promise to disrupt both the Asian balance of trade and the Asian balance of power, just as Germany's rise disrupted the European balance after 1866. Since the early 1990s, various theories such as the "China threat" and "containing China" have been developed in the West as responses to the rise of Chinese nationalism.

These theories, however, are based on some Western perceptions of Chinese nationalism. Is Chinese nationalism aggressive? Does it pose a major threat to international peace, especially to east Asian security? Should China be contained? It seems to many in the West, like any other nationalism of major powers such as Japan and Germany, that Chinese nationalism is a destabilizing force for the international peace and security, and needs to be contained so that the existing international peace can be maintained. Such perceptions of Chinese nationalism in the West in turn result in strong nationalistic reactions in China.[1]

Chinese nationalism has been mis-perceived to a great degree. Without doubt, mis-perceptions have contributed to the rise of what the Chinese government calls "anti-China" theories in the West. As a matter of fact, what China regards as "anti-China" theories such as "China Threat" and "Containing China" have been controversial in the West. While many argue that China's growing strength portends a threat, others disagree (see, for example, Kristof 1993; Munro 1992; Shambaugh 1994; Kurth 1996; Bernstein & Munro 1997). The revival of nationalism in China can be attributed to, among other things, its rapid domestic development and the consequent resurgence of Chinese power in the nation–state system. While the Soviet Union and other Eastern European communist powers collapsed, China has managed to achieve high economic growth for two decades. Individual Chinese have received enormous economic and other types of benefits in the course of this rejuvenation. A strong sense of national pride comes to average Chinese citizens, a sense probably as strong as, if not *stronger*, than what they felt when Mao Zedong declared the establishment of the People's Republic in 1949. The Chinese leadership certainly welcomes this resurgence of nationalism because a new ideology is necessary as faith in Marxism or Maoism declines, and nationalism, if handled properly, can justify the political legitimacy of the leadership. In other words, nationalism can become the ideological basis of a transitional regime that turns away from totalitarianism but is not yet democratized. The leadership, aware of the danger of an ideological vacuum, often consciously appeals to nationalism to legitimate its political governance. Furthermore, owing to rapid economic growth, for the first time in modern history, China is increasing its capability to bring different parts of China together, including Hong Kong, Taiwan, and Macau. A Chinese tradition-based new nationalism can be a theoretical foundation to serve such a united Chinese nation.

But many in the West, especially in the United States, perceive China's new nationalism in a very different way. They view the rise of China as a threat to the existing international system, especially to the US interests in Asia. When the 1995–96 Taiwan Strait crisis resulted from Taiwan President Lee Tung-hui's visit to Cornell University and the missile exercises over the Taiwan Strait, China claimed that its missile exercise was to prevent Taiwan's Lee Teng-hui from declaring independence. But according to the Americans, what China did was to "crack down" the island's democracy as it did in Tiananmen Square in 1989. Indeed, many in the United States have long regarded China as a potential enemy since the collapse of the Soviet Union. It seems to them that the United States needs to contain Chinese power by all possible means such as the issues of Taiwan, Hong Kong, Tibet, South China Sea, human rights, MFN (most favored nations), WTO (World Trade Organization), arms sales and so on. With such perceptions, various myths have been created about China's threats. Swaine (1997) has identified five myths about China:

1 China's recent attempt to intimidate Taiwan through military force proves that it intends to threaten all of Asia.
2 China is pursuing a crash program of military modernization, spending, by various estimates, $80 billion to $150 billion per year on defense.
3 China has already acquired advanced military systems that greatly augment its ability to project beyond its borders and thereby alter the basic balance of power in Asia.
4 Even if China does not have potent offensive capabilities now, it surely will within a decade.
5 China's modernization effort is primarily intended to challenge US capabilities across Asia.

With the rise of various "anti-China" theories and their publicity, many have become convinced that China is a monster. According to a poll conducted towards the end of 1994, 57 percent of the American public regarded the "development of China as a world power" to be a "critical threat" to the United States – up from 40 percent in the previous poll in 1990 (John E. Rielly 1995; cited in *The Economist* 1997a). Another poll in August 1997 found that China remains, by a substantial margin, the country that Americans most commonly view as unfriendly or an enemy.[2]

On the other side of the Pacific Ocean, many Chinese have seen how the United States has transformed itself from China's "friend" in the 1980s to its "enemy" in the 1990s: it issued a visa for Taiwan's Lee Teng-hui to upgrade its relations with Taiwan; it almost passed a bill to send an ambassador to Tibet and thus treat it as an independent country; it supported Britain's efforts to make last-minute political changes in Hong Kong that China opposed. The Chinese could not see any valid connection between MFN deprivation and human rights policy. What they saw was that the United States was manipulating human rights policy to serve its Realpolitik. When the United States initiated a campaign against China's bid for the 2000 Olympics, a dramatic change occurred on the Chinese streets: ordinary Chinese people expressed their anger to American tourists. Indeed, one observer pointed out that "in the past five years, much of the knowledgeable citizenry of China has shifted from idealization of the United States to a view that Washington is determined to make China the enemy" (see Overholt 1997: 5). It is in this context that we can understand why many Chinese intellectuals tend to be so nationalistic towards the West, especially the United States, as shown in the two recent best-sellers, *The China that Says No* and *Behind a Demonized China*.[3] A recent article published by an official English newspaper *China Daily* compared anti-China sentiment in the United States to McCarthyism in the 1950s.[4] It is worth noting that a strong nationalistic sentiment is also found among Chinese scholars and college students in the United States.[5]

Mis-perceptions and nationalism often reinforce each other. The result could be a tragedy. A new cold war between China and the United States or the West is not impossible. Indeed, many in both China and the West believe that a Second Cold War is taking place. According to William Overholt:

> The emergence of the Second Cold War is increasingly difficult to reverse because it is emerging not just in national policies but also in the hearts of the American and Chinese peoples. Citizens of the United States increasingly see China as dangerous, aggressive, and militaristic. Citizens of China see the United States as determined to use any means necessary to suppress China's revival. In both cases, these perceptions are close to the opposite of the truth. But the perceptions go very deep (1997: 4).

A right perception of Chinese policy needs to be based on a correct perception of China's nationalism. This study attempts to show the nature of China's new nationalism in a period of transition and its implications for the outside world through a detailed examination of Chinese perceptions of various important domestic and international issues. China's new nationalism needs to be re-interpreted if the West wants China to play a positive role for international peace. This re-interpretation of Chinese nationalism cannot be based on Western understandings of the development of nationalism, but on the Chinese context of Chinese nationalism. This book aims to (1) present a Chinese understanding of Chinese nationalism, (2) examine how the new nationalism has presented itself through different outlets, (3) explain why it manifests itself in the way it does, and (4) discuss its impact on China's international relations.

Realism, Liberalism, and Chinese Nationalism

The mis-perceptions of Chinese nationalism in the West are embedded in various theories of international relations that are based on the Western experience of international relations. Among others, realism and liberalism have had a profound impact on people's perceptions of the international implications of Chinese nationalism.

The realist model simplifies reality so that the international geopolitics and power configuration become most obvious.[6] The rise of great powers can be interpreted as a structurally driven phenomenon. The interaction of two factors; that is, differential growth rates and international anarchy, determines whether great powers will rise or not (see Layne 1993: 5–51). Because of uneven economic growth, great powers rise and fall over time. According to Robert Gilpin (1981: 13), "the differential growth in the power of various states in the system causes a fundamental redistribution of power in the system". Paul Kennedy (1987: xv–xvi; xxii) also notes that "the relative strengths of the leading nations in world affairs never remain constant, particularly because of the uneven rates of growth among different societies and of the technological and organizational breakthroughs which bring a greater advantage to one society than to another". Uneven growth rate will give rise to new great powers "which one day would have a decisive impact on the military/territorial order". Rapid economic growth can lead to dissatisfaction with the *status quo* on the part of the rising power. It may challenge the existing power distribution among nations. As Gilpin (1981: 95) argued, the significance of uneven growth rate is that "it alters the cost of changing the international system and therefore the incentives for changing the international system". A second fact that drives the emergence of great powers is international anarchy. According to Waltz (1979) the international system is characterized as a self-help system in which states must be concerned with survival and provide for their own security. Layne (1993) observes that the international system is a competitive realm in which every eligible state must attain great power status in order to avoid punishment.

From this realist perspective, the rise of China's nationalism is due to the end of the Cold War, which "has released indigenous conflicts that were previously suppressed" and created a "power vacuum" in East Asia (Buzan & Segal 1994).[7] Roy defines "power vacuum" as follows:

> As the influence of a dominant country is seen to recede in a given region, at least one of the other regional states, previously restrained by the erstwhile hegemon, attempts to expand its power . . . [A] power vacuum means that natural forces draw in a new hegemon to replace the old one. The new dominant power may not yet be as strong as the former hegemon in its heyday, only stronger than any other country in the region (1995: 46).

China is likely to fill this power vacuum due to its rapid economic development and modernization, which has given rise to new nationalism. It is argued that China's nationalism will change the power distribution among east Asian nations and pose a great threat to the region; that

China is ready to be a regional hegemon (Roy 1995; Kristof 1993); that even a hegemonic war is not impossible between China and Japan (Roy 1994).

Roy goes on to state:

> China's growth from a weak, developing state to a stronger, more prosperous state should result in a more assertive foreign policy . . . A growing economic base will increase opportunities for China to establish greater control over its environment, while simultaneously decreasing the costs of doing so. An economically stronger China will begin to act like a major power: bolder, more demanding, and less inclined to cooperate with the other major powers in the region (1994: 159–60).

Moreover, the danger that China's growing strength poses a threat to world peace is reinforced by Chinese traditional culture. Earlier on many diplomatic historians like John Fairbank (1968) argued that China's "Middle Kingdom syndrome" affects China's modern foreign policy behavior. Nevertheless, both Chinese and foreign scholars believed that although Chinese traditional culture inhibits realist behavior, it is radically different from other cultures in the way of thinking about war and violence. Confucianism has been long regarded as a philosophy of peace and the Chinese rate the utility of force very lowly and give high marks to deception, stratagem, and other psychological means. This is what Sun Tzu's phrase "win without fighting" means. But for the new generation of scholars, the traditional Chinese approach to force is indeed close to what Western scholars call "realism". Based on his reading of traditional Chinese military texts for warfare and the Ming history (1368–1644), Alastair Iain Johnston (1995) argued that Chinese realism reflects not simply pragmatism and expediency in response to events, as many have argued, but rather Chinese culture itself. What underlies Chinese realism is a hard Realpolitik strategic culture; that is, "the best way of dealing with security threats is to eliminate them through the use of force". Because Chinese Realpolitik behavior is strategic-culturally rooted, what predisposes the Chinese state to use force to cope with security issues is "not anarchical structures generating Realpolitik self-help impulses, but rather the Chinese strategic culture" (Johnston 1995). Thus, warfare is regarded as a relatively constant element in international relations, stakes in conflicts with the adversary are viewed in zero-sum terms, and pure violence is considered highly efficacious for dealing with the threats that the enemy is predisposed to make. According to Johnston, this explains the fact that compared to other major powers, China (PRC) is more likely to restore violence to cope with foreign-policy crisis (1995: Chapter 8).

Liberals believe that democratic states do not go to war against each other. Countries whose citizens choose their leaders are more likely than those with other forms of government to be reliable partners in trade and diplomacy, and less likely to threaten peace. An authoritarian regime with rapid economic development could become a major threat to world peace (Doyle 1983, 1986; Russett 1993; Owen 1994). Peace in Europe can be attributed to the fact that most European states are stable democracies with relatively low social and economic stratification. This is not the case in Asia. Asia lacks stable democratic states with relatively equitable internal distributions of wealth and income. Also, there is a diversity in the range of the regime type, including Stalinist North Korea, South-east Asia's mix of modernizing and authoritarian governments, the liberal democracies of Australia and New Zealand, and China's evolving mixture of communism and capitalism (Friedberg 1993–94). China's authoritarian regime, with its membership in the nuclear club, is without doubt a great threat to east Asian security (Segal 1995; Buzan & Segal 1994; Roy 1995).

Liberals also believe that international institutions can facilitate international cooperation and help prevent unilateral military attempts against others. This is also not the case in Asia, however. Asia's economies are far less interdependent with one another than are Europe's; there are few strong regional institutions that provide a basis for pan-Asian cooperation, and that can constrain the rise of a great power like China (Friedberg 1993–94).

More importantly, China has been reluctant to join multilateral security arrangements. This is because:

> The Chinese belief in the essential impermanence of relationships requires maintaining independence and maximum flexibility. Alliances and binding commitments are to be avoided because they limit independence and freedom of maneuver . . . Alliances with foreign nations are distrusted because the partner frequently has its own agenda that it wishes to pursue, attempts to manipulate China for its own purposes and draws China into extended disputes with the partner's adversaries (Shambaugh 1994: 45).

Consequently, by nature, China's international behavior is uncooperative. China's reluctance to participate in regional security regimes is likely to pose a threat to the region's security.

How should China be treated? Both realists and liberals believe that the West needs a grand strategy to cope with China's rise. Nevertheless, because they perceive the "China threat" differently, their proposed strategies are rather different. Realists argued that China's nationalism must be constrained and Chinese power must be balanced. This realist view is expressed in the recent debate of "containing China". Hard-core realists argued that it is in the interest of the United States and other Asian Pacific powers to seek to weaken China by isolating it economically and choking off its growth in the means of, for instance, withholding trade and technology.

Krauthmmer (1995: 72) states that undermining China's pseudo-Marxist but still ruthless dictatorship should be a goal of US policy towards China and that the United States should intensify the struggle "in the public arena" to realize respect for human rights in China. The Heritage Foundation (1995; cited in Metzger & Myers 1996: 18) also regards China as a delinquent nation "defying international norms of behavior" with regard to the whole range of human rights, security and economic issues, and recommended that the "US must make clear to Beijing that such behavior is unacceptable to the entire international community".

According to *The Economist* (1995: 11–12) containing China "should not mean ringing China with nuclear weapons, as the West did the Soviet Union", but the Western countries should form a united front in dealing with China and "gradually . . . expand ties with Taiwan". The realist also suggests that the West should aim at weakening China's central power by encouraging localism or regionalism in China, and design a strategic economic engagement to treat China's provinces or regions as more independent levels of government, to encourage China's provinces to feel more confident about their own position and their ability to deal with the outside world (Segal 1994).

Segal (1995a: 73) also argues that the best way to constrain China is to tie it into the international system, because the more "China is tied into these relationships, the less heavy the chip on its shoulder will become, and the less ready it will be to use force to settle disputes".

On the other hand, liberals believe that continuous economic and cultural development in China will eventually lead to democratization. According to Strobe Talbot (1996: 57), Deputy Secretary of State, based on the experience of political development in other east Asian nations, "promoting economic growth while monopolizing political power is an almost impossible balancing act over the long term, especially in a world increasingly linked by communications and trade. As people's income rises and their horizon broadens, they are more likely to demand the right to participate in government and to enjoy full protection under the rule of law". In the first news conference of his second term, President Bill Clinton said that the impulses of society and nature of the economic change will work together, along with the availability of information from the outside world, to increase the spirit of liberty over time. China could not hold back democracy, just as eventually the Berlin Wall fell (Lee Siew Hua 1997). An engagement strategy has been proposed based on this liberal assumption, aiming to integrate China into the existing world system (Clinton 1994; Nye 1995; Kissinger 1995; Vogel

1997). Yet, engagement is conditional. Whether China can be accepted by the West depends on whether China will accept existing international norms and institutions first (Shinn (ed.) 1996; Kornberg 1996).

Neither the realist nor liberal approach to China's nationalism catches the nature of China's new nationalism. Their mis-perceptions about China's nationalism and its impact on international politics have only resulted in strong nationalist reaction in China. Under the influence of their nationalistic emotion, Chinese also often mis-perceive the United States' China policy. Indeed, the mis-perceptions of Chinese nationalism in the West is likely to become a major force that pushes China's nationalism towards more aggression.

A Chinese Understanding of China's New Nationalism

In his *Orientalism*, Edward W. Said discusses how mis-perceptions can occur when Western scholars attempt to understand non-Western cultures. According to Said (1979: 272), there is no simple one-to-one correspondence between reality and the way in which reality is presented. This is because "all representations, because they are representations, are embedded first in the language and then in the culture, institutions, and political ambience of the representater". With a similar line of thinking, Paul Cohen (1984: 1) argued that "the supreme problem for American students of Chinese history, particularly in its post-Western impact phase, has been one of ethnocentric distortion". Indeed, Said has been a popular figure among Chinese intellectuals, and "orientalism" has become a way that Chinese intellectuals construct their discourse of nationalism against the West (Zhang Kuan 1993: 3–9, 1994: 8–14; Wang Mingming 1995: 5–18). It is not necessary, however, to go along with Said to present a Chinese understanding of Chinese nationalism. It is impossible for us to eliminate all ethnocentric distortion in interpreting foreign cultures, but it is not impossible to reduce such distortion to a minimum. As Cohen (1984) pointed out, the main feature of a China-centered approach is "that it begins with Chinese problems set in a Chinese context. These problems may be influenced, even generated, by the West. Or they are Chinese problems, in the double sense that they are experienced in China by Chinese and that the measure of their historical importance is a Chinese, rather than a Western, measure".

He goes on to say that a China-centered approach possesses four distinct characteristics:

- It begins Chinese history in China rather than in the West, and adopts internal (Chinese) rather than external (Western) criteria for determining what is historically significant in the Chinese past.

- It disaggregates China "horizontally" into regions, provinces, prefectures, counties, and cities, thus making regional and local history possible.
- It also disaggregates Chinese society "vertically" into a number of discrete levels, facilitating the writing of lower level history, both popular and unpopular.
- It welcomes the theories, methodologies, and techniques developed in disciplines other than history and strives to integrate these into historical analysis (Cohen 1984: 186–7).

A Chinese approach to China's new nationalism requires discovering China's nationalism in China rather than in the West, and to "dig out" Chinese internal forces of nationalism rather than those perceived by many in the West. It also requires identifying the major theme of China's nationalism by examining how it formed, what remains intact, what changes have occurred, and why and how these changes have happened. This does not mean that different Western approaches cannot be used to understand China's new nationalism. Rather, it means that these Western approaches cannot be used to "construct" or imagine a Chinese nationalism. This study thus can be regarded as an effort not to "construct," but to present or crystallize a Chinese approach to China's nationalism.

National Identity and International Behavior

How does national identity link to China's international behavior? Recent literature of international affairs, especially national security, goes beyond the traditional focus on power and national interests to include sociological considerations of culture and identity, and shows the importance of cultural factors in influencing a given State's domestic and international behavior (see Katzenstein 1996a; Klotz 1995). Cultural norms or identities can affect behavior by providing individuals, in Ann Swidler's (1986) term, a "tool kit" of habits, skills, and styles from which people construct strategies of action. In other words, "norms shape behavior by offering ways to organize action rather than specifying the ends of action. They create habits of interpretations and repertoires of practice grounded in experience" (Katzenstein 1996b: 19). Furthermore, "what matters is not only the compliance of political actors with social standards that shape their interests and behavior but the competence of actors to (re)interpret their identities and thus to (re)define their interests and behavior" (Katzenstein 1996b: 19).

Nationalism is a collective identity. A study of the psychological or "ideational" basis of Chinese nationalism – national identity – and its impact on China's international relations or foreign policy-making can take many directions. Chinese scholars have long noticed the role of culture, ideas, identities and individual perceptions in affecting China's foreign policies (see Kim 1994; Bin Yu 1994). Mark Mancall (1984: xvii) wrote, "Policy is made and executed by people who define the world and themselves in terms provided to them by the world view within which they lead their daily lives. The intellectual assumptions, emotional pre-dispositions, cognitive maps, and perceptual structures of the foreign policy-makers are all rooted in the prevailing world view of his society". The works of Gilbert Rozman (1984), Allen S. Whiting (1989), and David Shambaugh (1991) explored how elites' perceptions of a given foreign country affected China's foreign policies towards that country.

For example, in exploring changes in China's Japan policy, Whiting focused on Chinese elite and popular perceptions of Japan, and found out two contradictory images about Japan. The positive one regarded Japan as a developmental model that China's modernization should fol-low, while the negative one viewed Japan as a ruthless historical enemy and predator. Both images affected Sino–Japan relations between 1982 and 1987. Through a detailed examination, Whiting reached a conclu-sion that is contrary to the realist conventional wisdom that post-Mao Chinese foreign policy is driven by the rational pursuit of national eco-nomic and strategic interests. Chinese ignorance, misunderstanding, mis-perception, and mistrust of Japan among the elite and students, all stand in the way of stable, cooperative Sino–Japan relations.

Through an examination of scholarly writings on changes in Chinese perceptions of Soviet socialism, Rozman (1984: ix) attempted to explore "the Chinese worldview on sensitive matters critical to domestic and international affairs" in the period 1978–85, and thus the inner dynam-ics of the foreign policy-making process. In the same vein, Shambaugh focused on the changing perceptions of the United States articulated by China's "America Watchers" and found that Chinese elites were still heavily influenced by their Marxist–Leninist worldview when they analyzed foreign countries like the United States.

These works show how an examination of elites' worldview can improve our understanding of China's foreign policy and international behavior.

More recent works by Johnston and others have put much emphasis on how ideational factors affect China's foreign behavior. Johnston (1995) shows how Chinese strategic culture has oriented Chinese deci-sion-makers in their international behavior throughout different histor-ical periods. In their edited volume on China's national identity, Lowell Dittmer & Samuel Kim (1993: 240) discussed this collective identity in the context of China's relations to other nation–states, noting that embedded in national identity is a sense of a distinctive international mission. Both the editors and many other contributors found that the

Chinese tradition, whether "big traditions" like traditional culture and values or "small traditions" like the culture of the Chinese Communist Party (CCP), has played an important role in shaping Chinese national identity since the reform began in the late 1970s. However, national identities have become diversified. Edward Friedman has developed a similar perspective on China's national identity, which he calls de-nationalization. This means that post-Mao reforms have pluralized the Chinese society, and national identity has been weakened rather than strengthened. Friedman (1995) believed that two different national identities already existed within China; that is, north Chinese identity versus south Chinese identity. He (1997) implicitly argued that it is the chauvinistic north China identity that has given rise to China's aggressive nationalism.

While these studies have enriched the study of China's national identity and nationalism, some important aspects are ignored or under-emphasized. First, not enough attention has been paid to changing aspects of Chinese national identities and nationalism. Some authors overwhelmingly emphasized the continuity of Chinese national identities. Yes, new ones have to be built within the traditional framework of Chinese nationalism. But they have to be in concert with changes in China's domestic and international environments in order to survive this competitive world. In other words, ideational factors matter and have an important role in affecting China's foreign behavior, but they are under continuous change. Without paying enough attention to ideational changes, it is hard to understand changes in China's foreign behavior.

Second, the role of institutions, especially the State, in reconstructing a new national identity and nationalism has been under-emphasized. Most authors noticed that China's post-Mao reforms have given rise to different types of local identity such as regionalism and ethnic nationalism. Local identity and national identity, however, are not necessarily exclusive of each other. The weakening of national identity is not a result of the rise of localism, but because of the decline of Marxism–Maoism-based communist national identity. This is the rationale behind the efforts by the State and other social and political groups to construct a *new* national identity. Most scholars believe that changing identities and a rising civil society will undermine State power and the people's identification with it, but they have underestimated how reforms have brought about new national identities and how the State and other institutions have redoubled their efforts to incorporate such identities into a new nationalism.

Third, although Chinese national identities have diversified, the way different groups with different national identities influence China's foreign policy behavior is another matter, and the linkage between the new nationalism and China's foreign policy-making needs to be scrutinized. This study aims to examine the way the State and other institutions re-construct new national identities and the impact this has had on Chinese identity in relation to China's position in the nation–state system.

The role of the State and other institutions in shaping nationalism has been emphasized by recent scholarship on nationalism. Ernest Gellner (1983) sees nationalism in terms of the logic of industrialism. Because the segmentary form of communities in pre-industrial societies was not adequate for creating the homogeneous and mobile workforce required by industrializing societies, the State came to play the role of creating the requisite workforce through its control of education. As the primary identification of individuals was transferred from segmentary communities to the nation–state, nationalism came into being to supply industrializing societies with linguistic communicability and cultural uniformity through state power. While Gellner only points to the functionalist nature of the State, others focus on the subjective nature of nationalism as shown in Anderson's (1991) conception of nationalism as an "imagined community", and in recent efforts to explore the "invented" nature of national tradition (Hobsbawn & Ranger 1983).

The State and other institutions change or re-construct their culture or identities to cope with changing domestic and international environments. Changes in their national and international identities are significant for China's international relations. On the other hand, changes in China's international environment also have a major impact on Chinese national identity. The literature of international politics has shed light on how domestic and international politics are linked together. Since James Rosenau (1969) initiated the study of "linkage politics" decades ago, scholars have paid close attention to this area. The regional integration school, represented by the works of Karl Deutsch (1957) and Ernst Haas (1958), puts particular emphasis on the impact of domestic politics on international affairs. While these authors focus on the domestic determinants of foreign policy, others (Katzenstein 1985; Gourevitch 1986) have emphasized the impact of the international economy on domestic politics and domestic economic policy. Still others such as Robert Keohane and Joseph Nye (1977) emphasized interdependence and transnationalism. Peter Katzenstein (1976) and Stephen Krasner (1978) not only show the importance of domestic factors in the formation of foreign economic policy but also stress that central decision-makers must be concerned simultaneously with domestic and international pressures. Robert Putnam (1988) and others (Evans, Jacobson & Putnam 1993) attempt to establish a more dynamic model of domestic–international relations by focusing on the role of government agents in linking domestic and international politics.

Although most of these authors do not deal with nationalism directly, their diverse approaches are useful for analyzing the rise of China's new nationalism and its implications for the outside world. Three general points can be made here. First, since identity affects behavior, the implications of the new nationalism need to be examined in the context of changing national and international identities of the State and other institutions. Second, changes in China's domestic and international environments can lead to changes in the State's and other institutions' national and international identities. Thus, it is important to examine the rise of China's new nationalism in the context of China's internal and external developments. Moreover, with increasing interdependence between China and the outside world, foreign countries' China policies and strategies tend to have an increasing impact on Chinese perceptions of national and international identities. Third, the State and other institutions can change their perception of national and international identities in order to adjust themselves to changing domestic and international environments. Reforms have changed the basis of Chinese nationalism. With identity changes, a transformation from communist nationalism to post-communist nationalism has occurred, and the State and other key social and political groups have changed their perceptions about China's rightful place in the world.

Chinese Problems and Nationalism

The new nationalism is about the State, national identity, and national sovereignty, and it needs to be examined in the context of China's internal and external developments. Internally, China is experiencing a profound social, economic, and ecological transformation that is underlying its position in world politics. Externally, the global system in which China is now anchored is also undergoing a structural and political metamorphosis. Both internal and external changes have driven the rise of the new nationalism. In this context, there are several meanings of the new nationalism. First, it is about how the Chinese State should and can be reconstructed in accordance with changing domestic and international circumstances. Second, it is about state sovereignty and people's perceptions of China's proper position of power in a world of nation–states. Third, it is about people's perceptions of a "just world order", an international system that accords with China's national interest.

The links between these problems and Chinese nationalism can be examined from these perspectives. According to Wang Gungwu (1996: 8), Chinese nationalism has many faces including the concerns over the form of the polity, the recovery of sovereignty, the unification of divided territory, national self-respect, moral order and the preservation or rediscovery of traditional values. Furthermore he states: "What I call restoration nationalism combines elements of both preservation and renewal, but ties in the faith in a glorious past more directly with a vision of a great future" (Wang 1996b: 7). We have seen that throughout modern China, when the above-mentioned issues (that is, state power, national identity, and national sovereignty) became problematic, nationalism arose to provide people with different solutions.

The Chinese have used the term *neiluan, waihuan* (literally, civil chaos and foreign aggression) to refer to the severity of the crisis that China as a nation–state encounters. *Neiluan* and *waihuan* are interconnected. A weak centralized State and divided nation often invites foreign aggression. Hence, a strong centralized State is a precondition for China to be strong and independent in the nation–state system. "Chinese problems" therefore can be defined in the context of domestic–international linkages. Only in this context does nationalism make sense and influence both China's domestic policies and international relations.

Modern Chinese history has evolved with a variety of crises caused by both domestic and international factors, and the resolution of all these crises required a strong State. First, the intrusion of Western influences coincided with the decline of a dynastic state structure. The decline of the traditional state structure, symbolized by rapid decentralization of central power to local strong men and the failure of establishing a new state structure, was a result of the iron law of "the rise and fall of imperial power" (*wangchao xunhuan*, or literally the circle of dynastic State) and not by the intrusion of Western powers. But the latter without doubt accelerated the process of the collapse of the old state structure.

Second, with the intrusion of Western forces, China became increasingly semi-peripheralized or semi-colonized. Semi-colonization weakened state power domestically and made China's sovereignty problematic internationally. Meanwhile, it forced China to modernize in order to survive. Modern Western institutions and concepts flowed into China and began to influence the path of China's development.

Third, revolution also played a part in modern Chinese history. The aim of all revolutions was to establish a new polity. For the Chinese only revolution could destroy the old socioeconomic and political structure that had existed for thousands of years and pave the way for a new strong state structure. Revolution became the most effective means for various political parties and groups to realize their own ideals of what form of polity China should have in order to be strong (see Luo Rongqu 1996: 43–53).

Semi-peripheralization triggered off China's modernization. It was in this aspect that China was deeply dependent on the West. For many Chinese political leaders, westernization and modernity were identical;

the West was the standard that China should aim for; and only by west-ernization could China develop a strong nation–state and become an equal member in the nation–state system.

Nevertheless, both modernization and the inflow of Western influ-ences inevitably resulted in very conflicting nationalistic reactions in China. While Chinese leaders saw how learning from the West could make China strong, the intrusion of Western powers was accompanied by successive Chinese military defeats and consequent humiliation and unequal status in the world system.

> [Chinese] leaders looked for an alternative to the mainstream Western model, which was seen as an exploitative system that was impoverishing China. Ironically, they looked to the West for an ideology that was more pow-erful than orthodox capitalism and liberal democracy, something that would help China stand up against the West itself. Some found it in Mussolini's fas-cism, others in national socialism, and yet others in anarchism, socialism, and communism (Wang Gungwu 1995: 47).

Consequently, anti-Chinese tradition coincided with anti-foreignism and, anti-westernization with westernization.

Though before the coming of Western powers, China formed its cul-tural nationalism through its frequent contact with those it traditionally called "barbarians". China as a cultural nation was never challenged. "Barbarians" (minorities or ethnic groups in peripheral areas, especially in the north) were never successful in using their own approaches to rule China. Instead, they had to give up their own means and accept the Chinese way. For centuries, the Chinese believed that their country was the Middle Kingdom of the world and was thus without any boundaries. The tributary system reflected the perception of the Chinese world order (Fairbank 1968). The intrusion of Western powers forced the Chinese to change their perceptions of state power and world order. They began to feel that their cultural nation was seriously threatened. It was against this background that China's modernization and national-ism began. The goal of both modernization and nationalism was a strong State and national survival.

National survival is the theme of Chinese nationalism proposed by Sun Yat-sen, the founder of the Republic of China. For Sun, national-ism's chief concern was to ensure the survival of the Chinese nation because it had suffered from foreign aggression. According to Sun, the meanings of Chinese nationalism were multifold. First, nationalism was the equivalent to the doctrine of the State as China had developed as a single State out of a single race ever since the Qin and Han dynasties. Second, nationalism was the key to the development and survival of the Chinese nation, and third, nationalism called for the equality of all races and was the way to restore freedom and equality to China (Chou Yu-sun 1996: 68). Throughout modern Chinese history, building a strong State was a consistent theme of Chinese nationalism, and waves of nationalistic movements led to the formation of a "strong State complex" among social and political groups. Whenever the State was challenged, or people perceived that it was challenged, nationalism rose.

From this perspective, the rise of nationalism in post-Mao China was not only a result of China's rapid economic growth and its growing muscle. Of more importance, it is a response to the "Chinese problems" that post-Mao China has encountered. In other words, the new nationalism can be understood in the context of the "Chinese problems", symbolized by the decline of central power, the weakening of national identity, and actual or perceived external threats. It is also around these problems that Chinese nationalists construct their discourse of nationalism.

The interaction between China and the outside world has resulted in the Chinese perception that poor and weak central power is the main reason for China's humiliation by foreign powers, and the only solution is to build a wealthy and strong central government that could defy such victimization. Furthermore, an approach that Mao Zedong called "politics in command" would enable the regime to mobilize all domestic resources to catch up with advanced Western powers and prevent China's further victimization. This perception began to change only after Deng Xiaoping came to power. Deng had a more realistic vision of world politics and saw economic wealth as the foundation of Chinese power. According to Deng, whether China could have a rightful place in the world of nations depended on China's domestic economic development. Great leaders before Deng Xiaoping saw national unity as a source of China's wealth and power. But Deng argued that national unity depended on whether China could catch up with the developed countries. This meant that prerequisites for national unity were China's wealth and power. Though Deng (1984d) did not give up the principle of "politics in command", he insisted that "politics" had to serve the principle of economic priority (*jingji youxian*). Deng was successful in establishing economic modernization as the Chinese Communist Party's basic principle and insisted that those who were not able to promote economic modernization should step down. This "economics in command" without doubt is a new idea in modern Chinese history, and its impact on China's internal and external developments cannot be underestimated.

Nevertheless, the implementation of this new idea was not without its costs. China has achieved a high rate of economic growth. Rapid growth, however, does not make the Chinese State stronger than before. State power has been in decline ever since Deng's reforms. This decline was a consequence of Chinese-styled modernization; that is, decentralization. In the West, especially Japan and Germany, modernization and centralization were almost two identical processes, and modernization generated centralized states. But in China, the regime initiated modernization by decentralizing state power to lower level polity and society, and state power was often weakened.

The decline of central power resulted in the weakening of national identity for a variety of reasons. First, decentralization gave rise to strong local governmental states that became the locomotive of China's rapid economic growth.[8] The socioeconomic welfare of local residents is linked with these local states. Local residents' identity has thus moved away, to some extent, from the national government to local units. Second, decentralization meant the withdrawal of institutionalized central power from local societies. Consequently, the national government gradually lost its "touch" with local societies. As long as the national government is not capable of delivering socioeconomic goods directly to local residents, national identity will be problematic. Third, traditionally, Marxism or Maoism as an ideology was the most powerful weapon for the national government to regulate or coordinate local societies. With the decline in Marxist or Maoist faith, foreign ideas, such as capitalism, individualism, and political liberalism, gradually took over the ideological vacuum among local residents.

Deng's reform has also affected China's external environment. Since the late 1970s China's economy has maintained an annual growth rate of more than 9 percent. According to the World Bank, China is set to become the world's largest economy in 2010, or even 2002 if "Greater China" is included. The International Monetary Fund reported that based on the "purchasing power parity" calculations of gross domestic product (GDP), China already had the world's second largest economy in 1994 (*The Economist* 1992; Garnaut & Guonan Ma 1993). Many world powers began to feel that their positions in the nation–state system could be threatened by China's rise. The development of various "anti-China" theories in the West thus coincided with a growing crisis of state power and national identity within China. While many in the West see the actual and potential "negative effects" of China's modernization and rapid growth, the Chinese feel that China will not be able to avoid the iron law of modernization – a crisis of state power. Furthermore, with the rise of various anti-China theories, the Chinese have begun to fear that their process of modernization is being interrupted by external forces. Again, nationalism rises as a response to China's changing international environment. The Chinese increasingly believe that the West does not want China to develop and become an equal player in the international community as Western countries do, nor does it want to recognize Chinese power. This is the perceptional basis of the new nationalism.

It would be sensible for the Chinese government, as many have argued, to appeal to nationalism to reconstruct national identity at home and to counter the "China threat" abroad. The rise of the new nationalism, however, does not mean that China will become aggressive towards the existing world system. This study will show that nationalism is a double-edged sword. It could be used to strengthen the political legitimacy of the regime, but it also could result in political chaos. What the leadership wants is not to simply appeal to popular nationalism, but to reconstruct an official nationalism that can strengthen its political legitimacy while maintaining socio-political stability. In terms of foreign policy-making, changes have occurred to China's national and international identities. It seems to many Chinese political leaders that only by integrating China into the world system can it become a strong state and world power. What the leadership wants is not to overthrow the existing system, but the recognition of Chinese power and its rightful place in the world system by other major world powers.

Conclusion

Many factors have contributed to the rise of the new nationalism in the People's Republic of China. Since the 1980s the Chinese Communist Party has consistently experienced crises in faith in Marxism and Maoism. The 1989 Tiananmen Square pro-democracy demonstration showed that the political legitimacy of the CCP's rule had become doubtful among different social and political groups. With the collapse of the former Soviet Union and the end of the Cold War, China found that it was suddenly pulled by the West to the front of great power competition. For the first time in its modern history, China encountered an opportunity to be a real great power in the world system. But China also found great challenges from the international community since the West doubts China's international intentions. However, with rapid economic growth and modernization, the Chinese felt more confident in dealing with the outside world and required a higher level of respect from the international community.

For all these factors, since the early 1990s the regime has allowed the rise of nationalistic voices among different social and political groups despite its strict control over other aspects of political discussions. Chinese intellectuals gained relative freedom to express their opinions on China's domestic reform and its international affairs. Regarding the rise of nationalism, many new journals such as *Zhanlue yu guanli* (Strategy and Management) and *Dong Fang* (The Orient) were established. Various academic journals, such as *Shijie zhengzhi yu jingji* (World Economics and Politics), *Dangdai guoji guanxi* (Contemporary International Relations), *Xiandai guoji guanxi* (Modern International

Relations), and many others also began to publish articles on national-ism. With the approaching of Hong Kong's return to China's sovereignty, more and more mainland scholars managed to publish their opinions in various Hong Kong-based journals such as *Shehui kexue jikan* (The Social Sciences Quarterly), *Xianggang shehui kexue xuebao* (Hong Kong Journal of Social Sciences) and *Ershiyi shiji* (Twenty-First Century). Also, various extreme nationalistic works such as *A China that Says No* and *Behind A Demonized China* were allowed to be published. More importantly, ever since the reform began in the late 1970s, China has become increasingly open to the outside world and scholars are rel-atively free in conducting research, including interviews on the main-land. These developments make it possible to carry out a detailed examination of China's new nationalism in the 1990s.

CHAPTER 2

Nationalism and Statism: Chinese Perceptions of the Crisis of State Power

Chapter 1 argued that throughout its modern history, China has developed a very persuasive idea that a strong central government was a prerequisite of a strong China; that whenever central power was actually weakened, or people perceived it as weakened, nationalism arose. Thus, Chinese nationalism is not only a reaction to China's international environment. More importantly, it is a response to the decline of central power caused by domestic modernization. This chapter attempts to shed light on how Chinese nationalists have perceived the crisis of state power caused by rapid modernization in the post-Mao era.

In many other countries, modernization and centralization were almost identical. But in modern China, modernization was characterized by decentralization. While decentralization created dynamism for socioeconomic development, it often resulted in the decline of state power and a crisis of nation–state building. This is what has happened in post-Mao China. Decentralization promoted rapid economic growth and dramatic social changes on one hand, and led to a nation–state crisis on the other. Furthermore, like many other multinational states, China's modernization does not always imply nation-building, but nation-destroying; not centralization, but de-construction.[1] Modernization and economic development have also given rise to ethnic nationalism in China's peripheral areas. This crisis of nation–state in turn leads to the rise of statism. For the proponents of nationalism, the ultimate aim of China's modernization is to build a strong nation–state, rather than to weaken it, let alone to destroy it. Statism therefore consists of a mainstream of China's new nationalism in post-Mao China.

This chapter is divided into three parts. The first part examines why and how nation–state building has become the most important theme of nationalism throughout modern China. The second part discusses the impact of post-Mao decentralization on China's communist state. The third part examines how China's nationalists have perceived the nation–state crisis and what statism means for China.

Nationalism and Statism in Modern China

A brief comparison of the development of nationalism in the West and China will throw light on how statism became a main theme of China's nationalism. Modern Western nation–states were created by the interplay of two types of sovereignty; that is, national and popular, and nationalism played an essential role in the development of popular sovereignty. According to Hans Morgenthau (1957: 481), the idea of nationalism is intimately connected with the idea of freedom. "Nationalism as a political phenomenon must be understood as the aspiration for two freedoms, one collective, the other individual: the freedom of a nation from domination by another nation and the freedom of the individual to join the nation of his choice". Nationalism first meant that the nation itself was called on to defend its freedom. But more importantly, it meant the triumph of individual liberty. The rise of nationalism occurred not only because the absolute monarchy betrayed the nation abroad, but also because it oppressed the individual at home. Morgenthau elaborates that:

> Individual freedom was taken as a precondition of national freedom and the latter, in turn, was regarded as a mere extension of the former to the international scene. The political and legal principles, originally formulated to support and guarantee the freedom of the individual, were applied to the nation (1957: 482).[2]

Without the rise of popular sovereignty, it is hard to understand the evolution of modern Western nation–states.

In China, the modern concept of the nation–state was "imported" from the West and nation–state building was influenced significantly by Western nationalism. Nevertheless, when nationalism came to China, a grand transformation occurred: national sovereignty was separated from popular sovereignty; the former was given the highest priority, the latter was replaced by state sovereignty, and individual freedom by national freedom. Consequently, even though Chinese political elites were fascinated by the new ideas emerging from foreign countries such as national identity, nationality and nationhood, their interest was in strong state power, not in the question of citizenship and political participation (Wang Gungwu 1995).

The formation of a Chinese "strong state complex" occurred because China encountered a different international environment and domestic political structure when modernization began than the West did when it began to modernize. Throughout the modern era, Chinese political elites attempted to build a new nation–state and a new type of national identity. But in doing so, they were constrained by both China's international environment and domestic political structure. Facing various constraints, Chinese political elites realized that to build a strong nation–state, China's nationalism had to be transformed and emphasis had to be put on state sovereignty rather than popular sovereignty.

In the late 19th century, when Chinese leaders began to struggle to modernize China's political institutions, they found that they had to give priority to military modernization since the international system was characterized by "an age of imperialism". Among the European nations and the United States, a nation's power was measured almost invariably in terms of its ability to wage war successfully (Kennedy 1987). The intrusion of Western powers into east Asia shattered the traditional Chinese idea of a world order based on the Middle Kingdom. Western powers brought the idea of nation–state to China, but they were not prepare to recognize China as a sovereign State. As Theodore Friend contended:

> In the tradition of Renaissance diplomacy, the Western imperial powers treated each other as legal equals; but in the tradition of social Darwinism they treated Asian polities as legal and moral inferiors unless counterforce proved otherwise" (1988: 54).

This international system had a significant impact on China's choice of modernization alternatives. Marius Jansen argued:

> In both China and Japan, modernization had to be carried out under the shadow of the economic and military power of the West, and this produced distinctive elements in the drive for change. In both cases the basic motives were defensive in nature. Modernization came to East Asia at the point of guns . . . This outside challenge meant that an emphasis on national survival would take first place in all efforts to modernize. There was not a free choice, for the alternative to modernization was extinction (1975: 3).

Only a modernized military force could prevent further intrusion of Western powers. According to Iriye, both China and Japan:

> saw the mighty nations of the West primarily as military powers, with strong arms, a powerful class of military leaders, and overseas bases, colonies, and spheres of influence. Such perceptions made a decided impression on the elites . . . and they became convinced that their countries should develop similar feature (1992: 8–9).

Chinese leaders soon realized that if China was to gain respect abroad and to protect itself, it had to first strengthen its armed forces. Military modernization was given the highest priority. Li Hongzhang's Huai army was equipped with rifles and cannons imported from Europe. Foreign language schools were established and Western books on military, business and scientific affairs were translated. A modern navy came into being, and a navy office was established in order to centralize naval policy and administration.

Despite all these efforts, China was defeated in the Sino–Japanese war (1894–95). The two countries had begun military modernization almost at the same time, but China's domestic structure seriously constrained its military efficiency. China's initial impetus for military strengthening came from the authorities' need to preserve domestic order. Li's Huai army was first organized by the scholar-gentry as a provincial force to combat the Taipings; it then gained official recognition as the armed power of the country and went on to constitute the core of the fighting force against the Japanese army in 1894. Although Li's army was formally nationalized, it was still characterized by regionalism (Mccord 1993). General Yamagata, the builder of the Japanese armies and a leading commander in the Sino–Japanese War, attributed China's defeat to the localism that characterized Chinese land forces. He said:

> I discovered a great weakness in the army of Li Hung-chang, and one which I could appreciate from its resemblance to a weakness which had been encountered at the time of the Restoration in Japan, which consisted of the feudal retainers under different feudal lords. This weakness was that Li Hung-chang, besides drawing a considerable portion of his soldiers from his own native place, also obtained his officers there. Thus, when anything happened to an officer in his army, he could not be replaced from among the troops under the command of other generals. Thus it was necessary to send to Li Hung-chang's native province for all new officers (cited in Jansen 1975: 17).

Without a centralized modern state, military modernization alone would not save China. Creating a strong nation–state through government reforms was not ignored by the Chinese, at least not within the intellectual circles. With the incursion of the Western powers, the concept of popular sovereignty, a theme of nationalist movements in the West, also spread among the Chinese (Schrecker 1971). Even before the Sino–Japanese War, many Chinese had criticized the self-strengthening approach to China's modernization, which put emphasis on military modernization (Hunt 1993: 65). Knowledgeable intellectuals like Wang Tao saw that if China wanted to catch up with the power of the Western states, more emphasis had to be placed on "the people". The self-strengtheners were not able to win popular support for government policy. Wang wrote in 1893, "Of all the great evils in the world, the greatest is when the people lack confidence in their rulers". China suffered from precisely that evil – "the failure of communication between ruler and ruled and the distance separating the sovereign and the people" (Cohen 1974: 227, 229).

Earlier reform programs of viceroys like Li Hongzhang had attempted to utilize the machinery and weapons of the West, but the fact that China was defeated by Japan made many Chinese realize the importance of a strong State. According to Yan Fu, there could be no *way* without a State and a people to sustain it (Schwartz 1964). Kang Youwei argued that if China wanted to stem the rush of foreign demands, the State would have to undergo extensive renovation, including a new bureaucratic system, a top-to-bottom revision of economic and educational policy, a popular army equipped with the most advanced equipment, a new taxation system, and the development of an extensive railway system. But central to all these programs was to foster the Chinese people. Kang believed that "if we cannot think how to foster those people, then we ourselves destroy our own foundation" (Hunt 1993: 66). Liang Qichao also argued that although the traditional Chinese imperial system was highly centralized, it did not play the role of a modern State. The Chinese people were patriotic, but they were not nationalistic and their national identity was very weak. According to Liang, a strong modern nation–state required a transformation of emperor-identity to state identity (Levenson 1970). High officials also began to talk about "the people". In responding to the argument that the central government could not rely on the Boxers to resist foreign intrusion, the empress Dowager Cixi (Hunt 1993: 67) said, "if we cannot rely on the supernatural formulae, can we not rely upon the hearts of the people? China has been extremely weak, the only thing we can rely on is the hearts of the people".

After the Sino–Japanese War, official policies continued to make efforts to modernize China's military. Even though institutional reforms, especially the popular base of the State, were also emphasized, compared to other aspects of China's modernization, political reforms were much more constrained by China's traditional political structure. China had a very centralized political system, but the central government was extremely weak. Laws were made by the central government, but could not be implemented. China lacked a strong emperor when foreign powers intruded. What Japanese leaders did was to centralize their political system. However, in China, the centralized national government was too weak to implement various modernization programs by itself, thus it had to decentralize its power in order to create local initiatives, which often further weakened the center. Moreover, the weakness of the center gave local elites opportunities to seize power, dealing with local affairs independently and influencing national affairs. As local elites expanded their power, they wanted not only to manage local affairs, but also for the national government to consider their opinions when national policies were formulated (Rankin 1971). Decentralization thus introduced changes to state–society relations. Local participation in national politics meant that the national government had less autonomy in decision-making. This in turn constrained central power in dealing with domestic and international affairs. The center therefore had to recentralize its power.

Theoretically, popular sovereignty could strengthen China's power in international arenas. But in practice, it did not. As political reforms went on, Cixi feared that the national government was losing its control over the formulation of national policy and called for a halt to the radical political reforms in the summer of 1898. What the central government needed was the type of political reforms that could strengthen central power while promoting local initiatives. As Paul Cohen (1988) pointed out, the real issue in Chinese politics was not reform versus no reform but what kind of reform there was to be and who was to have primary control over its implementation. Cixi attempted to establish a constitutional monarchy so that central power could be strengthened while popular sovereignty and political participation could be expressed to some extent.

Nationalism means that ethnic or national communities desire their own independent state. With the spread of nationalism in China, "ethnicity", in addition to "popular sovereignty", came to influence Chinese people, especially radical revolutionaries. While many measures towards a constitutional monarchy were being implemented by the Qing court, many Chinese began to doubt whether the Qing State was an adequate foundation for renovation. For radicals, China should not only be a strong State, but also one that was based on Chinese ethnicity rather than Manchurian ethnicity. Reforms within the existing Qing State would not help save China and the Chinese people.

This version of Chinese nationalism was shared by many Chinese political activists at home and abroad, and even existed among Chinese officials. For nationalistic revolutionaries, constitutional monarchy was not enough; only a republic purged of all traces of the self-serving and inept Manchus could make the State strong and bring about their patriotic goals. Only Chinese nationalism could forestall racial destruction by foreign powers and build a strong China. They began to organize their own armed units against the Qing court.

Sun Yat-sen and other revolutionaries attempted to use two principles of nationalism – that is, statehood based on ethnicity and popular sovereignty based on democracy – to reorganize China. However, the 1911 republic revolution itself was a product of decentralization.

State-making, which required a centralized political force, became difficult. After the revolution, the forces of decentralization became dominant in Chinese politics. Local elites at all levels benefited from the revolution simply because they had played a crucial role in it. Provincial officials, who had acted autonomously during the revolution, sought to strengthen their autonomy and block the resurgence of an all-powerful and autocratic center. The State itself was no longer monolithic, but comprised of competing levels of authority. Below the provincial level, local elites dominated the self-government organs that proliferated after 1911, expanded control over local finances, and attempted to exercise sway over the appointment of local officials (Kuhn 1975; Young 1977).

Great political liberalization convinced Yuan Shikai, the most powerful military man in China, that "the devolution of power from the center to the provinces and localities was inimical to the restoration of Chinese national strength" (Cohen 1988: 522). Following the advice of Frank Goodnow[3] that a constitutional monarchy was more appropriate to China's tradition than republicanism, Yuan became determined to reestablish the political dominance of the center. Yet, Yuan's various attempts to restore the monarchy failed because of political opposition from all sides. By the early 1920s, the Republican State began to disintegrate as a constitutional and parliamentary entity, and as a bureaucratic force. China entered a period of chaos and warlordism.

In his early days as a revolutionary, Sun Yat-sen stressed popular sovereignty and believed that republic government, based on the western European and north American multiparty model, would provide a channel for political participation. However, the 1911 revolution did not help China build a strong democratic State. New democratic political arrangements "failed to bring unity and order, not to mention legitimacy. Representative government degenerated rapidly into an autocracy hostile to popular participation and ineffective in foreign policy" (Hunt 1993: 68). Sun reconsidered the problem of "popular sovereignty" and realized that without strong political institutions, any type of democratic regime would not be stable and China would not become a strong State. Sun thus turned to the organizational side of state-building. His strategy now became "state-building through party organization", which he learned from the Russian revolution. Sun argued:

> Why has not our party engaged in organized, systematic, and disciplined struggle before? It was because we lacked the model and the precedent . . . The Russian Revolution took place six years later than in our country, and yet after one revolution the Russians have been able to apply their principles thoroughly; moreover, since the revolution the revolutionary government has daily become more stabilized. Both are revolutions: Why have they succeeded in Russia, and why have we not in China? It is because the Russian

Revolution owed its success to the struggle of the Party member: on the one hand the Party members struggled, on the other hand they were aided by military forces, and so they were able to succeed. Therefore, if we wish our revolution to succeed, we must learn the methods, organization, and training of the Russians; then there can be hope of success (Teng & Fairbank 1979: 265).

According to Sun, Russians placed the Party above the State; the Russian model was more appropriate to China's modernization and state-making than the European and American model. China should follow the strategy of "governing the state through the party", whose first priority would be to establish a new state structure. "We now do not have a state to be ruled. What we need to do is to construct a state. After the construction of the state, we can govern it" (Sun Yat-sen, 1986, vol. 9: 103). Only after a strong and highly organized party had been built could China begin to make a strong State. Only a strong State could lead to a working democracy. Sun thus proposed three stages of China's political development: first, military government; second, authoritarian government; and third, constitutional government (Chen Runyun 1988).

The Nationalist Party was reformed and became highly organized and centralized. Sun's successor Chiang Kai-shek kept to that course and used the Party to restore unity and order, end foreign humiliation, abolish unequal treaties, regain lost territory, and ultimately restore China's lost grandeur. During the 1926–28 Northern Expedition, China was recentralized under the Nationalist Party regime. A centralized State was established through two primary methods. In the military sphere, the regime maximized the center's control over the instruments of force while in the civilian sector it extended and deepened the national government's penetration of local society by quasi-fascist projects such as the Blue Shirts and the New Life movement, and self-government reforms like new country campaigns. The nationalist regime put much emphasis on the control of urban areas. The regime did not realize that "in a predominantly rural society the sphere of influence of cities was much more severely circumscribed than in the West where such a strategy might well have proved successful" (Whitney 1970: 71). Local elites, on whom the regime heavily relied, were not able to succeed in fundamentally transforming the lives of the peasant (Averill 1981).

More importantly, as Whitney pointed out (1970: Chapter 2), the nationalist government was not capable of providing a viable state-idea. As a ruling party, the Nationalist Party stressed a centralized state structure and limited political participation. Nevertheless, the idea of popular sovereignty was spreading in China. At the societal level, the idea of popular sovereignty was very appealing. By contrast, the Chinese Communist Party transformed the idea of popular sovereignty and used it to mobilize urban people and intellectuals against the Nationalist regime. Joseph

Levenson (1964) showed that the Communist version of the state-idea was more appealing to Chinese intellectuals than the Nationalist version. Also important was that the Nationalist regime lacked any effective means to spread its nation–state ideas among the Chinese. The regime's urban-centered modernization strategy left rural areas untouched. On the other hand, by sending its officials to rural areas, the Communist Party successfully transmitted its nation–state ideas to Chinese peasants. The rise of peasant nationalism finally led to the failure of the Nationalist government and pushed the Communist Party into power.

The Chinese Communist Party (CCP) was successful in using the idea of "popular sovereignty" to mobilize urban citizens against the Nationalist regime. Nevertheless, once it came to power, it put much emphasis on organizational and ideological control. Franz Schurmann revealed the nature of the Chinese Communist State:

> Chinese communism came to power and created the present People's Republic of China through revolutionary struggle. The last decade and a half in China have witnessed a human drama played out by great and small men who have used organized political power for many different ends. They have rebuilt a great country, disciplined its people, improved the conditions of life, and laid the foundations for growth . . . Communist China is like a vast building made of different kinds of brick and stone. However it was put together, it stands. What holds it together is ideology and organization (1968: 1).

Decentralization and Development

Without doubt, organization and ideology were the two pillars of the Communist State. The Communist Party regime effectively eliminated local political forces through the land reform campaign of the early 1950s. The movement removed a major obstacle in the path of China's state-building efforts. The Party–State was successful in establishing a hegemonic regime and achieved an overall control over local society through its coercive organization and ideology. The dominion of the State, however, does not necessarily mean that it will be able to modernize the country. The State's capacity to develop the economy depends not only on the will and skill of the top leadership, but also on lower level state organizations and social institutions. Without the initiative and cooperation of the latter organizations, the leaders can hardly get their job done or get people in society to do what they want them to do.

So, once centralization was achieved it quickly became apparent that the highly centralized regime carried its own burden of problems, that there were distinct advantages to decentralization and societal initiatives. Mao Zedong realized that China needed to achieve a degree of power balance between State and society, between statism and democracy. In other words, the "democracy" component of the democratic centralism principle needed strengthening. In the wake of the unparalleled centralization achieved in the early and mid-1950s, Mao began to focus on local initiatives. How to arouse local enthusiasm towards the new State became a major concern in the central regime. Mao argued:

> [The central government] should enlarge local power and give localities greater independence and let them get more things done . . . It will be much better to have two initiatives [local and central] than one initiative [central]. We cannot follow the Soviet Union, centralizing everything and leaving no leeway for localities (1976: 11).

The CCP regime initiated two waves of rapid decentralization during the Great Leap Forward and the Cultural Revolution. But Mao did not prepare to let local elites have a say in national decision-making. He initiated decentralization mainly because he disliked the Soviet type of strong central bureaucracy and favored a mass mobilization strategy. Once Mao felt that central power was challenged by local elites, he turned to attack them. Mao believed that localism must be eliminated or constrained so that a strong Chinese State could be built and a unified China could be maintained. So, centralization often followed decentralization. Moreover, because of waves of radical decentralization, geographical immobility, and enforced self-reliance, the Chinese State became fragmented. Power was centralized, but was less effective since land, labor, and capital were generally under the control of local states, rather than the central State. The "fragmentation" of the regime led to a growing disjunction between the State and society, and the decline of local and societal initiatives led to the decline of state capacity (Shue 1988). By the late 1970s China fell into severe crises.

After Deng Xiaoping came to power in the late 1970s the regime attempted to change China's worsening situation by decentralizing power to society and local government. Many leaders realized the importance of social and local initiatives in promoting economic development and thus alleviating the tension between the State and society. Though the new regime did not oppose some limited political reform, economic decentralization was given the highest priority. Major leaders saw the necessity of de-politicization of people's daily lives:

> Like Germany after World War II, Chinese people after the Cultural Revolution were no longer interested in politics. They were more interested in food, clothing and housing. They needed to take care of themselves rather than the country. Many old leaders would reject any radical political reform. Most people would also oppose it because they were already tired of political movements. So, economic reforms first became the basic consensus among reformist leaders and social groups (Chen Yizi 1990: 12).

While political elites in the Soviet Union and east European countries implemented a top-down reform strategy, the reformist leadership in China identified the decentralization of economic decision-making power as a major strategy for reforming the economic system and achieving economic development. Under the auspices of Deng Xiaoping, reformist leaders decentralized essential decision-making power, together with *de facto* property rights and fiscal power, to local governments at different levels. An institutional setting was created for the rise of the local developmental State, which was also known as development-oriented local government (White 1984).

The rise of local developmental states accelerated local economic growth (Oi 1993, 1996; Walder 1995).[4] Due to great diversity among Chinese provinces, the State had difficulties implementing unified policies. Only after each province was assigned enough power to make its own economic policies could China achieve fast economic growth. This was especially true in coastal provinces such as Guangdong, Fujian, Zhejiang, Jiangsu, and Shandong. Indeed, decentralization became local government officials' catch-cry to justify their local policies. The coastal provinces were assigned overall decision-making power and took initiatives to promote radical decentralization. As a result, significant changes occurred to the State's power structure. As one Guangdong author contended, "decentralization meant that Guangdong people were to manage Guangdong affairs by themselves" (Yan Changjiang 1993: 21).

With great local autonomy, provincial government officials want to integrate their economies with the international economic system, at least with the economies of their foreign neighbours. As a Guangdong author asked, when China opened its door, when provincial leaders in Guangdong saw rapid development in Hong Kong, why should Guangdong not integrate its economy with Hong Kong (Yan Changjiang 1993: 20)? Provincial governments one after another seized the initiative to develop provincial foreign economy. The significance of intensive competition for rapid development among provinces is far reaching. As *The Economist* explains:

> Every Chinese province has been transfixed by the success of Guangdong . . . All realize that Guangdong has had the incomparable advantage of being next to Hong Kong. But most now realize as well that Hong Kong would not have knocked on Guangdong's door had it not been for the province's pro-business government and the small share of state-owned firms there. The result is that provinces are striving for and carrying out models of reform (1992: 7).

Decentralization resulted in rapid economic growth and a dramatic improvement in people's living standards. The Chinese economy chalked up an average annual growth rate of 9.5 percent during 1978–92, and double-digit rates for three consecutive years from 1992 to 1994 (Wong 1996b). Ironically, however, rapid economic growth did not make the Chinese State stronger than before. Indeed, growth has led to the decline of the power of the State. The impact of economic development on the nation–state and thus Chinese perceptions of the nation–state crisis cannot be underestimated.

The Formation of Economic Localism

Without doubt, radical decentralization bears its costs. First of all, it has rendered the state structure chaotic. Power has shifted from the national State to local governments at different levels, but local–central relations have not been institutionalized (Wu Guoguang & Zheng Yongnian 1995). Without effective institutional constraints, localism or regionalism often becomes uncontrollable and poses a serious challenge on central power. One observer argued that Beijing can only now pretend to rule the provinces, and the provinces only pretend to be ruled by Beijing, and that China as a nation–state needs to be redefined. Decentralization has transformed China from a Middle Kingdom to a muddle state (Segal 1994).

One sign of the crisis of central power is the decline of the fiscal and financial power of the State. Since the reform began in 1978, central revenue has declined continuously. Initially, the national government decentralized fiscal power to local governments in order to motivate local economic initiatives. Central officials, however, find that once power is decentralized, it is rather difficult to collect fiscal revenue from the provinces, especially from booming coastal areas. Central revenue shrunk from 34 percent of GDP in 1978 to 6 percent in 1995 (Hu Angang 1996: 2). The provinces even began to resist new fiscal policies initiated by the central government. When the national government asked rich provinces to pay more taxes, resistance from rich provinces was very strong. These rich provinces were able to challenge central authority because of their wealth generated by decentralization.

Economic decentralization widened diversities among provinces and regions. In coastal areas such as Guangdong, Zhejiang, Jiangsu and Shandong, local officials developed very strong non-state sectors including collectives, private economies, and joint ventures, each of which was very profitable and beyond the control of the national government. In inland provinces, owing to the lack of financial resources and skilled personnel, local governments had difficulty pushing local growth, let alone adjusting the local industrial structure. Consequently, some provincial governments achieved a high capacity to lead local development and improve local residents' living standards, while others did not. Due to local diversity, the national government often failed to implement unified policies to lead and constrain local governments, and local officials could easily nullify central policies. The national government was thus unable to bring local governments in line with the national interest.

The decline of central power and authority gave rise to local protectionism and the national government was no longer able to coordinate local economic activities effectively. During Mao's time, a rigid planning system was not able to coordinate local behavior effectively and it was undermined by the Cultural Revolution. Once this rigid system stopped functioning, there was nothing left to coordinate local behavior. Rich provinces were reluctant to cooperate with one another when they could design local development independently. Even below the provincial level, coordination was also very poor. One study talks of "the fragmentation and lack of coordination" in the well-developed Pearl River Delta region of Guangdong province (Taylor 1990). Another study indicates very poor coordination among the three richest areas within the Jiangsu province: Suzhou, Wuxi, and Changzhuo (Ding Jinhong & Luo Zude 1993).

Poor and rich provinces were also reluctant to cooperate. They have similar industrial structures; however, the attitude of the local officials in poor provinces was important. For instance, local officials in Anhui province did not cooperate with neighboring Shanghai because they believed that they had been victimized by Shanghai, and they regarded it as a colonial center. Hunan was unwilling to cooperate with Guangdong because of a similar belief of being victimized, and its leaders once blocked grain shipments to Guangdong. Local governments competed with one another for local development and used all possible administrative methods to protect local industries (Zheng 1994b).

Economic decentralization also resulted in a relatively greater increase in interdependence between Chinese provinces and the outside world, and a surprising decrease in interprovincial interdependence. According to the World Bank, as of the early 1990s, internal trade as a percentage of GDP among Chinese provinces was 22 percent, which was lower than the European Community's 28 percent, and the 27 percent among the republics of the former Soviet Union before it was dissolved. The World Bank thus warned that individual provinces have the tendency to behave like independent countries, with an increase in external (overseas) trade and a relative decline in trade flows with each other (Kumar 1994).

Enormous unwanted consequences of economic decentralization gave rise to nationalistic sentiments among local officials and brought great pressure to the national government. Uneven development among regions became one major issue on China's political agenda.

Local officials in poor areas called for recentralization and asked the national government to pay more attention to their areas. Obviously, local officials felt great pressure from local residents concerning increasing diversities among regions. According to a survey among government officials at the provincial and prefectural levels in 1994, 84 percent of government officials believed that great regional income disparities would cause social instability, and 16 percent contended that they would lead to national disintegration, especially in minority areas. The same survey also showed that nearly 64 percent of local government officials believed that reducing regional disparities should be the most important political agenda for the national government (Hu Angang 1994).

Then, what does economic decentralization mean for local–central political relations? With rapid local economic development, local officials strengthened the economic base of their political power. Hegemonic rulers in Mao's time were able to remove or constrain local forces easily. Post-Mao economic decentralization, however, transformed hegemonic rule into interdependence between the center and the provinces. With great local economic initiatives, the central government gradually found that it could not remove locally elected officials easily.

Local leaders were increasingly important even in the national political arena, and their political interests had to be satisfied to some extent. Since the establishment of the reform regime, local interests have been increasingly reflected in the personnel arrangements at the central government level. Many local leaders have been recruited to the most important positions in the central government and central party committee. Such recruitment has been institutionalized to an extent. During Mao's time, the majority of party elites came from central China, especially Hunan, Jiangxi, and Hubei. Since 1978, more and more power elites in the Central Committee are from the eastern coastal areas, where rapid economic growth has occurred. A leadership transition in terms of geographic distribution has also occurred. It has been noted that Hebei, Jiangsu, Shandong, and Zhejiang provided nearly 45 percent of the Fourteenth Central Committee (1992), while cadres from Hunan, Jiangxi and Hubei made up only about 9 percent of the party leadership (Zang 1993: 794).

Although local power in the central government and party committee should not be overestimated, local leaders' recruitment into the top leadership is significant. As one observer commented:

> this change [the recruitment of more local leaders into the top leadership] first means that economic reforms have led to the rise of local force, and that rising local force is recognized by the central leadership. Local force must have more say in top decision-making from now onward (Wu Guoguang 1993: 14).

The power of provincial leaders was reflected in the composition of the 11th, 12th and 13th party committees, where they formed the largest bloc.

The Rise of Ethnic Nationalism

Since the 1978 reforms, moderate and tolerant policies have been implemented towards minority peoples in order to recover their confidence in the government (Gladney 1991). According to Gladney:

> By the mid-1980s, it had become clear that those groups identified as official minorities were beginning to receive real benefits from the implementation of several privileges including permission to have more children (except in urban areas. Minorities are generally not bound by the one-child policy), pay fewer taxes, obtain better education for their children, have greater access to public office, speak and learn their native languages, worship and practice their religion (often including practices such as shamanism that are still banned among the Han), and express their cultural differences through the arts and popular culture (1995: 5).

To some extent, economic growth can constrain or alleviate ethnic nationalism by allowing greater economic initiatives to minority nationalities. However, ethnic nationalism can be intensified by changes resulting from economic development.

Economic changes are often accompanied by the development of media, transportation, school enrollment, and urbanization. These factors do not necessarily favor a homogenization of society. On the contrary, they objectively unify styles of living while providing minorities with the means of subjectively recognizing themselves as conscious entities (Dogan & Pelassy 1984: 52)

This is what has happened in China. Reform policies have led to the rise of ethnic consciousness and thus the emergence of ethnic nationalism as exemplified in Tibet. In 1980 two top leaders, Hu Yaobang and Wan Li, made a highly publicized personal visit to Tibet and announced a six-point program for Tibetans. The major measures of this program provided for increasing the number of Tibetan cadres in local government and withdrawing a substantial number of Chinese officials, dissolving collectives, exempting Tibetans from state taxes and requisitions for a period of time, permitting commerce along the borders, and promoting the native economy. Hu also encouraged a moderate cultural policy that permitted a renaissance of Tibetan tradition, designed to spark greater tolerance for Chinese rule and greater political stability. Nevertheless, these policies did not lead to expected consequences, but rebellions and riots (Karmel 1995–96).

The central government's moderate policies also resulted in a strong reaction from other major minority areas such as Xinjiang and Inner

Mongolia. In these areas, the nationalities constantly expressed their dissatisfaction. In Xinjiang, minority groups claimed that the Chinese were exploiting them by taking away their resources and giving them to the rest of the country. Various riots and rebellions occurred. In Inner Mongolia, it was reported that some grassroots organizations, aimed at independence, were crushed by the regional government in 1991. Given the fact that these minority nationalities inhabit China's border areas with neighbouring countries, ethnic nationalism is frequently influenced by forces out of China's control. With the collapse of the Soviet Union, the newly independent status of the Central Asian states has allowed separatist groups in Xinjiang to locate some sources of support, leading to over 30 reported bombing incidents in Xinjiang in 1994. These were claimed by groups militating for an "Independent East Turkestan" (Gladney 1995; Wang 1998).

The economic reforms have generated many problems that have significant consequences for ethnic groups. The central government's policies further deepened "uneven development" between the Han majority and minority nationalities. Many local officials argued that a typical colonial economy has been developed in terms of minority–majority relations because minority groups sell their raw materials at a cheaper price and then have to pay a higher price for their consumer goods (Hu Angang 1994: 90). Ethnic groups feel "relatively deprived" and they have become politically restless in certain circumstances. In some areas, ethnic groups demand favorable policies from the central government in order to improve their economic situation. In other areas, as noted above, people express their dissatisfaction through rebellions and riots. The rise of ethnic nationalism without doubt has posed a serious threat to China as a multinational State.

Political Disconnection Between the State and Society

Throughout modern Chinese history, one major difficulty facing state-making movements has been the issue of establishing a relationship between the State and society. Popular sovereignty was a major theme of China's modern nationalism, even though it never became dominant. Many political elites as well as intellectuals saw that a strong State had to be based on people. The lack of institutional connections between the State and people could only weaken state power. Even though post-Mao reforms have introduced changes into the relations between the state and society, the disconjunction between the two still continues.

The post-Mao Chinese leadership's reform strategy has been regarded as "economic reform without political reform" (Shirk 1993). The regime gives economic growth the highest priority rather than political reform in terms of democratization. Deep commitment to a strong State made the reform leadership conclude that political liberalization should be subordinated to economic growth. The State has to constrain civil society or spontaneous social forces as long as they endanger political stability. Meanwhile, the State has to use various administrative mechanisms to promote economic development, making it difficult to succeed in bridging the gap between itself and society.

Like many of his predecessors, Deng Xiaoping emphasized the importance of popular sovereignty or democracy in building a strong China after he came to power. Following a visit to the United States in 1978, Deng noted that intellectuals and students there had the freedom to engage in various social and political activities, which in turn created favorable circumstances for democracy. Deng thereby implied that the Party–State's control over social groups, especially intellectuals, needed to be loosened (Chen Yizi 1990: 10). In early years of reform, many top Chinese leaders expressed their support for democracy. Deng even argued that "without democracy, there will be no socialism and socialist modernization" (Deng Xiaoping 1983b: 154). Encouraged by such an idea, many autonomous social groups and associations were established. For these groups, the official four modernizations of industry, agriculture, the military, and science and technology were not enough for China to build a strong State. A fifth modernization – democracy – was imperative. This collective identity finally led to the "Democracy Wall Movement" of 1978–79 (Nathan 1985).

Again, after Hu Yaobang and Zhao Ziyang were assigned great responsibilities in initiating and handling China's overall reforms, they attempted to narrow the gap between the State and society. Substantial academic and cultural freedom was encouraged by the new reformist leadership. Hu and Zhao realized that in order to make decisions scientifically, certain forms of policy debate were necessary. With regard to such decisions, the reformist leadership also aimed to establish its legitimacy among social forces. When the conservative faction, a group of senior leaders and Party ideologues such as Chen Yun, Hu Qiaomu, and Deng Liqun, initiated the campaign against "Spiritual Pollution" between 1983 and 1984, and then the Anti-Bourgeois Liberalization Campaign in 1985, the reformist leaders attempted to limit its scale within the Party.

Without doubt, all these efforts were favorable for the development of non-government organizations or civil associations. However, the regime became intolerant when social groups attempted to influence national political agendas. In many aspects, Deng's reform shows similarities to the political programs of Chiang Kai-shek, Yuan Shikai, the empress Dowager Cixi, and the Self-Strengthening Movement, who proposed a series of reforms to strengthen China in the late Qing dynasty. All these leaders shared "a profound commitment to order and stability and abiding aversion not only to uncontrolled change resulting from mobilization from below in the social arena, but also to pluralism in the political realm, in the sense of constitutionally safeguarded opposition and dissent" (Cohen 1988: 533). China's political elites, especially Sun Yat-sen, believed that, as a late-developing country, if China wanted to catch up with the advanced countries, it had to create a strong State that could play an important role in promoting modernization. For Deng, an overriding aim of reform was to strengthen the State. Strand observed that:

> Deng Xiaoping's political reforms have focused mainly on the manner in which policy is made and executed within the state apparatus. In other words, political reform has been practically synonymous with administrative reform. Reform of participation in the sense of broadened or expanded involvement by citizens in policy-making and implementation has been strictly limited (1989: 1).

If political participation is needed, it has to be administered and licensed by the State. This was one major reason for the regime's crackdown of the 1989 pro-democracy movement, as Deng Xiaoping argued then that China was no longer be able to bear more political and social chaos (Fan Shen 1992).

The Perceptions of the Crisis of State Power and the Rise of Statism

The rise of statism in the 1990s is not only a response to enormous unexpected consequences generated by widespread decentralization in the 1980s, but also a result of the strong State complex among various social groups. This complex often leads the new nationalists to mis-perceive or exaggerate the crisis of state power in an attempt to justify their call for strengthening central power. No doubt, the reform of the 1980s aimed to build a strong State. This is true for both reformist leaders and the proponents of democracy. An important question facing both the State and society was how the Chinese State could become stronger. While reformist leaders gave the highest priority to economic development, many social groups, especially Chinese intellectuals, argued that only democracy could make a strong State. From this perspective, statism was a consensus among different social groups. But for the proponents of the new nationalism in the 1990s, the issue is no longer whether a strong State must be based on popular sovereignty. They argued that a strong State is imperative if China wants to remain integrated. Economic growth and democracy can strengthen the State, but if they challenge or endanger state power, they have to be subordinated to it.

Statism in the 1990s finds many outlets among social and political groups, especially those based in Beijing and Shanghai. In the context of nationalism, two arguments form the notion of statism; both concern how a strong State can be created through centralization.

First, the proponents of statism argue that the survival of a strong State is a prerequisite to the survival of the Chinese nation. During the 1980s many Chinese argued that an authoritarian State was a major barrier to Chinese economic liberalization and political democratization; that political reforms were necessary in order to decentralize state power. However, according to the proponents of statism, this perception was proven "wrong" by changes in China's international circumstances. The break-up of the Soviet Union and Czechoslovakia, and the civil war in Yugoslavia all revealed that the weakening of state power could lead to the collapse of the nation–state; that the collapse of the authoritarian or totalitarian states would not necessarily lead to the transition from dictatorship to democracy, and from a command economy to a free market. Both political democratization and economic liberalization have to take place within the framework of the nation–state. An absence of such an institutional framework would only lead to chaos.

As discussed above, economic decentralization resulted in enormous undesired consequences in China. Indeed, as early as the late 1980s, many Chinese and government officials began to see the negative impact of economic reform. During the debate of neo-authoritarianism, many proponents presented arguments for the role of the national government in maintaining China as a nation–state because they perceived that economic decentralization was leading to political and economic disintegration, and eventually the disintegration of the nation–state. Wang Huning (1988: 35–6), one major proponent of neo-authoritarianism in the late 1980s and who was summoned to Beijing as an advisor to Jiang Zemin in the early 1990s, in Shanghai argued that decentralization would result in political disintegration between the center and localities:

> With decentralization, plus many measures of redistributing fiscal power [between the central and local governments], the sense of local interests is increasingly stronger than that of national interests . . . With the improvement of democratic institutions, local residents will vote for local officials who can satisfy their demands . . . Local leaders must consider local interests first if they want to be elected . . . Coordination among localities is constrained. If further decentralization occurs, localities will become important political and economic entities (1988: 35–6).

Many leading Chinese intellectuals believe that national disintegration has come into being, that economic decentralization not only has become a major barrier for central authorities to implement their policies and for central power to reach grassroots societies, but also it has resulted in the rise of "dukedoms" (*zhuhou*). "Dukedom" refers to a situation under which the regional nobility arrogated power to themselves as central power waned.

Two well-known Chinese economists Shen Liren and Dai Yuanchen wrote:

> Economic circles describe the result of economic decentralization during the economic reform as a new economic phenomenon – "an economy of dukedoms". That means, 30 provinces are big dukes, 300 prefectures and cities are middle dukes, and 2000 counties are small dukes. Those dukes have their own domains and political regimes, and seek to develop independently (1992: 12).

During Mao's time, Chinese reformers such as Chen Yun advocated Yugoslavia-like decentralization. By contrast, the proponents of statism now argue that if decentralization goes further, China will follow Yugoslavia; that is, break-up. This argument gained popularity through an extensive debate of "state capacity" in the early 1990s. In 1993, two scholars, Wang Shaoguang (a Cornell University-trained political scientist) and Hu Angang (a member of the National Conditions Research Group at the Chinese Academy of Sciences in Beijing), published a report about the danger of weakening central power symbolized by the decline of its ability to amass revenue. The two authors argued that China's state capacity or state power had been seriously weakened as a result of Deng Xiaoping's economic decentralization. As the central government's "extractive capacity" fell, other aspects of state power would inevitably fall. If this situation continues, the break-up of China as a nation–state is not impossible. Ethnic conflict played an important role in national disintegration in the Soviet Union and Yugoslavia, but according to Wang and Hu, the break-up of Yugoslavia cannot be blamed on ethnic hatred, but rather on the fiscal weakness of the State. By arguing that, they provided a theoretical legitimacy for recentralization measures by the central government. Wang Shaoguang (1991) warned that "the weakening of state capacity in China should not be read as a good sign. Rather than bringing about Swedenization, as most of us have hoped, it may, at best, lead to the creation of a stable but weak democracy, or Indianization. At the worst, the collapse of the central authority may even lead to a disintegration of the nation, or economic Africanization, plus political Lebanonization". Indeed, "while an over-centralized system may result in huge efficiency losses, an overly decentralized system is very likely to end up with the dissolution of the state *per se*" (Wang Shaoguang 1995: 37).

Huang Yasheng (1996) provided a different picture in terms of central control over localities. Huang argued that even with radical decentralization, the central government is still capable of bringing local officials into line through a variety of bureaucratic means.

However, Wang and Hu's argument is similar to that raised earlier by Chen Yuan, Vice-Governor of the Central Bank. Chen Yuan believed that economic decentralization would lead to the division of China as a nation–state. In 1991 he wrote:

> If we consider the relationship between economy and politics, the necessity of recentralization will be more obvious. China is such a huge country, and its economic development is very uneven. Nothing can be done without a centralized central government. If we allow the current decentralized situation to continue, the economy will break down. Then, we will encounter a split and divided politics. The central government requires enough power to guarantee economic development, political stability, and national unification. Except for that, we have no choice.

In the 1990s the fear that China as a nation–state could be endangered by economic decentralization becomes popular not only in the intellectual circles but also among government officials of different levels. Wang and Hu's report soon drew much attention from high authorities. Chinese economic czar, then Vice-Premier Zhu Rongji warned that "once the central government becomes poor, China will be divided" (Hu Angang 1996: 2). Local officials, especially those in minority areas, are afraid that the weakening of central power will result in national disintegration. Many argued that if the central government is not able to promote economic development in poor and minority areas, conflicts between nationalities and socio-political instability will follow. Therefore, to strengthen the State through recentralization is the key for both China's continuous economic growth and its survival as a nation–state (Hu Angang 1994: 88–90).

This fear of national disintegration was reinforced further by the impact of rapid decentralization on the People's Liberation Army (PLA). The PLA has been the most important national institution in the People's Republic and played an important role in maintaining regime stability. It saved the regime in the 1960s, when the country was in chaos due to the Cultural Revolution, and Mao Zedong used the PLA to maintain stability and save the regime from a bitter political struggle. And in 1989 Deng Xiaoping asked the PLA to crack down on the pro-democracy movement and restore an authoritarian political order for the regime.

Military modernization has been one of China's four modernizations. Since the end of the 1970s, the Party–State has made enormous efforts in modernizing the PLA as a modern national institution.[5] Many new developments within the PLA such as geographical reorganization, professionalism, and the establishment of the Rapid Reaction Force and the acquisition of tactical nuclear weapons tend to strengthen national integration (Lin 1994). However, many Chinese began to doubt whether the PLA could continue to play an integrating force (Wu & Zheng 1995: 117–35).

According to Wang Shaoguang, the decline of central fiscal power resulted in a crisis of national defense. The national government could not afford to finance the country's armed forces and had to allow the military to engage in economic activities to compensate the insufficient living expenses of the PLA. The PLA had become one of the few armies in the world that traded in all areas of the business world. This had resulted in low morale. The military that is engaged in economic activities cannot take on the responsibility of protecting the nation and the people, and it also might rely on its monopoly of violence to intervene in economy and politics (Wang Shaoguang 1995).

Without doubt, the military's economic involvement was very damaging to the PLA as a military organization and had posed a danger to its combat capability, professional ethic, internal cohesion, and subordination to the central leadership (Yang et al. 1994; Joffe 1994, 1995; Dreyer 1994; Goodman 1994; Mcmillen 1994). More importantly, through deep economic involvement the PLA had succumbed to regionalism. In many places, especially in coastal areas, the military's economic welfare was related closely to local economic development. The relationship between local military forces and local governments became interdependent. Local military forces often helped local government officials engage in illegal economic activities. The interdependence between the two tended to reinforce localism (Wu & Zheng 1995: Chapter 8).

How can central power be strengthened? Traditionally, organization and ideology were two major means for the Chinese Communist Party to consolidate its power. The proponents of statism argued for recentralization, but this does not mean that they want to return to this tradition. Instead, they emphasize institutional initiatives by learning from the West since they have realized that the Chinese State as an organization is not modern enough. Accordingly, traditional means will not enable China to become more centralized, and thus modern methods have to be introduced or initiated. While political centralization is still too sensitive for public discussion, the proponents of statism have overwhelmingly focused on fiscal centralization and other related economic means.

Indeed, according to the proponents of statism, whether China can remain unified and integrated as a multinational State depends, to a large extent, on whether the national government is able to recentralize its fiscal power (Chen Yuan 1991). These proponents attributed China's enormous problems to fiscal decentralization and the weakening of central fiscal capacity. According to Wang Shaoguang, China's fiscal system is overdecentralized and the central government is no longer able to exercise its power. The weakening of central power has led to a series of economic, social, and political crises. Due to the shortfall of central revenue, the national government cannot adequately provide national public goods and services. A deficient infrastructure has become a bottleneck in China's economic development. Moreover, China now encounters a dangerous ecological and environmental crisis. Rapid development has been achieved at the expense of ecological balance and the environment. Acid rain not only threatens China's economy and ecology, and the health of its population, but also causes dissatisfaction and protests from neighboring countries such as Japan and Korea. Since the fund for pollution control has not increased, China's environment is degenerating rapidly.

In the early 1990s the national government began to design a federal type of fiscal system in order to recentralize its fiscal power. The system was implemented nationwide in 1994. But because of strong local resistance, the central government had to revise its initial plans in order to satisfy local demands. Consequently, the national government was not able to achieve what it had expected. Central revenue continued to decline. In 1993, central revenue was about 5 percent of total GDP. The figure increased to 6.5 percent in 1994, and then declined again, to 5.7 percent in 1995. Central expenditure declined from 5.7 percent of total GDP in 1993 to 3.5 percent in 1995, lower than that of Yugoslavia before its collapse, which was 5.3 percent (Hu Angang 1996: 2). Hu Angang thus warned that the national government is on the verge of bankruptcy (1996: 2). The central government is no longer able to support the army, police and government officials. Furthermore, both local residents and government officials seem to have lost confidence in the central government. These developments will endanger not only China's further development, but also pose a great threat to the survival of China's multinational State. From whatever perspective, fiscal recentralization should be the most important political agenda for the central government.

How can central fiscal power be recentralized? According to the proponents of statism, besides continuously improving and strengthening the federal type of fiscal system, it is of vital importance to implement other aspects of institutional reform in order to centralize central fiscal power. Institutionally, fiscal power needs to be recentralized not only in terms of local–central relations, but also in terms of the State Council's relations with its various bureaucracies. Although fiscal power has been relatively centralized owing to the implementation of the new fiscal system, it is still very diffused at the national level. Various bureaucracies and departments, not the State Council, share great fiscal power. So, fiscal recentralization first means to centralize power to the State Council, especially in the hands of the Premier. Intense competition among bureaucracies for fiscal power often gives rise to departmentalism, and fiscal centralization becomes impossible (Hu Angang 1996: 5).

Furthermore, changes also need to be introduced into sub-provincial levels. Since the reform began, many cities have been promoted to such levels (*jihua danlie shi*). These cities should normally be directed and their economic activities planned not by the provincial government, but the national government. In effect they are controlled neither by the national government nor the provincial government, but independent kingdoms with great fiscal power. If these independent "kingdoms" cannot be eliminated, it will hard for the national government to become powerful in terms of fiscal capacity (Hu Angang 1996: 8).

Conclusion

In the first half of the 20th century, a major theme facing Chinese nationalists was to transform the Chinese State from a traditional dynastic State to a modern one. Many Chinese intellectuals then realized that the Chinese cultural State, or dynastic State was different from modern European nation–states. The dynastic State was very centralized, but the national government was too weak to develop the country, let alone to defend the nation. If China wanted to be strong, the first step was not democratization and welfare, but to build a modern State. How could a modern State be created if China did not have one? Many believed that it was necessary to establish a dictatorship first because only a highly centralized dictatorship would be able to build a strong State. This argument was popular even among liberal intellectuals. It was this statism that became the foundation of the Nationalist Party regime in the 1930s (Lei Yi 1995).

The proponents of the new nationalism in the 1990s still encounter the same theme as their predecessors in the 1930s; that is, how a State can be transformed. The Communist Party established a highly centralized State. Yet, it was not capable of transforming a country that has great diversities. Economic decentralization became the regime's only alternative to modernize China, but resulted in the weakening of central power. For the new nationalists, a strong State is crucial for China to survive as a unified nation–state. The survival of the State is the first priority regardless of whether it is a dictatorship or anything else. Only with this precondition is it worthwhile to discuss the transition of the State.

This is the logic for the proponents of statism in the 1990s who believe in giving the highest priority to building a strong national State through recentralization. However, this does not mean that China needs to return to a totalitarian regime. For the advocates of statism, it is possible to build a strong State by using *modern* methods. Without the introduction of such methods, it will be hard to modernize the Chinese regime and to transform the State from a traditional totalitarian type to a centralized modern one.

However, once power is decentralized, it will be hard to regain. The national government's various institutional initiatives have met strong resistance from local governments of different levels and central bureaucracies as well. Facing strong resistance, the national government often had to modify its initial plans to accommodate local and departmental interests. Thus, even though the proponents of statism see the importance of a strong State, whether their dream can be realized is still a problem.

CHAPTER 3

Identity Crisis, the "New Left"
and Anti-Westernization

Nationalism is about *us against them*. It is important to sharpen the sentiments about *we-ness versus they-ness* when nationalism is constructed. In other words, the creation of in-group identities can lead to the devaluation of out-groups (Mercer 1995). From this perspective, nationalism often contains elements of anti-foreignism. This is why nationalism as a form of national identity is so important for a country's international behavior.

The idea of national identity was a major discovery by Chinese intellectuals at the turn of the century. After China was defeated in the Sino–Japanese War of 1894–95, Chinese intellectuals realized how important a strong national identity was for constructing a strong Chinese nation–state. They began to introduce such modern terms as *minzu* (literally, "clan people") from the writings of the Japanese Meiji period. Nevertheless, the international environment in which the Chinese national identity (including that in the People's Republic) formed, by and large, determined that it connoted a strong sentiment of anti-foreignism (Liao 1984). It is argued that the current nationalism still has this characteristic (Barme 1996).

It was found that Chinese nationalism was formed in the context of anti-imperialism (Schrecker 1971), and that the term *Zhonghua minzu* (Chinese people or nation) was closely associated with nationalistic writings warning of the clear and present danger of national annihilation under external invasion (Dittmer & Kim 1993: 252). Wang Gungwu succinctly summarized the impact of external factors on the formation and development of Chinese nationalism:

> The idea of nationalism itself was an inspiration for all Chinese who felt humiliated by the successive military defeats that led to unequal status for

Chinese everywhere, to extraterritorial privileges for foreign residents within China, and to the increasing dominance of foreign enterprises on Chinese soil. Nationalism was tied to anti-imperialism and anti-colonialism as the key to almost all of the political struggles of the 20th century. Both Chiang Kai-shek and Mao Tze-tung were propelled into politics by their nationalistic urges. And, despite the romantic internationalist slogans after the communist victory in 1949, national pride and interest remained in the forefront of the goals of the People's Republic (1995: 47–8).

The question is how the rise of anti-West sentiments in the post-Mao reform era should be understood. Is this a continuation of the old anti-foreignism? If the answer is "yes", then China's new nationalism can be regarded as aggressive and aiming to form a new type of hatred towards foreign powers, especially those that have "unfriendly" foreign policies towards China. Or is it a new form of anti-West sentiment? If it is, then the question becomes: is it because China wants to flex its growing muscles due to its rapid modernization as Germany and Japan did before the Second World War? Or is it a response to the "Chinese problems" resulting from rapid modernization?

Although China's new nationalism still tends to be characterized by anti-foreignism, the former can no longer be equated with the latter. The new nationalism of the Deng era, as opposed to that of Mao's era, is a reaction to China's international environment. But more importantly, it is also a reaction to China's domestic modernization in the 1980s. According to the new nationalists, China's modernization in the 1980s was westernization-oriented and resulted in various forms of crises such as the decline of national identity, the decline in traditional values and in Marxist or Maoist faith. If westernization continues, China's modernization will go nowhere. If China wants to be a strong State, its modernization has to be based on nationalism. Nevertheless, unlike traditional anti-foreignism, the new nationalism aims to build a new national identity for China by emphasizing the "Chineseness" of China's post-Mao reform and differentiating between Chinese civilization and Western civilization.

This popular nationalism of anti-westernization has presented itself in two forms. The first form is what Chinese commentators called the "New Left",[1] and the second is anti-Western civilization. The New Left criticized various versions of China's reform theories that they believed were influenced by the Western debate on economic reform. Central to the anti-Western argument is the notion of why and how a Confucianism-based Chinese nationalism could be established in order to resist the intrusion of Western influences.

Chapter 3 will discuss the arguments of China's cultural nationalism in terms of Chinese criticisms of Western civilization. This chapter attempts to show how Chinese nationalists construct a Chinese discourse concerning China's modernization. It is divided into two parts. The first gives a brief discussion on the "New Left"; that is, the nationalists' perceptions of China's westernization in the 1980s. The rest of the chapter examines various arguments of the New Left of anti-westernization, and how the proponents construct a local (Chinese) discourse of China's reform and development.

Search for New National Identities: Modernization vs "Westernization"

It is hard to say whether China's modernization in the post-Mao era was characterized by westernization. As a matter of fact, "westernization" has been a cultural construct created by Chinese nationalists in their efforts to search for a new cultural and national identity. The crises of cultural and national identity resulted from Maoist radicalism and were a reaction to Deng's reforms. The proponents of the new nationalism, however, regarded China's modernization in the 1980s as westernization-oriented. According to them, it was this modernization that led to various forms of national identity crises. Thus, if a new national identity is to be established, anti-westernization seems an effective way.

Without doubt, China's reform aimed to alleviate an identity crisis resulting from Mao's radical development policies. But the reforms created new identity crises while resolving old ones. When the Maoist leftist policy led the country to chaos people began to doubt Maoism. When post-Mao reform promoted rapid economic growth, while rejecting political democracy, a new crisis occurred and people began to doubt the Deng model of reform.

While there remains a controversy over whether China was experiencing a serious economic crisis after the death of Mao Zedong, there is no doubt that an identity crisis occurred. In Chinese commentary, there was a "belief crisis" (*xinnian weiji*). This crisis existed among different social groups, especially among young people, who were described by the media as "a contemplative generation", "a wounded generation", "a wasted generation", "a lost generation", and "a fallen generation".

In the late 1970s, a debate about the "meaning of life" was carried out in the journal *China Youth*, the organ of the Communist Youth League. In 1978, the journal published a letter from a young female writer, entitled, "Ah, The Path of Life: How Is It That It Gets Narrower and Narrower!" The writer believed that everyone is selfish. "When it comes to a crucial moment, everyone acts according to his selfish instinct . . . Everyone, on the surface, acts altruistically but, deep down, seeks to benefit himself" (Pan Xiao 1981). This letter led to an enormous response from the young generation. Within twenty-five days, the editors of *China Youth* received 18 603 letters in response (*RMRB,* June 10, 1980: 1). Furthermore, many young people had begun to doubt socialism. One student wrote,

> So far as our generation is concerned, we have been taught, ever since primary school, how good our socialist motherland is and how bitter and hard the lives of the people are in capitalist nations. [Now] we see from television the skyscrapers, modern facilities, parks and cultural centers in foreign countries. Compared with that, our country is backward. How can you expect us to turn our thinking around to continue believing in the superiority of socialism (*RMRB*, May 18, 1979: 3; cited in Liu 1986: 332)?

The peasantry also expressed their dissatisfaction with the government. In Guangdong, peasants told reporters, "In the past thirty years (1949–78), the CCP did mainly two things to us. First, it did not allow us to have enough food, and second, it did not allow us to speak out" (Chen Yizi 1990: 18). Many old peasants believed that they had a better life in the 1920s and 1930s under the rule of "warlordism". In Shandong, peasants also believed that their lives in the 1930s and the 1940s were better than in Mao's time. Indeed, such perception became prevalent in rural China (Chen Yizi 1990).

Furthermore, the identity crisis also had an impact on the attitude of local government officials towards the central State. Many of them, especially in coastal provinces such as Guangdong, Fujian, Zhejiang, Jiangsu and Shandong, became doubtful about the State's development goals and its capability of achieving these goals, and thus called for greater decentralization and autonomy in their dealings concerning local economic affairs. For example, in April 1979, Xi Zhongxun (cited in Yan Changjiang 1993: 21), the first Party Secretary of Guangdong claimed that "many comrades in Guangdong have discussed the problems in the province. We feel that our advantages cannot be used. Where will our (local) economy go? . . . We have to ask for power from the central government. We need the central government to liberalize its policies to let us export more so that we can earn more foreign exchange for the central government". Xi even argued that "if Guangdong was an independent country, we would develop ourselves in a few years. Under the existing system, we cannot go forward. Thus we ask the central government to give us power" (1993: 21). While it is clear that Xi did not mean that he wanted Guangdong to be independent from the rest of the country, he certainly cast doubt on a highly centralized regime and asked for a power-sharing arrangement with the central government.

The crisis at the end of the 1970s stemmed from a loss of faith in the existing ideology, the regime's development goals, and the political legitimacy of leadership. Without doubt, Deng Xiaoping's modernization program aimed to make China stronger and richer, but its immediate goal was to alleviate the tension between the State and society. Throughout the 1980s, China was successful in achieving rapid economic growth and improving people's living standards.

According to *The Economist* (1992: 3–4), real GNP grew by an average of almost 9 percent a year. Between 1978 and 1991 grain consumption on average went up by 20 percent. In 1981 every 100 urban households averaged less than one color television set among them; ten years later it was seventy. In 1981 there were six washing machines per 100 city households, in 1991 there were more than eighty.

With the implementation of reform and opening policy, Western ideas rapidly flowed into China. Chinese leaders were also influenced by the Western experience when they made decisions on reforming China's economic system.[2] As one Chinese scholar pointed out, "at the beginning of China's reform and opening policy, Western social and institutional structures and its value system had an important impact on our line of thinking about China's future" (Sun Liping 1996a: 17). In the mid-1980s, most Chinese showed their strong preference over Western cultures. According to a nationwide survey in 1987, 75 percent of Chinese were tolerant of the inflow of Western ideas, and 80 percent of Chinese Communist Party members showed a similar attitude (Min Qi 1989: 128).

Unfortunately, these developments did not lead to the improvement in State–society relations. Instead, they resulted in a new crisis of national and cultural identity, especially among young people and in the intellectual circles. Throughout the 1980s, individuals' loyalty to the socialist State was weakened seriously as shown in a national survey. When interviewees were asked, "Do you think that 'love the socialist motherland' is the most important basic morality?" the distribution of those who answered "yes" was only 28 percent among people aged 18–30 years of age; 38 percent among those aged 31–45 years of age; 46 percent for persons 46–60 years of age; and 52 percent for those 61 and over. At the same time, the Party–State faced serious criticism from individuals. Only 30 percent believed that the Party's performance was satisfactory, and 62 percent thought otherwise (Zheng 1994a: 243, 245).

Furthermore, rapid economic development led to intellectuals calling for China to be democratized. Initially, the regime attempted to make efforts to reform China's political system. But it was almost impossible for it to carry out any radical political reform. For major leaders, the aim of China's political reform was to strengthen rather than weaken the Party. Democratization would necessarily weaken the Party's power. When the regime was unable to satisfy the people's demands, the intellectuals lost faith in the Party–State.[3] For many, the reasons for China's difficulty in democratization lay in its traditional culture. Thus, in order to democratize China, it was the first priority for the intellectuals to criticize this. The theme of the TV series "River Elegy", whose authors ascribed China's authoritarian regime and its backwardness to Chinese traditional culture and believed that only through wholesale westernization and the introduction of advanced Western cultures could China develop itself, highlighted this (Su Xiaokang et al. 1988).[4]

The nationalistic voices began to appear in the late 1980s as shown in their call for neo-authoritarianism; that is, the recentralization of power, which had been weakened by the reformist leadership. It was not until after the Tiananmen Incident, especially after Jiang Zemin took over power in 1992, that nationalism became a dominant discourse among Chinese intellectuals. The major causes were the enormous changes that occurred to China's internal and external environments, and Chinese perceptions about China's interplay with the outside world. Four issues have been identified.

First, the end of the Cold War led to the rise of nationalism in the former Soviet Union and Eastern Europe, and nationalism replaced the old communist ideology in these countries. The collapse of European communism had an important impact on Chinese nationalists. According to Sun Liping, what happened in the Soviet Union and Eastern Europe led Chinese intellectuals to believe that social disintegration is a more serious threat to China than social stagnation and conservatism, that political and social chaos will follow the decline of the traditional ideology and the worsening of social crises. Therefore, it is necessary to promote nationalism as a new ideology (1996a: 17).[5]

Second, with China's integration into the international system, especially with the continuous inflow of information about the Western world, Chinese intellectuals began to reflect on Western culture. In earlier stages of the reform, the West was regarded as a model for China to follow. But now many Chinese felt that the West did not want China to be strong and the inflow of Western influences had a "negative" impact on Chinese traditional culture.

In other words, the rise of nationalism resulted from the Chinese's reflections on Western cultures and ideas. In the early days of the reform and open-door policy, the Chinese regarded the West as a symbol of a comfortable material life, a spirit of initiative, rational institutional arrangements, and advanced technologies. Nevertheless, a decade later, when China was increasingly integrated into the world system, the Chinese found that the West was not perfect, that it was far from their original high expectations, and that its practices were unfair towards

China's national interests. When the West imposed high conditions on China's entry into the World Trade Organization, the Chinese began to doubt the West's motives towards the rise of China (Sun 1996a: 17).

Third, China has been increasingly integrated into the international system, but it is unwilling to identify with the existing international rules and norms. This leads to China's exposure to various forms of international pressure. Nationalism becomes a spiritual force for China to resist foreign influences. As one Guangdong author pointed out:

> Although China had already abandoned the use of its ideology as its guideline and turned to a pragmatic approach, it was unwilling to adapt itself to the Western value system. China thus encountered external ideological pressure. Facing all internal and external changes, nationalism became a "candidate" for replacing the old ideology (Chen Shaoming 1996: 74).

Fourth, with the transition from a planned economy to a market one, China's economic power was strengthened and the old ideology was no longer effective to manage a changing society. The regime thus needed a new spiritual instrument to guide the reform and to control the enormous changes resulting from the reform policy. Without doubt, nationalism became such a spiritual instrument (Chen Shaoming 1996: 74).

The Rise of the New Left

For the proponents of the new nationalism, China's modernization can be simply understood as a process of westernization. It is westernization that has led to the crises of national and cultural identity. If this process continues, China as a nation–State would be in crisis. The task of the new nationalism is to resist China's westernization. Nevertheless, resisting westernization does not mean that China's modernization would be slowed down. Instead, it means that the revival of the national and cultural identity on which the Chinese nation–state is based should be given the highest priority. Any reforms, if they pose a threat to the nation–state, will be undesirable. Furthermore, if new cultural and national identities are to be established, China's reform needs to be interpreted not in terms of westernization, but in terms of "Chineseization". In other words, China's modernization and westernization should be de-linked, while the "Chineseness" of China's reform process needs to be enhanced. In this sense, the new nationalism is also regarded as a movement of the New Left to be distinguished from the old Left which is mainly referred to Party ideologues associated with either Maoism or Marxism.

A major theme of modern Chinese nationalism was to make China strong and rich. Since China's modernization was parallel to the incursion of Western powers and the inflow of Western ideas, Chinese political and intellectual elites encountered a dilemma between modernization and westernization. For radical reformists, in order to save the nation, China had to become more cosmopolitan. They believed that to cope with the crisis of national survival, the Chinese should not overemphasize defending Chinese tradition or Chineseness, but appeal to a universal value system that was prevalent in the West. China should and could adapt itself to such a value system by reforming its existing system. On the other hand, fundamentalists and conservatists opposed China's westernization and argued that China needed to appeal to its traditional value system in order to revive the people's national confidence.

This theme also appeared in the early stages of China's post-Mao reform. While radical reformists proposed that China needed to follow various Western models of economic and political systems, conservatives or leftists appealed to China's traditional value system, even to Maoist ideology. It is hard to put the New Left in this dichotomy, however. Unlike the old Left, the New Left does not oppose the reform and opening policy, even though it opposes introducing any radical reforms to the political and economic system. The old Left put much emphasis on strengthening the Communist Party. In contrast, the New Left argued that the Party should put China's national interest above itself and reform itself so that it would not become a major barrier to China's modernization. What concerned new leftists was how China could avoid the loss of national and cultural identities in its process of rapid modernization.

Against Institutional Fetishism

As mentioned above, in the 1980s many Chinese intellectuals called for the introduction of Western-style institutions such as market systems and political democracy to reform Chinese traditional systems such as the planned economy and authoritarian polity. Although top leaders were reluctant to follow any Western model to reform the political system, they were willing to liberalize it to some extent. Deng Xiaoping emphasized that political reform was necessary to facilitate economic development. Under the auspices of Deng Xiaoping, Hu Yaobang and Zhao Ziyang regarded political reform as one of the major agendas of China's reform (Goldman 1994; Harding 1987; Hamrin 1990). Economically, major leaders believed that it was the goal of China's reform to withdraw the State from economic affairs and to establish a market system.

It is worthwhile to note that Chinese intellectuals began to reflect on this "westernization"-oriented reform strategy before the collapse of the communist states in Europe as shown in the debate of so-called neo-authoritarianism in the late 1980s (Liu Jun & Li Lin 1989; Petracca & Mong Xiong 1990). The collapse of communism in Europe convinced

Chinese intellectuals that "westernization"-oriented reforms would lead to both economic and political chaos. This was one major reason why Chinese intellectuals turned to conservatism after the 1989 pro-democracy movement. The New Left thus came into being, opposing any forms of radical reform and justifying the importance of a centralized State in guiding China's development.

One major school of the New Left is anti-institutionalism or new conservatism. While the reformists in the 1980s believed that China could use Western-style institutions to replace the old Chinese system, anti-institutionalists argued that it would be impossible for any such institutions to take root in China. If China's modernization aimed to introduce Western-style institutions, political and economic disasters would follow. *Gaige* (reform) only means to reform existing political and economic systems, rather than to replace them with any forms of alien institutions. Xiao Gongqin, one major proponent of the New Left, argued that China's modernization should not be westernization-oriented; that is, a political democracy and a free market economy. Democracy and the free market system function well in the West because there are various supporting socioeconomic and cultural factors there. Neither democracy nor a free market system will work in China because there are no such supporting factors (1996b: E2).

According to Xiao, it was understandable that Chinese political elites looked to Western systems because the traditional planned economy could not be reformed by the forces that were generated by this system. The problem was that when radical reformists wanted to follow Western models, they ignored that these models developed in the context of Western socioeconomic and cultural circumstances, and would not survive in the Chinese context. The crisis of national identity would occur when the linkage between the old and new systems could not be established (Xiao Gongqin 1989).

The proponents of the New Left argued that the difficulties that China's reform encountered in the 1980s resulted from radical reform policies or policy proposals raised by those who idealized Western systems. In the late 1980s, reformist leaders proposed to promote economic reforms by a method called *jiage chuangguan* (overnight price liberalization). Under the influence of Western liberal economists, some reformist leaders even believed in the "shock therapy" that had been used in the Soviet Union and eastern Europe. Meanwhile, many Chinese intellectuals, backed by major reformist leaders, argued that China needed to introduce Western democracy in order to provide an institutional foundation for a free market system. It was these westernization-oriented reform measures that eventually led to China's political chaos as exemplified by the 1989 Tiananmen demonstration (The Department of Thought and Theory of China's Youth 1991).

The collapse of east European communism and consequent economic chaos pointed to the significance of a centralized regime. Once the regime collapsed, the nation–state would be in crisis, and both economic and political reforms would have to take place within it. The survival of the nation–state was the most important prerequisite of China's reform. According to the proponents of the New Left, a "wrong" perception that became prevalent among Chinese intellectuals and political leaders in the 1980s was that economic and political reforms needed to go together. Therefore, with the introduction of a free market system, the regime had to be liberalized and democratized. In effect, a centralized regime is necessary for China's economic reforms. Without such a regime, it will be hard to cope with various unexpected consequences resulting from rapid economic growth. If the regime is weakened, economic modernization will lead to a crisis of national survival rather than political democracy.

According to Xiao Gongqin, to promote economic modernization, an authoritarian regime is needed. He goes on to state:

> The growth of modernization would have to rely on a powerful state; that is, through the effective government of a "strong man", to maintain the order and peaceful stability of the entire society's development, and create a steadier social environment for the prosperity and growth of the economy and the growth and maturity of the middle class (Xiao Gongqin & Zhu Wei 1989. For the translation see Rosen & Zou 1990–91).

In the West, a free market system or an "invisible hand" developed without state interference. But in China, the visible hand; that is, the State, has to play an important role in creating an "invisible hand" or a market system.

Therefore, instead of political democratization, China's political reform has to aim to establish a neo-authoritarian regime (Petracca & Mong Xiong 1990). According to Xiao (Xiao & Zhu 1989), the new authoritarianism would borrow from the traditional value system as a pillar for galvanizing the social spirit. Because the traditional value system had a powerful implication of a trend towards autocracy, and implied the concentration of power and a personality cult, it would be possible for a new authoritarian regime to emphasize coerciveness and pursue the personification of power, and thus lead to the abuse of power and political corruption. In this sense the new authoritarianism could become a major barrier to political democratization. The new authoritarianism, however, Xiao argued, could provide a solid political framework in which China's economic modernization could take place. This was because, first, the new authoritarian rulers must possess certain predilections for modernization. Since the political legitimacy of the new authoritarian regime was derived from nationalism and its appeal to modernization, it would "emphasize economic development, popular education, and other such goals to obtain the support of the vast majority of the population". Second, the new authoritarian regime would rely on a vast and yet efficient bureaucracy, and a powerful military to establish a top-to-bottom system of government. And, third, the new authoritarian regime would use such powerful administrative forces to adopt an open-door policy towards Western capitalism and advanced technologies to promote the development of domestic capitalism (Xiao & Zhu 1989; see Rosen & Zou 1990–91). This argument was shared widely among Chinese intellectuals.

"Localizing" Chinese Discourse of Economic Reforms

A second school of the New Left attempted to localize theories on China's economic reform. In other words, a new paradigm of China's reform needed to be established both theoretically and practically (Cui Zhiyuan 1995). In the 1980s, China's reformist leaders did not have a clear line of thinking on economic reform, but they were willing to listen to, if not to follow, the suggestions by Western economists and international economic organizations as exemplified by Milton Friedman, who visited China in 1980 and 1988, and who became influential among Chinese intellectuals and many reformist leaders (see Friedman 1991). In 1988 Zhao Ziyang, General Secretary of the Chinese Communist Party, discussed China's economic reform with Friedman. Later, with Zhao's fall, Friedman was also criticized.

For the proponents of the New Left, China's reform succeeded because China was successful in resisting Western influence and because Chinese reformist leaders were unsuccessful in carrying out westernization-oriented economic reform. How should China's economic reform be explained? This is a major task for the New Left in their efforts of anti-westernization.

Radical reform measures such as "shock therapy" and "big bang" led to economic and political chaos in the Soviet Union and eastern Europe. The failure of economic reform in these former communist countries was due to the fact that their political leaders attempted to use Western neo-classical economic principles to reform their economies. Nevertheless, it is impossible for the Western models to function in an alien system. On the other hand, China's economic reform did not follow any model. The existing Western economic paradigm is not able to explain China's success. According to Cui Zhiyuan:

> The old paradigm refers to the neo-classical economic theory. Central to this paradigm is "getting prices right" and "getting property rights right". The planners of economic reform in Eastern Europe were the faithful disciples of this paradigm. Various radical price reforms such as "shock therapy" and "big bang"

were the natural results of the neo-classical economic policies. On the contrary, China did not follow "one step" price reform . . . According to the neo-classical economists, China's reform has followed a wrong direction (1995: 2).

How could China's success be explained? Cui Zhiyuan, one of the major spokesmen of the New Left, asked.

According to the New Left, it is necessary not to think about Chinese practice in terms of Western social theories if a Chinese theory of economic reform is to be established. As Gan Yang, another proponent of the New Left, pointed out:

> What we call social sciences today is Western social sciences which were developed in the process of *Western* "social changes". [Social sciences] not only represented Westerners' self-understanding of social changes, but were also results of the interaction among various complex social and political factors in the process of social change [in the West] (1994: 50–7).

The New Left thus called for the localization (*bentuhua*) of China's reform theory. They have made efforts to theorize China's socioeconomic and political development, but it is hard to say that the New Left has developed a systematic theory. Some directions can be identified as follows.

"Catch-up" vs "Comparative Advantage"

In the 1980s many Chinese leaders believed that China needed to be integrated into the world economic system in order to be modernized. This was a major theme of China's open-door policy. Senior leaders such as Deng Xiaoping, Hu Yaobang and Zhao Ziyang recognized that one major cause of China's backwardness since 1949 was that Mao's leadership isolated China from the international economic system. According to Chen Yizi, an advisor to the government in the 1980s, by the end of the 1970s, various social and political groups increasingly realized that if China wanted to modernize it needed an open-door policy, and to use foreign technologies and capital; otherwise, China would be dismissed from its global citizenship (1990: 12).

With the development of the open-door policy, China's economy was increasingly integrated into the world system. As of the late 1980s, many Chinese intellectuals argued that if China could not be integrated with the outside world, it would lose its global citizenship (*qiu ji*). They began to theorize about China's export-oriented economic performance and provided various alternatives for China's further integration into the world economy. Liberal social scientists proposed different theories; for example, the theory of international circulation (Wang Jian & Pei Xiaolin 1988), the theory of comparative advantage (Zhou Xiaochuan

1990), the theory of the international division of labor (Yuan Wenqi 1990), and the theory of overseas investment (Wei Dakuang & Dao Liang 1988). Central to these theories was that only after China was integrated into the world economy could it use its comparative advantage and compete with other countries in the world market. Without doubt, Zhao Ziyang's proposal of the export-oriented development strategy was influenced by these theories (*RMRB* 1988).

After cracking down on the pro-democracy movement in 1989, the leadership in Beijing became more conservative and economic reform lost momentum. In 1992 Deng made a high profile trip to Guangdong, aiming to initiate a new wave of reform from below. After this southern tour, China accelerated its international economic development. Chinese intellectuals also made great efforts to theorize new economic phenomena. Among others, Lin Yifu, a Chicago University-trained economist, and his collaborators, proposed a theory of comparative advantage (Lin Yifu, Cai Fang & Li Zhou 1994a, 1994b, 1995 & 1996). According to them, the failure of China's economic system during Mao's time was due to the implementation of the strategy of catching-up and surpassing. Central to this strategy was a highly centralized planned system in which government at different levels entered economic activities. This system led to China's backwardness characterized by a low level of living standards, irrational economic and social structure, low economic efficiency and an irrational welfare system, and inflation and the shortage of central revenue. On the other hand, the success of the economic reform in the Deng era was due to the implementation of the strategy of comparative advantages. Domestically, economic decentralization led to a far greater autonomy for local government officials and individuals to promote local development. Internationally, the open-door policy made it possible for China to make use of its advantage to compete with other countries in the international market system.

Why does China still encounter enormous difficulties in its economic reform? According to Lin, this is because the government's economic policies are still under the influence of the catching-up and surpassing strategy. If China wants to deepen its economic reform, the strategy of comparative advantage needs to be implemented further. The implementation of this strategy requires that the government establish various supporting institutions for a free market system (Lin, Cai & Li 1994a).

The comparative advantage strategy led to an enormous reaction from the New Left and other proponents of anti-westernization. There are three major arguments against the theory of comparative advantage.

First, the adoption of the comparative advantage strategy implies that China's economy needs to be fully integrated into the world system. Even though China can benefit from economic integration with other countries, it's political independence and national security will be undermined. Shi Zhong, also a major proponent of the New Left, argued that the danger of the comparative advantage strategy is that "it will allow other countries to determine China's fate; that is, China allows its economic future and national security to be dependent on other countries' strategic interests" (1995: 11). The integration of China's economy into the international system will have an impact on its domestic development and national security. Shi Zhong went on to state that:

> national security is not only about military, but also about a country's economy . . . Modern industrial technologies can be divided into two types: the first type can be used to control others and make others dependent; and the second type functions the opposite, i.e. leading the country to be controlled and to be dependent on others (1995: 12).

Modern Chinese history shows that dependence eventually leads to the loss of national sovereignty. Before the Opium War, China's economy was still more developed than most Western countries in many aspects. The West then became more advanced in certain key industrial technologies, such as naval and military, that eventually led to China's defeat. Therefore, for China as a late-developing country, the most urgent task for its political elite is to enforce a catching-up strategy to guarantee national survival.

Mao Zedong's catching-up and surpassing strategy brought about various economic crises. It was this strategy that made China more independent from the outside. Without a relatively independent economic system, China's sovereignty in the world system would be in doubt. Although China has achieved rapid economic growth since the 1978 reform, it is still backward in many key industrial technologies. Thus, according to Shi Zhong:

> If China cannot implement a catching-up and surpassing strategy, it will again be defeated by new technological revolutions, and its fate will be even more miserable than in the last century . . . To build an independent and self-sufficient industrial system should still be China's long-term development goal (1995: 11).

Due to China's overall backwardness, the strategy of comparative advantage cannot protect national industries from intensive international competition. A solid industrial base will enable China to become a great power in the international community. But the strategy of comparative advantage will weaken China's existing national industries. As a matter of fact, many Chinese have begun to believe that foreign capital is destroying China's national industries and weakening China's national power (Wu Yuetao & Zhang Haitao 1997).

Though a strategy of comparative advantage means following international rules and norms established by the developed West, it will not necessarily be in China's national interests. He Xin, a major spokesperson of the new conservatism, argued that the current leadership should learn from Mao Zedong's international policies; that China should make its own rules in the international community, and China's national interests should be given the highest priority (He Xin 1993).

Furthermore, whether China can utilize its comparative advantages depends on specific international environments. During the 1950s and 1960s, China's catching-up and surpassing strategy was partially attributed to a hostile international environment. Many proponents of the New Left argued that with the collapse of the Soviet Union, China's international environment would worsen. China would not be allowed to use its comparative advantages to compete with the advanced West. In fact, the West, especially the United States, has begun to feel "threatened" by China's comparative advantages. It is understandable why the West started to impose a technological embargo and economic sanctions to contain China's development (Shi Zhong 1995).

Second, the proponents of the New Left favor China's independence and oppose an export-led development strategy. During Mao's time, China implemented an import-substitution strategy. This strategy was gradually replaced by an export-led strategy in the 1980s when the open-door policy was promoted. As mentioned above, major reformist leaders, especially Zhao Ziyang, regarded the export-led strategy as the key to China's development. This development strategy was re-emphasized after Deng Xiaoping's tour in southern China in 1992 in which he strongly proposed that China should follow the east Asian model to deepen its economic reform. However, it seems to the advocates of the New Left that this strategy will have a negative impact on China's long-term development and national survival. One author saw an export-led economy as a dependent one and argued that "the most serious weakness of an export-led model is that a country's economy will be greatly influenced by international environments. Because of a great dependence on the Western (and the US) economies, a minor change in the international market will cause great fluctuation in the domestic market" (Liu Liqun 1994: 44). This has been confirmed by other east Asian economies. The existing international economic system was established and key economic factors, such as tariffs, credit and loans, investment, exchange rates, and so on, are controlled by the West. Almost all countries with an export-led strategy have to rely heavily on developed countries. Once their economic interests are in conflict with those of the West, they are subjected to sanctions imposed by the West (Liu Liqun 1994).

For the supporters of the New Left, though China has benefited from the export-led strategy in the past decade, whether it will be successful in the long run is still doubtful. If China does not subordinate its sovereignty to the West, the West will not allow China's export-led developments. According to Liu Liqun (1995: 44–5), in the Development Research Center under the State Council, the success of the export-led development in east Asia so far depends on three preconditions. The first is the political–military alliance with the West, who was willing to form such an alliance with east Asian countries during the Cold War because it accorded with Western countries' national interests. Second, local economic activities have to depend on those in the West. Third, local socioeconomic systems have to be reformed in order to fit those in the West. Apparently, if China continues to follow such a development strategy, its fate will be controlled by more advanced countries.

Moreover, it is difficult for China's export-led strategy to succeed. This is because, first, the above-stated conditions that led to the success of this strategy in other east Asian countries no longer exist. Second, the West is unwilling to see China's rise. Previously, the West was interested in seeing China's integration into the international economic system. With China's economy becoming more competitive, it is increasingly in conflict with the economic interests, even political and military, of the West, which has become determined not to let China develop into a superpower and will use all possible means to contain its development.

An export-led development strategy is thus in conflict with China's national interest. Once China's economy is integrated into the international system, more options will be available for the West to contain China. It is imperative therefore to rethink China's development strategy. Even if an export-led strategy has benefited China, "China's national interests will, in the long run, be better served by independence rather than dependence" (Liu Liqun 1994: 46).

Third, the proponents of comparative advantage argue that China's economic reform can be strengthened if the government is able to abandon the old system of a planned economy and allow market and economic factors to play a major role in economic activities. On the contrary, according to the New Left, for China's economic reform to succeed, the government plan needs to be strengthened rather than weakened. But this does not mean that the New Left proposes to go back to the old planned system. Instead, its proponents stress that a new type of economic plan is necessary for China's economic growth.

The advocates of comparative advantage and those of the New Left interpreted the east Asian economic miracle very differently. While the former attributed it to a comparative advantage strategy, the latter argued that the east Asian economic success was due to "plan rationality" by government intervention through planning in these countries (see Cheng Ming 1994; Xiao Gongqin 1994a; Yin Baoyun 1994; Jiang Shixue 1995). China's catching-up and surpassing development strategy during

Mao's time was also an example of plan rationality. One author argued that the failure of Chinese socialism was not because of its planned economic system, but because of its political system. Even during the Cultural Revolution, China's economic performance was still impressive. While the old planned system rejected a market economy, a new government plan must aim at establishing such a system. A market system will not come into being automatically. Russia's attempt to let "market rationality" function led to economic chaos. If China wants to avoid such a misfortune, government "plan rationality" needs to be introduced and strengthened (Hu Wei 1995: 75–6).

New Collectivism or Neo-Maoism

The proponents of the New Left aim to, first, show why China's reform cannot be guided by any Western models, and, second, provide an alternative explanation of China's rapid economic growth; that is, a Chinese discourse of economic reform. Neo-classical economists, including those who advocate a comparative advantage strategy mentioned above, attributed China's success to its Western-styled economic reform, and argued that further economic growth depends on whether China can achieve privatization and establish a free market system. By contrast, the proponents of the New Left argued that it was Maoist legacies rather than westernization-oriented economic reform that promoted China's rapid economic growth. While neo-classical economists are interested in how a dynamism of economic development can be created, the New Left sees the impact of rapid economic growth on social and political stability and national integration, and emphasizes social justice.

When Mao Zedong was in power, egalitarianism guided China's economic development. For Mao, social justice was more important than economic efficiency. But Deng Xiaoping's reform reversed this guideline. For Deng, economic dynamism only lies in individual and local initiatives. Without doubt, the policy of "let some people and regions get rich first" led to wide disparities between different social groups and between different regions. It seems to the advocators of the New Left that if this situation continues, China will not be able to avoid Russia's misfortune; that is, socioeconomic and political disintegration. For the New Left, Russia's disaster was a natural consequence of its "institutional fetishism"; that is, its leaders suddenly abandoned its socialist tradition and rapidly introduced Western economic principles to guide its economic reform. So, the New Left attempts to show that not only China's economic dynamism lies in Maoist legacies, but also that China has to follow Maoist legacies in order to avoid Russia's misfortune.

According to the New Left, Maoism's contribution to China's economic growth lies in its collectivism. This is especially true in rural development. In rural areas, growth gained a momentum during Deng Xiaoping's era. But rural growth did not begin with Deng's reform. In many parts of China, especially in coastal provinces, rapid rural development occurred long before Deng's reform, even during the Cultural Revolution. Also important is that even in Deng's era it was within the Maoist collectivist system that rural economic development occurred (Cui Zhiyuan 1994). In other words, Deng Xiaoping's reform only provided a political condition for Maoist collectivism to promote rural growth. Deng's reform did not lead to a Western style of individualism in rural areas. Indeed, there was no chance for Western individualism to influence China's rural development. Privatization did not spread in rural China. Even after more than a decade of reform, private ownership did not become dominant. Main economic players are not individuals, but local communities. For the New Left, all these factors contributed to rapid rural growth (Wang Ying 1994).

Since the reform began in the late 1970s, the Maoist ideology has more often become a target for social and intellectual criticism. But for the New Left the Maoist ideology cannot be simply rejected. In many areas, it is still capable of providing individuals, especially lower level government officials, with "spiritual" motivation to lead local development. In many localities, it is Maoist "good" leadership that provides economic dynamism. The proponents of the New Left believe without any doubt that Maoist ideology plays an important role in strengthening rural collectivism, reducing income disparities among farmers and thus maintaining rural stability. So, a precondition of China's further rural reform is not to abandon Maoist ideology. Instead, it needs to be developed in accordance with China's practice.[6]

The proponents of the New Left also argued that China should not follow any Western model if it wanted to further its industrial reform and improve the economic performance for enterprises in the state sector and the collectives as well. Institutional fetishism (westernization) led Russia and many former east European socialist countries to political and economic chaos. If China wants to avoid such a misfortune, it should not appeal to any Western ideas to guide its reform. Private ownership, privatization and other capitalistic means are the products of the Western civilization and are unlikely to bring good results for China. Neither "getting the price right", nor "getting property rights right" could promote rapid development and social stability (Cui Zhiyuan 1995). What is important for China is that it needs to have its own non-Western theories to guide its development. What has been wrong in China's industrial reform is that many leaders are too westernized in their economic decision-making. Various Maoist legacies were thus neglected. According to Cui Zhiyuan, China needs to look for Mao Zedong rather than the West for its industrial management and reform because Mao's industrial practice provided one, if not *the*, most important modern forms of industrial management; that is, management through workers' participation (Cui Zhiyuan 1996). Cui also argued that Maoist industrial management as shown in the Constitution of the Anshan Steel Company, for example, is equivalent to post-Fordism in the West (see Lee 1987).

Political and Economic Democracy

The New Left also called for China's democratization. While many Chinese emphasize various forms of freedom, political rights, and a multi-party system, the proponents of the New Left argued that democratization is not westernization; that is, following the Western models of democracy. Instead, they believe that Maoist practice contained various important elements of democracy. If these elements can be developed properly, they will contribute to China's democratization (Cui Zhiyuan 1996b).

According to Cui Zhiyuan, there are two forms of democracy: procedural and deliberative. The former regards democracy as a political method in which political elites "buy" votes from people and thus emphasizes formal elections. The latter emphasizes the substance of democracy and various forms of popular participation. It seems to the proponents of the New Left that because too much attention has been paid to procedural democracy, deliberative democracy is neglected among Chinese intellectuals. It was Mao Zedong who during his long political career, especially during the Cultural Revolution, developed a theory of deliberative democracy that was not systematic. Indeed, for the New Left, Mao's deliberative democracy was the origin of rapid economic growth in the post-Mao era. China's deliberative democracy was mainly characterized by decentralization. During Mao's time, both China's economic and political system were highly decentralized. This made it possible for local communities and individuals to participate in the process of development. China's township and village enterprises developed as a direct result of Maoist development strategy; that is, by mobilizing mass participation into the production process. Similarly, the Constitution of the Anshan Steel Mill also provided workers an institutional framework to participate in the production process (Cui Zhiyuan 1994). Deliberate democracy also made it possible for local governments at different levels to play an important role in China's economic affairs. It is this Maoist legacy that makes it possible for China to avoid the misfortune of the former Soviet Union. For the New Left, deliberative or economic democracy rather than private property rights and individualism should become China's guideline for its further economic reform (Cui Zhiyuan 1996b: 70–1).

Politically, the proponents of the New Left also proposed to draw lessons from the Maoist theory of "mass democracy", which was developed during the Cultural Revolution. In fact, to re-evaluate the Cultural

Revolution has been a major theme of the New Left. According to the New Left, Mao Zedong's main purpose of "mass democracy" was not political struggle, but a real democracy that was based on mass participation. Maoist mass democracy was a reflection of the crisis of Western modernity and aimed to provide an alternative to the Western democracy. What Mao wanted was to create opportunities for people to be a part of Chinese political and economic development. But for various reasons, Mao's mass democracy was "distorted" during the Cultural Revolution. The New Left thus called for a transformation and institutionalization of Mao's mass democracy. China needs democratization, but this does not mean that China should follow any single Western model for political democracy. The institutionalization of Mao's mass democracy will make it possible for China to restructure Western modernity based on its own political practice, to establish a democracy with Chinese characteristics, and thus to become a strong nation–state in world affairs (Cui Zhiyuan 1996b: 67–2).

Conclusion

The New Left is a reaction to the decline of national identity even though it strongly opposes China's westernization. This complicates China's new nationalism. The anti-westernization movement does not mean that the New Left wants to revive China's traditional anti-foreignism. Traditional anti-foreignism movements, especially those organized by political elites, aimed to resist the intrusion of foreign forces and the inflow of foreign ideas by whatever means. The New Left abandoned this type of anti-foreignism and believed that because of China's integration with the world system, foreign ideas would flow into the country. For the New Left, the question is not whether China should be integrated into the international system in spite of various negative consequences, but whether China's domestic development should be guided by westernization-oriented government policies.

As a result, in order to prevent westernization from becoming a dominant discourse of China's modernization, a new discourse based on China's own development experience needs to be developed. It was serious external threats that led to the rise of traditional anti-foreignism. But the rise of the New Left is largely due to China's rapid domestic development and its consequences. For the New Left, since China is growing strong in the world system, it is time to develop a new Chinese discourse against the Western discourse of development. By doing so, China's national identity can be enhanced, and its influence in the world system can be strengthened.

While many people see the linkages between reform and development, the proponents of the New Left perceive "westernization-oriented" reform as a major cause of the decline of national identity. Through the spread of reform and the open-door policy, traditional Marxist–Maoist ideology becomes increasingly ineffective. While many Chinese tend to favor Western ideologies such as the free market and democracy, the Chinese Communist Party strongly opposes such alien ideas. It thus becomes difficult to develop a new ideology. The New Left saw the importance of ideology in maintaining national integration and strengthening the people's national identity. For the New Left, a new ideology that opposes westernization and emphasizes China's own experience could become acceptable for government, and promote and strengthen national identity among government officials and different social groups as well.

Deng Xiaoping called for a liberation of people's "thoughts" and used all possible means, whether Western or oriental, to develop China's economy. For the New Left, a second round of liberation of "thoughts" is imperative in order to deepen China's reform. This needs to emphasize the *Chineseness* of China's reform to avoid the misfortune resulting from the westernization that occurred in the former Soviet Union. Existing Western theories, which focus on the free market, non-government intervention, privatization, and free trade, are not able to explain the process and dynamism of China's rapid economic growth (for example, Friedman 1991). Nor can they provide any guidelines for China's future reform and modernization. Western free market theories can deepen our understanding of China's traditional planned system but they cannot guide China's reform. When theories are not able to explain practice, it is time to reflect and challenge existing theories. In order to explain the success and failure of China's reform, it is necessary to establish new theories of reform based on China's reform experience (He Gaochao & Luo Jinyi 1995: viii). Without doubt, to influence the process of China's reform is a major goal of the New Left.

Practically, the New Left addresses many important issues in China's rapid development in the post-Mao era. As it appeals to anti-westernization and nationalism, the New Left also tends to be welcomed among many government officials, especially the old ideologues. Given the fact that the post-Mao reform has led to enormous negative consequences such as disparities among different regions and social groups, economic corruption, and money worship, the New Left does appeal to various social groups. The New Left, however, is unlikely to have a major impact on China's future development. After two decades of economic reform, liberalism has become one of the most important forces in China's political and economic arenas. The formation of a new middle-class and the establishment of capitalism as an official economic ideology and other drastic structural changes make it less likely for the New Left to change China's existing path of development.

CHAPTER 4

The Clash of Civilizations?
Confucian vs Christian Civilizations

Chapter 3 highlighted an important aspect of the new nationalism in China; that is, how Chinese intellectuals attempt to reconstruct a new national identity and nationalism by initiating an anti-westernization movement and localizing theories of China's post-Mao reform. This chapter emphasizes the civilizational or cultural aspect of this new nationalism. The revival of Chinese civilization has been one of the major themes in the discourse of the new nationalism. The chapter is divided into four sections. The first provides a brief examination of the role of ethnicity (Chineseness) in the development of modern Chinese nationalism. The second analyzes the meanings of so-called Confucian-nationalism. The third examines how a theory of "Chinese superiority" is constructed from the differences between civilizations; that is, Chinese civilization versus Western civilization. The fourth attempts to highlight the direction of the transition of China's nationalism.

Ethnicity and Nationalism in Modern China

Centuries ago, French philosopher Jean-Jacques Rousseau pointed out the importance of culturalism in national survival when he developed a constitution for Corsica. Rousseau said, "We have already done our best to level the site of the future nation: let us now try to sketch upon this site a plan of the building to be erected. The first principle to be followed is the principle of national character; if it did not [have it], we should have to start by giving it one" (Rousseau 1953: 293). According to Rousseau, a nation defined as a cultural or spiritual community could survive even foreign rule. Similarly, German thinker Johann Gottfried Herder argued that before Germany could emerge as a strong nation–state, it was necessary to formulate the idea of cultural nationalism. Without a strong cultural base, the nation–state would not go anywhere. Under Herder's inspiration, German nationalist thinkers such as Friedrich List understood nationalism in the context of "uneven exchange" or "uneven development" among nations. According to them, nationalism could be created and strengthened by putting an emphasis on the uniqueness of a given nation (Szporluk 1988).

How could cultural nationalism be created? This was also the theme of Chinese nationalists throughout its modern history. Ever since China began to come into contact with the West, Chinese political elites and intellectuals had learnt how to use ethnicity, or broadly speaking, differences among civilizations, to cultivate Chinese cultural nationalism (see Dikotter 1992). It was found that nationalism was built in Chinese traditional culturalism, and ethnicity has been a major discourse of China's modern nationalism.[1] As a matter of fact, the birth and development of modern Chinese nationalism was parallel to the inflow of foreign ideas and the incursion of foreign forces. The international environment determined that modern Chinese nationalists had to give the highest priority to the survival of the Chinese civilization.

As mentioned before, civilizational survival or national survival was the theme of Chinese nationalism proposed by Sun Yat-sen. For Sun, the chief concern of nationalism was to ensure the survival of the Chinese nation that had suffered from foreign aggression. It was an effective way to build a Chinese nationalism by elaborating the differences between the Han majority and other minority peoples within China, and between the Chinese as a whole and foreign races. If China was to be a strong and cohesive nation, Chinese nationalism had to be Han-centered. Furthermore, if China as a whole was to be strong and cohesive in the world, Chinese nationalism must be based on traditional Chinese culture and civilization.

Without racial solidarity within the Han majority, Chinese nationalism would go nowhere. Sun elaborated his rationale for a Han-centered nationalism:

> The Chinese race totals four hundred million people; of mingled races there are only a few million Mongolians, a million or so Manchus, a few million Tibetans, and over a million Mohammedan Turks . . . for the most part, the Chinese people are of the Han or Chinese race with common blood, common language, common religion, and common customs – a single, pure race (1927: 11–12; cited in Dikotter 1992: 124).

It seemed to Sun that only after a Han-centered nationalism was established, could real racial harmony among the Manchus, Mongols, Huis, and Tibetans be achieved, and a Chinese nation be built. Because the Qing Dynasty only caused China's humiliation by foreign forces and was not able to save China as a nation, the Manchurian rule had to be overthrown. Nevertheless, according to Sun (Chou 1996: 70), overthrowing the Qing Dynasty was a "negative" objective of nationalism. But only after this "negative" objective had been achieved could its "positive" objective; that is, to save the Chinese nation, be realized.

Furthermore, Sun also emphasized the differences between the Chinese and other major races:

> Mankind is divided first into the five main races – white, black, red, yellow, brown. Dividing further, we have many sub-races, such as the Asiatic races – Mongolian, Malay, Japanese, Manchurian and Chinese . . . Chinese belong to the yellow race because they come from the blood stock of the yellow race. The blood of ancestors is transmitted by heredity . . . making blood kinship a powerful force (1927: 8–9; cited in Dikotter 1992: 125).

Sun's nationalism became the doctrine of the Nationalist Party and played an important role in mobilizing people to oppose foreign imperialism and unifying China. Without doubt, the Chinese Communist Party (CCP) also utilized nationalism effectively in the struggle for a Chinese nation–state of its own version. Like the Nationalist Party, the CCP also used Chinese nationalism against imperialism. In its early revolutionary period, the CCP accepted the Marxist–Leninist doctrine of nationalism. Marxists regarded nationalism either as a disguised economic interest, or in Marxist terms as a form of "false consciousness" that misled people and stopped them from pursuing their "true" interests. Thus, on the matter of revolution, the CCP followed closely the Communist International, which in turn followed the Soviet Communist Party. Similarly, on the matter of the relations between the Han majority and minorities within China, the CCP emphasized liberal nationalism or national liberation. The Communiqué of the Second National Congress of the CCP (1922) declared that federalism would be used to unify China and integrate different ethnic groups into a Chinese nation. In 1931, the CCP again emphasized that minority peoples had the right to decide whether they wanted independence (Diao Dingtian 1989: 371).[2] However, the CCP did not go so far as true Marxists believed. Mao Zedong soon found that the Marxist paradigm of nationalism was in serious conflict with the goal of the Chinese nationalists; that is, a strong and independent nation–state. In the 1960s it was this nationalistic goal that led Mao to break China's close ties with the Soviet Union concerning the process of revolution. Nationalism became a major means for the CCP to mobilize the Chinese population to resist Japanese invasion and to compete for power with the Nationalist Party (Johnson 1962). Mao accepted and used the Marxist concept of class struggle in dealing with domestic affairs. But it is easy to exaggerate Mao's internationalist inclination in international affairs. In effect, like Chiang Kai-shek, Mao was a true nationalist in seeking China's status in international arenas. Regarding the relations between the Han majority and the other minorities, after the CCP took over power and established the People's Republic of China, Mao changed his early point of view that minority peoples had the right for independence. Instead, Mao used an institutionally vague concept – national autonomy – to deal with minority problems. Hence, ethnic nationalism was narrowly regarded. Meanwhile, the CCP used "patriotism" to replace the concept of nationalism, and emphasized that the Chinese nation as a whole should become the identity of all peoples within China.

Decades later, the concept of nationalism came back to China and became a major discourse of Chinese intellectuals in their design of a strong China. The previous chapter examined the background of this new nationalism and argued that the new nationalism can be regarded as a reaction to the post-Mao modernization movement. The remaining sections in this chapter aim to highlight how civilizational differences play an important role in the effort of China's intellectuals to construct a new nationalism.

Confucian Nationalism?

It is worth noting that the new nationalism has been constructed not in the context of the relations between the Han majority and minorities, but in the context of the relations between Chinese civilization and other civilizations. But this does not mean that ethnic nationalism is not important in China. In fact, rapid modernization has given rise to this phenomenon, especially in Tibet and Xinjiang (see Chapter 2).

The danger of raising the issue of "ethnic nationalism" is quite obvious. Nationalism could become a powerful weapon for ethnic groups to struggle for their own nationhood.

According to Wang Gungwu, although nationalism could inspire zealous support, it also could arouse open hostility and fear among different ethnic groups within the country. Therefore, if nation-building cannot be handled properly, problems of identity would lead to serious division among the ethnic groups within artificial boundaries that were not defined by national criteria (1995: 48).

Chinese intellectuals and government officials call China a "unified multinational" State. But many realize that China is still an empire or a dynastic State, not a modern one like those in Europe. Thus an emphasis on ethnic nationalism will lead to what happened in the former Soviet Union. Because there are different nationalities within China, the government and Chinese intellectuals believe that if ethnic nationalism is to be avoided and separatist movements are to be kept under control, the issue of ethnic nationalism should not be brought to any public debate. Indeed, ethnic nationalism in China is called "narrow nationalism" (*xia'ai minzu zhuyi*).

Therefore, what China needs is another type of nationalism. According to Xiao Gongqin, a major spokesman of cultural nationalism, this so-called "another type of nationalism" refers to "advocating that people ought to have concepts and feelings of loyalty for their own nation or nationality. The concept embodies the idea that people should serve national interests. Nationalism proposes that all people should hold their respective nations in the greatest sense of faithfulness and loyalty" (Xiao Gongqin 1994b: 150).[3] Nevertheless, by "nation or nationality," Xiao is referring to China as a multinational State. So, this new type of nationalism is similar to, but far beyond what has been called "patriotism" (*aiguo zhuyi*).

A major issue facing Chinese intellectuals is how the political legitimacy of government can be established. According to Chinese new nationalists, a new foundation of political legitimacy is essential to a strong government, which, in turn, is a prerequisite of national survival in a competitive world. As discussed in Chapter 3, with the decline of the CCP's traditional ideology, the crisis of national identity has become very severe, especially among Chinese intellectuals. At the societal level, with rapid modernization and economic growth, money worship has come to people's daily lives. When people get rich, they find that they are living in a moral vacuum.

The proponents of the new nationalism contended that this situation had become a major barrier to China's further development, and recreating an "ism" to fill the moral vacuum became the most important issue facing China. According to Kang Xiaoguang (1994), a spiritual vacuum is China's most serious current problem. In a country with a population of more than one billion, if people only follow what they feel, the country would be ruined. An example is the Soviet Union. It was once a great empire, but it disintegrated within days. The collapse of the Soviet Union was due to the decline of its ideology. Once all ideas, values, and "isms" embedded in that ideology could no longer provide the political legitimacy for the government, the collapse of the empire became inevitable. As a multinational State, China's survival depends on whether a new "ism" or ideology can be created.

Then, what is this "ism"? To some people, this "ism" should be democracy or liberalism. But more and more Chinese intellectuals believe that this "ism" should be Chinese traditional value-based nationalism, since nationalism, as the most powerful and intense ideology, can become the richest doctrine in emotional strength. Whenever a nation encounters external pressures or crises, its political leadership can evoke and stir up the people's nationalistic sentiments by appealing to the country's glorious history, culture, courage, and wisdom to gain a consensual acknowledgment of the legitimacy of their authority. According to Xiao Gongqin:

> it is nationalism that can produce the most direct and voluntaristic attraction and appeal to people . . . [A]s long as there remain different nations and nationalities within the human race, relative to the time-effectiveness of other ideologies, nationalism is the ideology that has the most long-lasting effect on history. From the perspective of the state and politics, the emotions and reasoned concepts stemming from nationalism compose an extremely valuable, "natural" political resource (1994b: 16).

What should the context of this nationalism be? How can it be created? Apparently, to create nationalism does not mean a simple return to traditional Confucianism or modern Chinese nationalism. According to Xiao, a new nationalism could be created by a creative explanation and combination of various existing elements, such as traditional Confucianism, the CCP's socialism, patriotism, traditional anti-foreign revolutionary ideology, China's international environment, and so on (Xiao Gongqin 1993).

Confucianism should be the foundation of the new nationalism (Xiao Gongqin 1994a, 1996b; Pi Mingyong 1996; Zhao Jun 1996). Nevertheless, it needs to be re-interpreted. Confucianism is in conflict with modern nationalism from various perspectives as Liang Qichao (one of proponents of modern Chinese nationalism) noted, and needs to be transformed in order to support nationalism (Pi Mingyong 1996). Xiao Gongqin argues that there have been two major schools of modern Confucian-nationalism; that is, Confucian fundamentalism and pragmatic nationalism. Confucian fundamentalism is a conservative, irrational and emotional force. Facing the incursion of foreign forces, it simply proposes to defend China by "going back" to tradition and resisting foreign forces by anti-foreignism. By contrast, according to the proponents of pragmatic nationalism, only by learning from the advanced West and by reforming China's traditional political and economic systems can China as a nation be saved (Xiao Gongqin 1996a: 59). What China needs today is this pragmatic or mainstream Confucian-nationalism.

Confucianism was China's traditional mainstream cultural form. Whether China will be able to modernize itself and achieve rapid economic growth while maintaining political legitimacy and stability depends on whether this mainstream culture can be carried forward and enhanced. According to Xiao:

> Mainstream culture is the foundation for a consensus among a nation's polit-
> ical elite, intellectual elite, and popular culture. As a nation's mainstream
> cultural values become a component part of a country's core symbols, they
> will have a major significance in the emergence of a coalescing force and
> consensus in that nation (1994b: 17–18).

Confucianism has had a major impact on China's coalescence because it
represents the collective experience of the nation formed through
China's long process of adaptation and response to the challenge of its
natural and social environments.

Apparently, in this context, Chinese nationalism is equivalent to what
Rousseau called "national character" (see the beginning of this chapter). As a matter of fact, Yan Fu, one of the modern Chinese reformers,
also elaborated the importance of "national character" (*guoxing*) in
national survival. One nation's character may differ significantly from
that of another, but all national characters present themselves as specific
cultures and teachings or values. National characters form over long
periods, often thousands of years, of gradual cultural growth, accumula-
tion and sedimentation. As long as a nation's national character survives, then even if the country is subdued by another race, its nation
cannot be destroyed. Yan Fu argued that China's national character
brought together different local territories and other major nationalities
to form today's China, and to face the outside world thanks to the teachings and acculturation of Confucius, which have been accumulating and
developing for several thousand years. As a result, what made China
"China" was its source and origin in the Confucian classics. Yan believed
that in a period of change and reform, and in a period of the intrusion
of foreign influences, Confucianism should be used to settle the minds
of the people and bring the nation together.[4]

Similarly, Xiao argues that what new nationalism needs are the
Confucian institutions, cultural traditions and relics that make up the
collective experience of the Chinese people. Since great changes have
been introduced to Confucianism throughout modern Chinese history,
Confucianism should not be in conflict with modern nationalism.
According to Xiao, this is due to the following two reasons. First,
Confucianism no longer has the characteristic of being "resistant to, or
antagonistic to modernity" (Xiao Gongqin 1994: 25). In modern China,
Confucianism became a fundamental point of support for the rejection
of modern Western civilization and played a negative role in resisting
modernization reforms because it was connected to and wedded to
traditional feudal and autocratic government. It also became the official
ideology. Now, this institutional base no longer exists. Second, the
importance of modern nationalism lies in its capability to bring people

together. This foundation can be performed by Confucianism, which emphasized moral autonomy as well as peace and harmony in terms of social relations. This is what a modern society requires. While individuals need to enjoy their opportunities of making their own choices among multiple possibilities, they also hold obligations and responsibilities to the society they live in (Xiao Gongqin 1994b: 25–6).

More importantly, both China's domestic development and international environment generate or require a Confucian-nationalism or modernizing nationalism. First, at the societal level, with rapid modernization and economic growth, individuals' belief systems have become more secularized. People now tend to identify national interest, which is the core of modern nationalism. Second, with the decline of the official ideology, nationalism can play an important role in national integration and solidarity, and political elites have to turn to nationalism for their political legitimacy. Third, China is facing a worsening international environment. Due to its rapid domestic development, the West has regarded China as a potential rival and has plans of containment. This will lead to a Chinese nationalistic reaction. In modern China, nationalism became powerful when China's survival faced severe external threats. External threats will cause individuals who share a culture, a religion, and a set of customs and history to become aware of the commonality of interests among themselves.

Moreover, history can be used to promote Chinese nationalism. According to Xiao, even though China today does not face direct and severe external threats, nationalism can still be promoted because of the historical experience of China in the past hundred years. "The profound sense of humiliation, including all the setbacks and frustrations that the Chinese have experienced, has planted in the Chinese people a certain complex that is accumulated and settled in the deepest recesses of the Chinese mentality. This complex can be called 'the dream of becoming a strong nation'" (Xiao Gongqin 1994b: 26; 1996a: 60).

· The promotion of Confucianism as the core of China's new nationalism also requires a re-evaluation of political and cultural radicalism and official patriotism. According to many intellectuals, China did not develop a Confucianism-based nationalism partly because of modern radicalism, which, by its nature, is a counter-mainstream cultural nationalism. China's radicals regarded Confucianism as a negative force and as an obstacle to national progress, and thus rejected Confucianism as the core of Chinese culture as exemplified by the New Cultural Movement and the May Fourth Movement initiated by Chinese intellectual elites in the late 1910s. Since the May Fourth Movement, Chinese political and intellectual elites viewed anti-traditionalism and rebellions against the traditions and legacies of their own mainstream culture as the basic means to make China rich and strong. Consequently, China lost its most important resource for the coalescence and cohesiveness of the nation.

From this perspective, the Chinese Communist Party (CCP) was also criticised by the nationalists outside the Party, since the Party once attempted to use Communist ideology to replace Chinese traditional culture. Since it came to power, the CCP – as a revolutionary organization – and its ideology inherited and carried forward elements of this radical anti-traditionalism. For Mao Zedong and many other leaders, Confucianism needed to be eliminated and purged as "the superstructure of feudalism". Furthermore, under the influence of the Soviet Union in the 1950s, nationalism was rejected and negated as a bourgeois ideology. In following the doctrines of Marxism and Leninism, the CCP regarded nationalism as an instrument that the newly emerging bourgeoisie employed as a means to oppose and stand against the regime of feudal aristocracies, and the nation–state as a historical product of the economic development of the early stage of capitalism. Nationalism was thus believed to die with the internationalization and monopolization of capitalism. Since Marxists believed that "the working class did not have a motherland" (Szporluk 1988), the CCP followed the principle of internationalism in dealing with international affairs. In some cases, internationalism was in accordance with nationalism or China's national interests such as the Korean War in the 1950s and the anti-US Vietnam War in the 1960s. But in most cases, internationalism was in serious tension with nationalism, that is, China's involvement in international affairs was not for its national interests.

It was against this background that the CCP has used patriotism as another means for the coalescence and cohesion of Chinese society since the 1950s. Because the CCP regarded nationalism as a bourgeois phenomenon, it did not allow nationalism to become an internal part of its ideology. Instead, patriotism became the pillar of the official ideology. Nevertheless, according to the proponents of the new nationalism, official patriotism does not contain any affirmation of mainstream Confucian values and symbols because it appeals to the marginal cultural elements. According to Xiao:

> [patriotism as an official ideology] was based on the wisdom of the lower echelon of laborers in traditional society, and the courage exemplified by historical resistance and struggles against invading aggressive tribes and races from outside China. It was also fashioned from the so-called "Four Great Inventions" of the Chinese and other ancient scientific and technological accomplishments (1994b: 22).

Without doubt, patriotism based on these non-mainstream cultural elements "could not serve as the core cultural symbols of the nation", and its role would be very limited in producing forces of coalescence and cohesion for the members of society in China (Xiao Gongqin 1994b: 23). Hence, patriotism needs to be re-interpreted if it wants to play an important role in solidifying China as a nation and strengthening the political legitimacy of government.

Socialism can also be an important element of the new nationalism. Socialism has been regarded by both political and intellectual elites as the only means to make China rich and strong. In this context, socialism is a Chinese version of nationalism. Second, socialism, as a part of the official ideology, has dominated China for decades and penetrated into people's daily lives. So, in the context of reform and development, socialism has an irreplaceable role and function to play in maintaining the historical continuity of the political order and upholding the legitimacy of authority.

Socialism can also be integrated into the new nationalism because the CCP has achieved rapid economic growth and social development under its banner. The government's economic performance can be a major source of political legitimacy. As long as the government sticks to developmentalism, its performance-based legitimacy will continue to grow. Unfortunately, according to Xiao Gongqin, developmentalism is:

> unable to provide sufficient control or regulation for goals such as orienting and targeting development and for resolving the specific form to bring about the integration in the relationships among the members of society. It is also unable to deal with the relationships of rights and obligations between the collective and the individual and between the state and society, the distribution of scarce resources, issues of spiritual life and ideals, and so on (1994b: 24).

In other words, the new nationalism should be Confucianism-centered. In order to establish a Confucian-nationalism, it is necessary to re-interpret Confucianism and modern Chinese nationalism. Creating a new nationalism does not mean a return to traditional Confucianism. Furthermore, without considering other elements such as patriotism, socialism, and the government's economic performance, a new nationalism will be impossible. An effective nationalism needs to integrate all these elements while a re-interpreted Confucianism can play an integrating role among these elements.

The Clash of Civilizations?

During the 1980s many Chinese intellectuals regarded westernization as the only means for China to modernize itself. Many intellectuals ascribed China's backwardness to its tradition. However, a dramatic change occurred in the 1990s when Chinese intellectuals attempted to make various efforts to promote Chinese traditional culture and civilization while attacking the West. First, as discussed in the previous chapter, the new nationalism was a reaction to the Western culture worship that became popular among intellectuals in the 1980s and resulted in a popular feeling of national inferiority. Many had lost their affinity for Chinese culture. One proponent of nationalism called such Western culture worship as "self-abandonedness" or "self-abasement" (Shi Zhong 1996: 98).

Second, the new nationalism is also a product of China's success in reform and economic development in the 1990s. Reforms in the Soviet Union and eastern Europe led to the collapse of communist regimes there. China became the only socialist country that was able to reform its planned system and achieve rapid development while maintaining a relatively stable regime. Many people began to argue that China owed its success to its great tradition. There was an air of national pride.

Third, the intellectuals' pride over Chinese civilization also resulted from their reaction to Samuel Huntington's "The Clash of Civilizations?". In his essay, Huntington offered a new paradigm for analyzing an increasingly multi-civilizational world order (1993).[5] Huntington's article was widely circulated among intellectual circles and government officials. It aroused intense debates. Huntington's theme stimulated nationalistic sentiments among Chinese intellectuals. According to Wang Hui in the Chinese Academy of Social Sciences, Huntington's essay has led Chinese intellectuals to believe "that they were alien to Western cultures" (1994: 19).

The impact of Huntington's essay on Chinese intellectuals is multifold. First, Huntington argued that Confucianism is becoming one of the major threats to Western Christian civilization. For many Chinese intellectuals this implies that Westerners now begin to believe that the Confucian civilization is at least equal to the Western civilization. Second, many intellectuals understand "The Clash of Civilizations" in the context of various anti-China theories such as the "China threat" and "containing China". It seems to them that defending the Confucian civilization should be their mission.[6] Third, Huntington argued that Western civilization has so far been a major promoter of democracy, human rights, the free economy, and so on. But many Chinese intellectuals saw a very different picture of the development and spread of Western civilization, and argued that it is not Western civilization but the Confucian civilization that can bring peace and harmony among nations. This leads to an implicit conclusion that the Confucian civilization is superior to the Western one. This section attempts to show

how Chinese intellectuals have constructed the argument of Chinese civilizational superiority. The two major arguments examined are: (1) international conflicts resulting from the expansion of Western civilization, and (2) the Confucian civilization's conduciveness to peace and harmony among nations.

Western Civilization and International Conflicts

Among others, Sheng Hong, an economist in the Chinese Academy of Social Sciences, became very influential among intellectual circles after he published two articles: "What Are Civilizations?" and "How Does Economics Challenge History?" in the two most important forums for the new nationalism, *Zhanlue yu guanli* (Strategy and Management), and *Dong Fang* (The Orient).[7] In these articles, Sheng attempted to develop a theory of the linkages between the expansion of Western civilization and international conflicts on the one hand, and between Confucian civilization and international harmony on the other.

What is a civilization? Sheng argues that any civilization must satisfy the following two assumptions. First, cooperation is better than non-cooperation, and second, costs and benefits are calculated through repeated games among civilizations or game players. Civilization is therefore a means to resolve conflicts among actors. Conflict resolution, in turn, will benefit the actors. The ultimate goal of any civilization is to reach peace and harmony among game-players. Because civilizations were formed at different times and locations and benefited different peoples, conflicts will occur when two civilizations meet. The more advanced a civilization becomes, the harder it will try to use peaceful means for conflict resolution. The question is how the conflicts are to be resolved. If Civilization A wants to use forces to eliminate Civilization B, then A is no longer a civilization because a civilization seeks to resolve conflicts and to achieve peace and harmony.

According to Sheng, modern Western civilization is based on social Darwinism, which has applied the jungle law of nature to human society and reached the conclusion that only the fittest will survive. Thus, as long as Civilization A is able to dominate Civilization B through whatever means, it is more advanced. Social Darwinism, however, is not able to distinguish human beings from animals; that is, animals are not capable of negotiating with each other, and cannot develop any civilization.

The expansion of a social Darwinism-based Western civilization would necessarily lead to conflicts among civilizations. It has been argued that the victory of the West in modern times depended on the rule of market economy, on the extension of free trade; that the West's military victory is a victory of one civilization over another. But Sheng reached a different conclusion from his reading of modern history. He argued that the victory of the Westerners over other civilizations was not achieved by peaceful free trade, but by advanced weapons (1995: 90–1). This is what happened in modern China. According to Sheng, the argument raised by Western mainstream historians that the Opium War occurred because Britain wanted to promote free trade in the world is not true. Sheng argued that the trade deficit between Britain and China led to the War. By initiating the Opium War, Britain attempted to reduce the trade deficit. Until now, many Western scholars are still reluctant to accept this fact because they believe that it is their civilizational mission to promote free trade among nations by whatever means (Sheng 1996b: 50). As long as they believe in their civilizational mission, the Western powers will be able to justify and legitimate their aggressive foreign behavior. Today, this is shown not only in the West's efforts to import its Christian democracy and human rights to other non-Christian civilizations, but is also exemplified by its differential attitudes and policies towards different ethnic groups in Algeria and the former Yugoslavia (Sheng Hong 1996b: 50).

It is impossible for a social Darwinism-based civilization to resolve conflicts within its boundary. The relations among Western nations are competitive, rather than cooperative in nature. International expansion became an important means for reducing their internal conflicts. According to Sheng:

> The external expansion by Western countries in modern times aimed to reduce conflicts among European nations and became an important factor in coordinating their behavior in external relations. The enormous interests that these nations gained from overseas colonies and semi-colonies alleviated interest conflicts among different groups within a given country. Nevertheless, with the end of colonial exploration, conflicts among these nations became intensified and international wars became unavoidable (1995: 93).

The worst scenario, however, is that with the expansion of the social Darwinism-based Western civilization, war and conflict rather than peace and harmony became the norms and rules among nations. By using the West as their model, other countries soon learned the rule of "victory belongs to whoever has advanced weapons". In east Asia, Japan was forced by the Western nations to accept their rule of game-playing and later became a war-maker in the region during the Second World War. Since then, east Asian countries rapidly developed their military forces by putting enormous natural and human resources into the military sector. As Britain is reluctant to admit its crimes over the Opium War with China, many Japanese are not only reluctant to acknowledge their war crimes in China and other Asian countries, but are also trying to distort their history and to make their war crimes disappear. The Western powers are now worried about nuclear weapons. But it was the expansion of the Western civilization that made people militant.

Modern Chinese history is a history of westernization, a history of Chinese adaptation to the Western rules of game-playing. China's modernization has had serious consequences for China itself and for the whole world as well.

The Chinese made great efforts to learn from the West and became a member of the nuclear club. What did this mean for the world and its civilizations? First, the Chinese were able to play games with the West, and well, by using Western rules. Second, the rule of "victory belongs to whoever has the more advanced weapons" has made international security more tenuous because another member has been recruited into the world nuclear club, which means that less resources can be used for world peace. Third, China has become a major power with nuclear weapons in east Asia that can compete for power with the West. But one can hardly say that Chinese civilization has become more advanced simply because it possesses nuclear weapons (Sheng Hong 1995: 95).

Similarly, after 1978, China again learned from the West. A market system was introduced and free trade was promoted. In a short period of time, China achieved great economic success and gained enormous benefits from foreign trade. China's success again showed the West that China could score a victory according to the Western rules of game-playing. Second, China is increasingly becoming a major rival competitor for resources and markets with the West. China's conflicts with other countries has also been intensified. Third, due to economic success, China will necessarily develop its military power and thus change the world power distribution. From whatever perspective, China's victory is a victory of the Western civilization. Many in the West now proposed various forms of anti-China theory. Facing threats from the West, China will again learn from the West and become a victor. International conflicts are the natural results of the expansion of the Western civilization. How could conflicts among nations be resolved? In order to resolve international conflicts, it is time to change the rule of game-playing produced by the Western civilization.

The Confucian Civilization and World Peace

According to Chinese cultural nationalists, the expansion of Western civilization will lead to conflicts among nations because, by its nature, the West is a religion-based civilization.

According to Sheng (1995: 96), religion regards moral education as its mission. In order to realize this, it has to be organized and ritualized.

But once it is organized, it needs people to devote themselves to engage in organizational and ritual activities. Religious interests are thus formed. Furthermore, the relations between different religions are competitive because there is only one God. Competition among religions, which civilian governments often were not able to regulate, eventually led to wars among nations that were based on different religions.

Since all religion-based civilizations would lead to conflicts among nations, a non-religion-based civilization is required to coordinate the different rules of game-playing resulting from different civilizations. The Confucian civilization can play such a role. Unlike other civilizations, the Confucian civilization is not religion-based. Sheng argued:

> The Chinese civilization also regards moral education as its mission. But it uses an ethical structure to resolve moral issues. The core of the Chinese ethical approach is its emphasis on personal relations among people . . . As long as personal relations between any two persons can maintain harmony and peace, the whole society can be in harmony . . . Owing to such a quality, the Chinese civilization will be able to create a buffer zone among different civilizations and to play an integrating role among them (1995: 97).

By its nature, the Chinese civilization will never bring about international conflicts. Confucianism is in conflict with modern Western imperialism. According to Yan Xuetong, a Berkeley-trained political scientist who has been influential in international studies in China, unlike their Western counterparts, Chinese rulers were historically non-imperialistic, declining to conquer surrounding "barbarian" countries even when they had the means to do so. Throughout Chinese history, international expansion occurred only when non-Chinese barbarians took over the Chinese throne. Chinese rulers regarded it as a shame to grab economic interests by force. Consequently, non-violent means were often used by Chinese rulers to extend the influence of their country. Even though in its long history China once attempted to expand its civilization, it was never done by military or with other coercive means. Instead, China's rulers often provided "barbarians" with material goods in order to disseminate its civilization as exemplified by the Zheng He journeys during the Ming Dynasty (Yan Xuetong 1996a: 51).

Unlike other civilizations, Confucianism does not have a strong sense of "salvation" because of its emphasis on "this world" rather than "the world beyond". Without a "salvation mission", the Chinese civilization appreciates rationality, peace, and the doctrine of the mean. Extreme emotion, irrationality and expansion are not and should not be justified (Xiao Gongqin 1996a: 61).

In its modern era China came to conflict with the Western powers. Chinese nationalism, however, has been reactive, and its intensity depends on the seriousness of the external crisis China encountered at a given time. It was the West that forced China to accept a Western style of nationalism. However, the peaceful spirit of the Chinese civilization still influences the Chinese rulers' mind-set when they make security strategy. Take China's nuclear weapons strategy as an example. The Chinese government has repeatedly emphasized the following principles. First, China will not be the first to use nuclear weapons against other countries. Second, China's nuclear weapons are used only for national defense. Third, the aim of China's development of nuclear weapons is the elimination of nuclear weapons. According to Sheng, these principles reflect the Confucian spirit.

> The first principle means "tit for tat". The second principle means that China will not appeal to its nuclear advantage to threaten any country that does not have nuclear weapons. In other words, China will not use the rule of "victory belongs to whoever has advanced weapons" to countries which do not have weapon advantages over China. The third principle means that China attempts to use peaceful means to resolve conflicts among civilizations (1995: 95).[8]

As long as China follows this Confucian spirit, it will not become an expansionist.

A Transformation of Nationalism?

The Chinese civilization emphasizes peace and harmony. But it was "defeated" by the Western civilization. The rise and formation of modern Chinese nationalism meant that China had accepted Western values regarding relations among civilization-based states. However, because modern Chinese nationalism was reactive, as long as China encountered a peaceful international environment, its Western style of nationalism would be less intensive. The rise of various forms of anti-China theories will necessarily lead to strong nationalistic reactions in China. How should China deal with a "bad" international environment? Should China promote the Western style of nationalism? Or should it retain its reactive nationalism? Or should it go back to the more traditional Confucianism?

It was found that with the spread of nationalism, China was transformed from a culturally defined entity to a politically defined one (Harrison n.d.; Levenson 1964; Schwartz 1964; Lin 1979). According to Joseph Levenson, modern Chinese national identity, which came to Chinese intellectuals around the turn of the twentieth century, is radically different from earlier forms of Chinese identity. The high culture and ideology in pre-modern China were principally forms of cultural consciousness – an identification with the moral goals and values of a universalizing civilization. Without regard to national boundaries, Confucianism was said to represent a universal ethic distinguishing a "civilized" way of life accessible to any population through education, virtue, and good government. On the other hand, modern Chinese nationalism sees the nation–state as the ultimate goal of the community. Culturalism is a natural conviction of cultural superiority that sought no legitimation or defense outside of the culture itself. Only when cultural-ism was challenged in the late nineteenth century was there a transfor-mation to nationalism (Levenson 1964).

Joseph Whitney (1970), Selig Harrison (1978), Ishwer Ojha (1971) and others also noted China's shift from a cultural entity to a political entity when the traditional Confucian idea of the State was replaced by an imported nationalism. Nationalism treats culture only as a means to aid the nation, while culturalism represents a non-territorial concept, a loyalty to and preoccupation with culture.

Wang Gungwu provides a different argument on the complicated relations between nationalism and Confucianism. According to Wang there is no contradiction between the two.

> For the Chinese, the two have been, and could again be, complementary . . . While Chinese nationalism could benefit from a deeper understanding of Confucianism, Confucian values do not depend on nationalism or on a nationalist government. In their original form, they have an autonomy which has survived violent attacks by the uncomprehending and also all kinds of governments. They do not necessarily have to depend on the support of the Chinese. Anyone can become a Confucian by studying the classics. Thus, Confucianism may contribute to nation-formation but it does not need nationalism for its perpetuation (1996: 24).

According to many Chinese intellectuals, it was the imported notion of Western nationalism that made China a major power in international politics. However, if China wants to seek international peace, it has to return to traditional Confucianism rather than to strengthen this "imported" nationalism. The aim of the new nationalism is to use China's power to revive Confucianism rather than to continue to pro-mote a Western style of nationalism in China.

If China wants to contribute to world peace and progress it has to put its emphasis on cosmopolitanism (*tianxia zhuyi*). Li Shenzhi argued that the Chinese traditional ideal is "cosmopolitanism" rather than "nation-alism". The emphasis of nationalism is on ethnicity and the State, while that of cosmopolitanism is on culture (Li Shenzhi 1994c). According to Li, nationalism often means a narrow national loyalty. Such a national-ism is undesirable since it produces parochial prejudices. China needs to be ready to borrow or learn from other cultures and integrate itself into

the international system in an age of globalization (Li Shenzhi 1994b).
While cosmopolitanism leads to peace, nationalism often leads to war
and conflict.

With the incursion of Western powers in China, the transformation from traditional cosmopolitanism to Western style nationalism
occurred. Because cosmopolitanism emphasized culture, China was not
a nation–state but a country without a modern government, territorial
boundary, armed forces, national emblem, national flag and national
anthem. Without nationalism, people did not have a national identity
and were hard to be mobilized. Without appealing to Western nationalism, China would have lost its opportunity to survive in a nationalistic
world. As a matter of fact, it was the West that "exported" nationalism to
China and forced China to accept it.

China was forced to give up its traditional cosmopolitanism. With the
disappearance of Chinese culturalism, nationalism spread, along with its
game-playing rule – "victory belongs to whoever has advanced weapons".
The rise of China was indeed a victory of Western nationalism. However,
if a strong China becomes nationalistic, Western interests will be threatened. In this sense, the West has reasons to worry about China and to
produce various anti-China theories. If China continues to promote a
Western style of nationalism, the Western civilization will be threatened
not by the Chinese civilization, but by a Western nationalism-based
Chinese nationalism (Sheng Hong 1996a: 18).

Nevertheless, modern Chinese nationalism still contains some elements of traditional cosmopolitanism. Apparently, the West's anti-China
theories will lead Chinese nationalism into a vicious circle; that is, China
will use Western nationalism to defend itself. A new cosmopolitanism is
necessary if the world does not want to be destroyed by nuclear powers.
According to Sheng, there are two ways to realize cosmopolitanism and
therefore achieve and maintain world peace. The first is the European
style, and the second is the Chinese style. European states attempt to
achieve integration through peaceful means. Nevertheless, it will be difficult to expand this model to other religion-based civilizations because
these European states belong to the same civilization. The Chinese way
is more reliable because it is not religion-based. In order to promote the
Chinese cosmopolitanism, China needs to return to or revive its traditional spirit. However, Chinese elites should not continue to promote
"imported" Western nationalism. Instead, they need to make efforts to
appeal to China's traditional Confucianism. The formation of modern
Chinese nationalism occurred because China had been repeatedly
humiliated by Western powers for more than a century. However, world
peace requires that China gives up using nationalism to avenge its

humiliation caused by the West. China's new nationalism should not aim at hegemonism, but the elimination of hegemonism (Sheng Hong 1996a: 19).

Conclusion

Chinese intellectuals appeal to the theme of the clash of civilizations to construct a new nationalism owing to a variety of reasons. As mentioned before, Chinese intellectuals do not have much freedom in doing so. They have to integrate different and even contradictory elements into one "ism". According to the proponents of the new nationalism, if China wants to become a real power it has to resolve the two crises it now encounters; that is, a crisis of national identity, and a moral crisis among its people.

Modernization did not strengthen the people's national identity. Even though the regime has made a great effort to promote rapid development, its political legitimacy seems to have declined drastically. On the other hand, rapid economic development has given rise to individualism and money worship has become popular. As a result, the foundation of traditional morality has been weakened. Chinese intellectuals believe that if this situation continues, China as a nation–state will face a crisis. To resolve these two crises, some look to traditional Confucianism while others to "civilizational clash". One author stated that the new Chinese nationalism must be based on three factors: the political regime as the institutional base of the new nationalism, comprehensive national power that enables the regime to cope with internal and external crises, and Confucian morality which enables individuals to overcome their excessive individualism and contribute more to the nation as a whole. This is where the meaning of Confucian ethic *tianxia weigong* (the whole world as one community) lies (Zhao Jun 1996).

Many intellectuals realized that Chinese traditional culture cannot result in a strong national identity among individuals. The formation of modern Chinese nationalism and thus the people's national identity occurred when the Chinese civilization was threatened by other civilizations. The meaning of resorting to civilizational clash lies in the fact that when people feel threatened by external forces, the solidarity among them will be strengthened. External threats also make it easy for the government to mobilize domestic resources to achieve its goal. Shi Zhong, one spokesman of the new nationalism, pointed out that one major function of civilizational comparison is ideological mobilization. In the 1980s intellectuals appealed to the West and argued that China's modernization could be realized by learning from it, developing foreign trade with the West, and even westernizing Chinese culture. This is the real origin of the crisis facing Chinese civilization (Shi Zhong 1996). Obviously, a new nationalism needs to be constructed to justify the superiority of the Chinese civilization.

From this perspective, the new nationalism is a reaction to rapid modernization and its consequences. Some scholars in the West regarded the new nationalism as anti-westernization and anti-foreignism (Barme 1996). Others even believed that the new nationalism will bring about China's aggressive international behavior (Segal 1995b). However, the significance of China's anti-westernization is complex. Chinese nationalists do not want China to return to its modern nationalism which is characterized by anti-foreignism. They regard the current anti-westernization movement as a "modernizer of nationalism" in order to distinguish it from its more traditional form.

Moreover, Chinese nationalists also realized that it is the Western style of nationalism rather than Confucianism that has made China a strong State. To promote Chinese traditional culturalism or cosmopolitanism, Chinese nationalists have to construct an image of the superiority of Chinese civilization. This is where the meaning of anti-westernization lies. Anti-westernization, however, is indeed in conflict with the goal of Chinese nationalists; that is, to make China stronger and richer. Yet, traditional Confucianism will promote world peace and harmony, but it did not, and will not, make China a strong nation–state and help it to survive in a competitive world. How can Confucianism and nationalism be conciliated and integrated? This most important question still remains unanswered.

CHAPTER 5

The Official Discourse of Nationalism: Patriotism and the Constraints of Nationalism

In their interpretation of China's new nationalism, scholars have had difficulties in distinguishing between two types of nationalism: official nationalism and popular nationalism. It is believed that with the decline of communist ideology and the loss of people's faith in Marxism–Maoism, nothing now stands in the way of the Chinese government to appeal to nationalism to strengthen its political legitimacy within the country and to seek China's national interests abroad. This argument has gained popularity not only among Western scholars, but also among Western-educated Chinese scholars. Yasheng Huang, a Harvard-trained political scientist, argued recently that "the post-Tiananmen regime has eagerly embraced Chinese nationalism as a new fount of legitimacy . . . The CCP (Chinese Communist Party) began in earnest to revive traditional values that the Maoist regime had tried for years to eliminate. The strategy has worked, as evidenced by the recently rising anti-American sentiment" (Huang 1995: 57). Similarly, Suisheng Zhao, a University of California-trained political scientist, contended that "the rapid decay of Communist ideology has led the Chinese Communist Party to emphasize its role as the paramount patriotic force and the guardian of national pride in order to find a new basis of legitimacy to sustain its role" (Zhao 1997: 725).

The argument suggested implicitly that popular nationalism among different social and political groups has been facilitated by the regime's efforts to strengthen its political legitimacy; that nationalist sentiments can be regarded as forces that will necessarily influence China's foreign policy-making.[1] As a matter of fact, Edward Friedman (1997) attributed the rise of nationalism to the post-Mao ruling groups' chauvinism.

Nonetheless, the argument missed two important points. First, it neglects, or at least underestimates, the contradictions between popular nationalism and official nationalism. The official discourse of nationalism has focused on patriotism that is rather different from popular nationalism. Nationalism can be used to strengthen the political legitimacy of the regime. But intensive nationalism can often destabilize Chinese society and thus is not in the regime's interest.

Second, the impact of nationalism on China's foreign policy-making is more complicated than what has been argued. In using nationalism to serve its foreign policy, the Chinese government encounters serious constraints. A given country's foreign policies can be viewed more or less as reflecting domestic public opinions. But the connections between public opinions and actual foreign policies are complicated even in democratic states where public opinions are believed to play an important role in influencing elected officials' foreign decision-making (Putnam 1988; Evans, Jacobson & Putnam 1993).[2] In China, owing to its authoritarian regime, the linkage between government foreign policy-making and public nationalistic sentiments becomes rather weak. This does not mean, however, that the government can ignore completely popular nationalism in China's foreign affairs. Nor does this mean that the government can utilize popular nationalism to serve its foreign policy.

This chapter aims to use the case of the Chinese government's campaign against "anti-China" theories to show the constraints the government encounters in dealing with popular nationalism. The rise of "anti-China" theories in the West, especially in the United States, resulted in strong nationalistic reactions in China. Different political and social groups expressed their strong disappointment with the United States. The government believed that both intensive popular nationalism at home and "anti-China" theories abroad would threaten China's modernization program. While nationalism at home can generate enormous political pressure for the regime and threaten its socio-political stability, "anti-China" voices abroad could worsen China's international environment. The regime thus initiated a campaign to counter "anti-China" voices in order to respond to the West. But in doing so, it did not want to appeal to popular nationalism that, the regime believed, if promoted, would become uncontrollable and pose a threat to political stability. The military was thus assigned a leadership role to initiate the campaign to counter the "anti-China" voices and to appease domestic nationalistic sentiments simultaneously.

This chapter presents the official discourse of nationalism – that is, patriotism – and its contradictions with popular nationalism, and then analyzes how the government initiated its official campaign against "anti-China" theories to show how the government is constrained in its use of nationalistic sentiments to deal with such sensitive issues.

Patriotism as Official Nationalism

A nation can be regarded as a group of people who actually belong to or who perceive themselves to be a community bound by the ties of history, culture, and common ancestry. Nationalism aims to seek a political expression for the nation; that is, statehood. The significance of the State to a nation lies in the fact that "nations needed stronger organizations to defend themselves or help them achieve more ambitious goals" (Wang Gungwu 1996c: 4). In the modern world, the most successful of these organizations are nation–states. When a nation's political expression cannot be realized, nationalism rises (Breuilly 1982; Kellas 1991; Guilbernau 1996).

Modern versions of nationalism did not exist in traditional China. Accordingly, the Chinese State was different from nation–states in the West. The traditional Chinese political system was a system of empires (Hsu 1960: 13). Unlike modern Western nation–states, an empire did not have territorial boundaries. China was regarded as the center of the world. The size of the country depended on the power of the central government; in other words, the wane and wax of central power largely determined the country's rise and fall. Moreover, while modern nationalism is an awareness of the nation–state as the ultimate goal of the community, Confucianism-based culturalism implies an identification with the moral goals and values of a universalizing civilization. Lucian Pye (1990: 1) thus argued that China is a civilization pretending to be a nation–state.

As discussed in Chapter 2, after the Western concepts of the "nation–state" and "nationalism" were imported to China, many Chinese intellectuals and political elites realised that China had to create a modern vision of nationalism and thus a modern nation–state in order to survive a Darwinistic world. China's defeat in the Sino–Japanese War of 1894–95 undermined the traditional Chinese world order and the Chinese were forced to accept Western concepts such as nation, sovereignty, race and citizenship, and to change their traditional cultural identity. Growing foreign imperial forces within China worsened the crisis of national survival. Consequently, Chinese nationalism tended to preoccupy with creating and maintaining a strong and unified State. Traditional culturalism was quickly replaced by statism. In the West, nationalism means people's awareness of its culture and nationality, and their affection for it. But in China, it implies strong State identity. It is in this sense that Michael Hunt argued that "nationalism . . . may not be the best term to apply to the Chinese case" (Hunt 1993: 63). After a long search for a Chinese equivalent to the Western concept of nationalism, Chinese intellectuals found that patriotism (*aiguo zhuyi*) was a better term to express loyalty to the State and a desire to serve it. Hunt (1993) argued that patriotism is a better term for describing and explaining the particular characteristics of the Chinese search for national identity. Nevertheless, it is not a simple linguistic translation, but a political reconstruct.

Over time and as a political construct, patriotism has changed considerably to meet the State's various needs in accordance with changing environments. Mao Zedong (1975: 196) argued that "the specific content of 'patriotism' is determined by historical conditions." But whatever changes have occurred, the theme of patriotism remains – that is, strong national identity – and the logic behind the construction of it remains the same.

Scholars have found how Mao tried to give a local interpretation of Marxism and used Marxist concepts such as class and socialism to build a strong Chinese nation–state (Munck 1986; Zwick 1983; Fitzgerald 1996). While patriotism and Marxism were regarded as contradictory in the West, Mao Zedong did not think that there was any contradiction between Marxism as internationalism and Marxism as a version of Chinese nationalism. "Can a Communist, who is an internationalist, at the same time be a patriot?" Mao's answer (1975: 196) is, "he not only can be but must be". How could this happen? According to Mao:

> Communists are internationalists, but we put Marxism into practice only when it is integrated with the specific characteristics of our country and it acquires a definite national form . . . For the Chinese Communist Party, it is a matter of learning to apply the theory of Marxism–Leninism to the specific circumstances of China . . . To separate internationalist content from national form is the practice of those who do not understand the first thing about internationalism (1975: 209–10).

What Mao said here indeed is the way that Chinese leaders have constructed patriotism in the post-Mao era. The past two decades have witnessed China's growing openness to the outside world and pragmatic leaders have utilized different mechanisms developed in the West to promote the country's development. Chinese leaders, however, are not ready to accept Western concepts in their rhetoric and ideology. Instead, they have created various "new" terms to characterize the country's development, such as "socialist market economy", "socialism with Chinese characteristics", and "democracy with Chinese characteristics". When they did so, their logic was the same as Mao's. Obviously, implicit in their efforts in creating these concepts were their concerns with the Chinese way to power and wealth, and their nationalistic or patriotic feelings.

This is the political logic behind the Chinese leaders' insistence on using the concept of "patriotism". On the one hand, the regime welcomes nationalism to fill the ideological vacuum left by the decline of Marxism and Maoism, and to strengthen its political legitimacy. This is the rationale behind the regime's acquiescence during the rise of various nationalistic voices. But to allow popular nationalism to rise does not necessarily lead to the strengthening of the legitimacy of the regime. On the contrary, popular nationalism can weaken the existing base of political legitimacy. This requires the regime not to simply follow the nationalistic themes expressed by popular nationalism, but to re-construct a new vision of patriotism.

Nationalistic voices have been pluralistic among different social and political groups. By contrast, the theme of patriotism has been rather consistent over the years. In constructing a new vision of patriotism, the regime has overwhelmingly emphasized three elements; that is, economic development, political stability, and national unification.

Economic development constitutes the base of China's wealth and power. While Mao Zedong attempted to use various political approaches to build China as a strong nation–state, Deng Xiaoping saw the importance of economic power in strengthening the nation–state Mao built. There was nothing inevitable about the decision of Deng Xiaoping and his comrades to put the highest priority to economic reform. What they saw was that Maoist "politics in command" had resulted in economic disasters and had posed a serious threat to everything that the Party leaders had fought for; that is, a strong Chinese nation and people's loyalty to the State. Economic modernization became imperative in order to provide a strong base for the nation–state and to win back people's confidence toward this State.

In the early 1980s Deng Xiaoping argued that the Party needed to focus on three important tasks; namely, anti-hegemonism, national unification, and modernization. Nevertheless, Deng contended that the highest priority should be on modernization, because:

> It is the essential condition for solving both our domestic and external problems . . . The role we play in international affairs is determined by the extent of our economic growth. If our country becomes more developed and prosperous, we will be in a position to play a greater role in international affairs . . . Therefore . . . the two tasks of opposing hegemonism and reunifying the country by achieving the return of Taiwan to the motherland both require that we do well in our economic development (1984d: 225).

Deng's logic between economic modernization and a strong nation–state has been widely accepted by the general public as well as government officials. In the late 1980s Paul Kennedy's *The Rise and Fall of the Great Powers* (1989) was translated into Chinese and his argument that economic power determines a nation's position in international affairs gained popularity. Almost at the same time, when China encountered difficulty in economic reform, a debate about China's "global citizenship" occurred in the intellectual circles and had an important impact on top leaders. Central to the debate is the argument that further economic reform needs to be implemented regardless of whatever the costs, otherwise there is no chance for China to be a strong nation–state in the world of nation–states.[3]

More important are the Party leaders' efforts in harmonizing socialism and economic modernization. Chinese leaders now use the concept "socialist market economy" to describe their model of economic modernization. For many outsiders, socialism and a market economy are contradictory. Apparently, it is because China became a victim of socialism that the post-Mao leadership turned to a market economy. However, from a patriot's point of view, embedded in this concept is the Chinese leaders' passion for a strong and unique China. When the transition from a planned to a market economy in Russia and eastern European countries resulted in social turmoil and economic stagnancy, the Chinese socialist market economy experience brought China wealth and power. By sticking to socialism the regime attempted to show that the Chinese way to a market economy was the best road to socialism, and that China's reform could become a universal model for other countries.

Such differences were highlighted for people to identify with China's uniqueness. In interpreting the Chinese use of "socialist market economy", Wang Gungwu correctly pointed out that it was not because the Chinese leaders wanted to hide their embarrassment that capitalism was now rampant in the country, nor because they did not understand modern economics and used the term incorrectly. Instead, the concept was seriously created to serve the regime's nationalistic goal. By considering divergent economic solutions to basic problems of livelihood, Chinese leaders attempted to develop a way to position China to play its rightful role in global affairs and thus establish a new basis for its future position in the world (Wang Gungwu 1995: 21). In other words, it seemed to the leadership that in order to strengthen popular national identity and the political legitimacy of the regime, they had to stick to the concept of socialism, which had directed the country's development for decades.

A second element the Chinese leaders have considered in their construction of patriotism is political stability. While economic modernization can provide an economic base for China's power position in the world of nation–states, political stability is *the* most important prerequisite for economic development. Deng Xiaoping (1988: 8, 13) repeatedly emphasized that China's modernization required two prerequisites: international peace, and domestic political stability. In this sense, patriotism means to help the regime to maintain stability, or at least, not to create troubles for the regime. Deng (1984d: 396) contended that the Chinese had their national self-respect and pride, and it was the highest honor to love their "socialist motherland and contribute all we have to her socialist construction. We deem it the deepest disgrace to impair her interests, dignity and honor". Patriotism here is viewed as loving China's socialist State. Deng contended that it is the socialist State, not any other forms of the Chinese State before, that has made China strong and wealthy (1984b; cited in 1993a: 60).

The meaning of political stability is twofold. First, the existing State is the result of the country's century long chaos and revolutions. Patriotism requires people to identify the State and pay it respect. Political reform is necessary to strengthen the State, but it does not mean introducing any Western styles of democracy. While many popular nationalists argue that democratization will be the way to strengthen China, the regime attempted to show that democratic institutions are not necessary for China to achieve rapid economic growth, or to guarantee stability and the people a decent livelihood. Thus, Chinese intellectuals regarded the 1989 pro-democracy movement as patriotic, but the regime perceived it as undermining China's stable development. Indeed, a deep fear of chaos and obsessive preoccupation with political stability constituted the rationale of the regime's crackdown of the movement. Like Deng Xiaoping, Jiang Zemin has also continuously emphasized that patriotism implies "loving the socialist state and the existing form of socialist democracy" (1990: 1, 3).

Furthermore, political stability means to constrain "narrow nationalism". Nationalism often occurs among people who have lived together in a territory with a shared history and a common culture, and assumes that every nation has the right to establish its own State. From this point of view, to engage in nationalism is a dangerous business for the regime. Given the fact that China has been a multinational State, nationalism can be destructive by provoking various ethnic groups within the country's boundary to pursue their own statehood as what happened in the former Soviet Union. Rapid modernization has given rise to various forms of ethnic nationalism in China's frontiers; for example, Tibet and Xinjiang. It is arguable that the fear of ethnic nationalism, more than anything else, pushed the regime to construct the new patriotism. While nationalism is based on a shared culture and ethnicity, patriotism does not necessarily need an ethnic or cultural base and can be regarded as encompassing all those legally entitled to be citizens, irrespective of their ethnicity, national identity, and culture. Patriotism thus attempts to downgrade ethnicity and culture, and emphasizes loyalty to the existing State (see Anderson 1991: Chapter 6).

In this situation, patriotism is similar to what Benedict Anderson called "official nationalism". According to Anderson, fearing the break-up of the State through nationalist separatism, the dynastic European states of the nineteenth century began a nationalism of their own and attempted to impose a particularly created national culture on the whole State and make that a condition for socioeconomic and political progress.

A third element of patriotism is national unification. At this level, patriotism is beyond its narrow definition; that is, statism or loyalty towards the State. In constructing patriotism, the Chinese leaders encountered a dilemma. On the one hand, they had to downplay ethnicity and particular national cultures in order to strengthen different ethnic groups' identity towards the existing State and to prevent the rise of nationalist separatism and thus the break-up of the existing multinational State. On the other, the reunification with different parts of China – Taiwan, Hong Kong, and Macau – requires the regime to appeal to the Chinese culture and ethnicity, and downgrade state identity. Owing to various reasons, the regimes of different parts of China have long formed different sets of economic and political institutions. In the early 1980s Deng Xiaoping (1984d: 225) contended that national unification should be one of the regime's most important agendas. However, Deng also realized how difficult it was to overcome institutional differences among different parts of China. He thus proposed a model of "one country, two systems" for national unification. Under this political framework, patriotism is given a particular set of meanings, different from that assigned to different groups within the boundary of the State. In interpreting "one country, two systems", Deng argued that:

> our standards for a patriot are: to respect one's own nation, to support earnestly and sincerely the motherland's sovereignty over Hong Kong, and not to undermine Hong Kong's prosperity and stability. As long as they meet these conditions, they are patriots regardless of whether they believe in capitalism, feudalism, or/and even slavishness (1984b: 61, vol. 3).

What Deng emphasized here is not the State, but the nation. Following Deng, Jiang Zemin also contended that patriotism means to promote national unification. According to Jiang (1990: 1, 3), from the perspective of national unification, patriotism does not require that "all those (overseas Chinese) who support the motherland's unification approve of the socialist system in the mainland", and "as long as they support 'one country and two systems', we can form solidarity with them". In effect, this theme is consistent throughout the whole reform period.

The above discussion shows how official nationalism or patriotism differs from popular nationalism. Both popular nationalism and patriotism aim at building a strong and wealthy China. But this does not mean there is no conflict between the two. While popular nationalists regard democratization as the way to a strong China, the regime puts its highest priority on economic development and political stability. Furthermore, patriotism requires all residents within the country to identify with the existing State, but ethnic nationalists aim at building their own states based on their culture. While the regime attempts to use the model of "one country, two systems" for national unification, ethnic groups want to use it to gain a *de facto* status of independence. An example is Tibet. The Dalai Lama contended that "one country, two systems" could be applied to Tibet. But the Chinese officials insisted that the model was only applicable to Hong Kong, Taiwan, and Macau (*Xinhua English Newswire* 1997).

The differences between popular and official nationalism impose serious constraints on the regime when it deals with popular nationalism. On one hand, many scholars have argued that the regime can use popular nationalism to create a base for political legitimacy. However, nationalism could become a dangerous Pandora's Box. Without constraints, it could release tremendous forces for unexpected consequences, such as popular political participation and national separatism, that oppose the regime's goal of nation building. Therefore the regime has to be cautious in promoting national pride and using popular nationalistic sentiments to consolidate its legitimacy. More importantly, it also has to constrain popular nationalism. The rise of this phenomenon can be beneficial for the regime, but it must stop at a certain point. In the following sections, I shall use the case of the regime's campaign against various "anti-China theories" to show why the government did not want to use popular nationalism to deal with such a sensitive issue.

How the Chinese feel Threatened

The rise of anti-China theories has resulted in a fear among various social and political groups in China that the West, led by the United States, is to contain China as it did the former Soviet Union. Senior Chinese political leaders, including President Jiang Zemin and many military heads, have used many public occasions to air their voices on this matter (Dong Liwen 1996; Zhang Yajun 1997). In the 1980s, the Chinese leaders believed that peace and development were two major trends in international politics. However, with the rise of "anti-China" theories, Chinese academic and policy-making circles increasingly believed that China's international environment has deteriorated, and that China's rapid modernization has only worsened its international environment. The end of the Cold War did not make the world more peaceful. Instead, with the decline of American hegemony and the polarization of world power, the original superpower constraints on international power distribution no longer exist, and international affairs again tend to be dominated by anarchy (Liu Jinghua 1994: 120).

Individual countries have already begun to use whatever means to expand their national interests outward. Nation–states again confront one another. This is what is happening to China.

According to Liu Jinghua of the Chinese Academy of Social Sciences, a situation of "soft containment" by Europe and the United States will appear early next century. It seems to Liu that "soft containment" refers to an environment in which China's development and survival will be controlled and contained by Europe and the United States through capital, market, high technology, Western values, and military forces (1994: 119).

The same analyst argued that China's clash with Europe and the United States is inevitable. The US engagement policy, emphasized by President Bill Clinton, cannot be a long-term international strategy with China. The engagement policy aims at, first, utilizing American capital and high technology to make huge profits and to occupy China's market before it develops, and second, to use Western values to influence Chinese development (Liu Jinghua 1994: 119). Similarly, Wang Jisi (1997: 7), Director of the Institute of American Studies of the Chinese Academy of Social Sciences, argued that Clinton's engagement policy is based on US strategic goals. He believed that the United States needs China's cooperation on a number of regional and global issues, and that the United States sought to influence China's domestic and foreign policy through engagement to pervade China with US economic, political, cultural and ideological influences. Wang Jisi (1997: 7) also argued that the United States hoped China would accept Western-led international norms.

Nevertheless, according to many, it is doubtful whether even such a limited cooperation between China and the West can survive for much longer. With China's rapid growth in its comprehensive national power (see Chapter 6), the law of diminishing returns will come to function; that is, China's markets will be less profitable for the West. Meanwhile, China will be more competitive in the international market, and the Western states will have to change their China policies to constrain China's rise. It is against this background that various "anti-China" theories were developed in the West (Liu Jinghua 1994: 119).

According to Wang Jishi, the United States will carry out a containment policy owing to conflicting national interests between the two countries (1997: 6). First, While the United States is a democratic State, China remains a "totalitarian" State. Since it is widely believed in the United States that democracies don't fight each other whereas "totalitarian states" are sources of evil, the United States will remain ideologically an anti-communist bastion to constrain the rise of a socialist China. Second, the rise of China will inevitably conflict with the existing international order dominated by the West. Third, China has made great efforts in exporting cheap products to the US market while restricting US access to Chinese markets. Fourth, in the post-Cold War era, religions and civilizations are replacing ideologies as the sources of international conflicts. Thus, the Confucian civilization, represented by China, tends to pose a threat to the Western Christian civilization. Fifth, China's growing military power is causing concerns for regional security among its neighbors.

Furthermore, China's inevitable conflict with the West is not only because of different national interests, but is also culturally and racially rooted. Shi Yinhong, a Professor at Nanjing University and who has maintained a high profile in China's international studies, stated:

> to explain the American animosity toward China, one has to take into account not only ideological, geopolitical and economic considerations but also cultural and racial factors. The West has never really been willing to accept a non-Western power as an equal . . . Conditioned by their centuries-old superiority, Westerners often subconsciously judge whether a nation is a friend or enemy by its racial or cultural attributes and national power (1996a: 11).[4]

The United States fought a protracted Cold War to contain the Soviet Union. It is still trying to expand NATO eastward to check Russia. The conflict between the West and Japan earlier this century had similar roots. Understandably, now that China is experiencing rapid economic growth, the United States has become even more hostile towards it. American media institutions rarely report China's progress. Instead, they focus on – and usually blow up, distort, or even fabricate – China's problems. Interpretations of China's domestic and foreign policies are absurd and odd. As shown in Samuel Huntington's thesis of the clash of civilizations, "West vs the Rest" has become a predominant thinking pattern for many Western states. It is perceived that Western countries are going to unite against the non-Western world.

A cold war between China and the United States seems unavoidable. Yet, the Clinton Administration has proposed an engagement strategy. However, it is hard to say whether engagement means containment. But apparently, a major goal of engagement is to contain China (Chu Shulong 1996).

How does the West, especially the United States, contain China? According to Chinese government analysts, the US containment strategy consists of various factors, including:

- The United States maintains its military presence in Asia as the base of containment. Even with anti-American movements and sentiments in Asia, the United States has decided to maintain about 100 000 military forces there in order to constrain China's rise in a regional setting. The United States has made it clear that its fundamental strategic interest is to prevent the rise of a hegemonic China. The United States has expressed its great interests in a range of issues related to China, including arms sales, arms purchases, military modernization, and so on. For the United States, engagement is about containment and the use of every possible means to promote its national interests against China.

- The United States has made efforts to strengthen its alliance with Japan. Japan has been China's major regional competitor and a potential major security threat. With its growing economic power, Japan has been seeking to strengthen its political influence in the region. It has made great efforts in developing sophisticated power-projection capabilities. Due to its sophisticated technologies, Japan could develop nuclear capabilities, missile expertise, and military aircraft in a short period. For many Chinese analysts, the United States has played a "pushing" role in the rise of Japan's militarism. The United States signed a new security treaty with Japan in 1995. US–Japan security cooperation might contribute to Japanese military expansion and is no doubt aimed at constraining China's rise. In other words, the US–Japan security alliance "gives the feeling" that the two countries "work hand-in-hand to dominate the Asia–Pacific region" (Zhang Guocheng 1996: 6).

- The United States has established various military alliances or cooperation with China's other neighbors to contain it (Yang Bojiang 1996; Xi Laiwang 1996). For example, the United States formed close military ties with Australia in 1996. However, the Australian government has claimed that it has made no attempt to contain China by forming an Australian–US alliance (*The Economist* 1996: 35). The United States also attempts to normalize and strengthen its relations with China's neighboring countries that have real or potential conflicts with China. It has perceived Vietnam as an important force to contain China and improved its relations with the former in the last few years. Meanwhile, the United States has made efforts to develop its relations with Mongolia and has integrated it into its security system of the Asia–Pacific region in 1994, and reaffirmed the military cooperation between the two countries in 1995.

- The United States attempts to interfere in issues concerning the South China Sea. In order to strengthen its influence in South-east Asia, the United States supported Malaysia and the Philippines in their territorial dispute with China over the Spratly Islands. Although US statements on the dispute have suggested neutrality on sovereignty over the islands, the United States expressed its willingness to side with ASEAN countries against China.

- More importantly, the United States has opposed mainland China's unification with Taiwan because it wants to retain access to its "unsinkable aircraft carrier". It has forced China not to use military forces in dealing with Taiwan. To maintain Taiwan's independence is obviously in the US's interest (Xu Yimin et al. 1996: 4). To do so, the United States continues to provide advanced weapons to Taiwan and tries to develop a relationship with it beyond an un-official level. In the summer of 1992 the Bush Administration agreed to sell 150 F-16 fighters to Taiwan. A few months later the Bush Administration sent Carla Hills, the US Trade Representative, to Taipei for the first cabinet-level visit since 1978. In the late spring of 1995, the Clinton Administration granted a visa to Taiwan's President Lee Teng-hui – the highest level visit from Taiwan since diplomatic relations were terminated at the end of 1978. The United States Congress even passed a provision that the Taiwan Relations Act "supersedes" (and thus nullifies) the August 1982 communiqué on US arms sales to Taiwan. All these actions by the United States violated its own earlier promises to China. Indeed, the American intention in upgrading its relations with Taipei was to endorse, even promote, Taiwan's independence.

- The United States policy towards Tibet also shows its intention to weaken China. Although the US government officially does not challenge Chinese sovereignty over Tibet, it has made great efforts to use Tibet against China's rise as shown in the greater willingness of top American officials to meet with the Dalai Lama, the regular Congressional resolutions criticizing the Chinese "occupation" of Tibet, and growing public support for the Tibetan government in exile. Moreover, the US Congress has introduced various bills concerning Tibet: a declaration that Tibet is a sovereign occupied country, and provisions that the President should appoint a special envoy to Tibet.

- In addition, the United States has also used the issues of human rights to foster China's disunity and disorder. The US government has condemned China's human rights violations repeatedly even though the Chinese leaders have made great efforts to improve the country's human rights record. On this regard, the US Congress has also introduced various bills: a provision that Radio Free Asia should draw on the "expertise" of Chinese dissidents overseas in designing its broadcasts to China; that funds should be provided to subsidize "freedom broadcasting" to China by private organizations, especially those connected with overseas dissident movements; and a requirement that the President provide a special report on the extent to which his policies for promoting human rights in China, announced when he renewed China's most-favored-nation status, have been effective.

- Overall, the United States attempts to use an engagement strategy to "pull" China into a US-centered international system and thus force China to subordinate to its interests. The US government tries to use this engagement strategy through political, economic, cultural, and ideological means to influence China and use so-called international norms and rules to contain it and constrain its domestic and international behavior (Wu Jiong 1996: 10). In terms of China's domestic politics, the United States claimed that it wants to promote human rights in China by supporting China's dissidents at home and abroad. Internationally, the United States has used so-called "international norms" on a variety of issues to constrain China's rise, including foreign trade, military, intellectual property rights, environment, arms sales, and so forth.

Although the "anti-China" theories remain rhetoric in the West, Chinese social and political groups, as well as government officials, believe that the United States is making efforts to contain China. The government's moderate US policy was criticized within the leadership, especially during the Taiwan Strait Crisis in 1996 when the United States warned China that it would interfere in the cross-strait affairs if China used force against Taiwan.

At the societal level, Chinese new nationalists called for the use of nationalism to counter the West's China policy. Popular nationalistic sentiments were confirmed by various surveys. It was reported in 1996 that almost 100 percent of the respondents suggested that they would support the government's decision of using force against Taiwan. Another nationwide survey conducted in September 1995 published by *China Youth* indicated that 57 percent of the respondents regarded the United States as the most disliked country and more than 87 percent regarded it as the most unfriendly country to China (Si Cheng 1996: 13; Ren Weiwen 1995a). Doubtless to say, the fact that the government allowed various nationalistic works such as *A China that Says No* and *Behind A Demonized China* to be published is not without any reasons.

The Chinese government believed that the "anti-China" theories have intensified nationalistic sentiments within the country and could become a cause of domestic instability. More importantly, they could be used by the West to constrain China's development and pose a threat to China's national strategy. An official campaign against these "anti-China" theories seems necessary. But this is not an easy enterprise for the leadership. How should the "anti-China" theories and domestic nationalistic voices be dealt with at the same time? For the new leadership, three major aims need to be achieved through such an official campaign. First, the leadership needs to show the international community that China's rapid domestic development will not pose a threat to world peace; instead, it will contribute greatly to international stability, and that the "anti-China" theories are only attempts by the West to constrain China's modernization. Second, domestic nationalistic sentiments must be appeased. If the nationalistic sentiments are too strong, they will hurt China's opening policy and its development. Third, nationalism needs to be used to consolidate the new leadership's political legitimacy. Economic growth becomes a major source of the political legitimacy of the new leadership. But it also generates enormous undesired consequences that pose a serious threat to the new leadership. The leadership recognized that nationalism could be carefully used to strengthen its political legitimacy. Thus, while it needs to constrain excessive nationalistic sentiments, it also needs to promote nationalism to some extent. This means that popular nationalism has to be transformed to justify the regime's political legitimacy.

Nationalism can be used to inspire the people's political awareness of China's external threats and to gain their strong support for the government's "nationalistic" foreign policy. But nationalism can also arouse the people's sense of democratic participation. The Chinese leadership realized that nationalistic foreign policies were not necessarily in accordance with China's national interests; and that a peaceful international environment is essential for China's continuous economic development and modernization. Domestic development should not be promoted by any international events if China wants to be a real great power in the world. Opening the country and learning from advanced capitalist practices are still the most important means for China to catch up. Therefore, a strong nationalistic reaction at the policy level could hurt China itself. As a matter of fact, to create and maintain a hospitable international environment is an important aspect of China's national strategy since the post-Mao reform began in the late 1970s.

Nevertheless, the leadership must make nationalistic responses from a political point of view. Jiang Zemin, General Secretary of the Chinese Communist Party, could hardly forget how former General Secretary Hu Yaobang's pro-Japanese policy aroused nationalistic sentiments among Chinese intellectuals and students. After he came to power, Hu Yaobang called for China to adopt a friendly policy towards Japan in order to improve and strengthen Sino–Japanese relations. Nevertheless, Hu's friendly stance provoked nationalistic anti-Japanese sentiments among Chinese intellectuals and students. Hu was forced to resign as General Secretary of the Chinese Communist Party in 1987 after the formation of two major student movements in 1985 and 1986. Indeed, Hu was criticized within the party for his pro-Japan stance, which was regarded a major factor that led to the rise of the 1985 anti-Japanese student movement. Though the fall of Hu can be interpreted differently, his moderate Japan policy without doubt is one of its major factors.[5] The lesson for the Jiang-centered leadership is that popular nationalistic sentiments cannot be ignored.

Civilian–Military Coalition and Official Campaign

The importance of a campaign against "anti-China" voices and the cautiousness of the leadership in dealing with popular nationalism led to a civilian–military coalition. The People's Liberation Army (PLA) has been involved in all major decisions, especially those related to China's foreign policy-making and sovereignty issues. Since the establishment of the People's Republic, the PLA has played an important role in maintaining the stability of the regime. When China descended into political chaos in the late 1960s and 1970s, Mao Zedong relied on the support of Defence Minister Lin Biao against other senior leaders such as Peng Zhen, Liu Shaoqi, and Deng Xiaoping. During the late period of the Cultural Revolution, Lin Biao and his lieutenants attempted to institutionalize the role of the military in civilian affairs. Although Lin died in 1971, after allegedly plotting against Mao, the PLA remained an essential part of the country's political system. When Mao Zedong died in 1976, the military's support was essential to Hua Guofeng in arresting Jiang Qing and the other members of the "Gang of Four". Even though there were serious political struggles within the military, it remained a relatively stable force compared to different social and political forces. When the anti-foreignism movements initiated by Mao caused serious socio-political chaos, the PLA played the role of stabilizer.

After Deng Xiaoping came to power, one of the major goals of reform was to restore the control of the civilian government over the PLA and reduce the military's role in civilian affairs. From an institutional point of view, Deng's military reform was successful. On his death, Deng had succeeded in retiring senior officers, reducing the number of military regions, reshuffling regional military commanders, and trimming military representation on the Political Bureau and Central Committee.

The military's role, however, has become more extensive. It has been one of the most important driving forces of China's modernization. Because the military officer corps is now drawn from a younger and better educated generation, and because the military is more sensitive to outside developments, it has been more sympathetic to economic modernization and its demand for military modernization remains high. This is especially true after the Gulf War when the military as well as the civilian leadership saw the awesome complexity of high-tech warfare and the chasm between the PLA and advanced armies. Thus, when the civilian government grew more conservative because of the fear of socio-political instability, the military became a driving force behind China's continuous modernization. It was reported that the Yang brothers (Yang Shangkun and Yang Baibing, the President of China and the director of the General Political Department of the PLA, respectively) argued that the PLA had to play a role that escorted the reform process (Ren Weiwen 1992). The Yang brothers' argument was seen as interfering with civilian affairs. They were removed from the Central Military Commission and replaced by two elderly military officers, Liu Huaqing and Zhang Zhen in 1992. But this move only meant that Deng was uncertain about regime stability. With the passing of the old generation of revolutionaries, whether the new generation of leadership will be able to maintain socio-political stability and exercise civilian control over the military becomes doubtful.

Since becoming the General Secretary of the Party and the Chairman of the Central Military Commission in 1989, Jiang Zemin has made enormous efforts to improve his relationship with the military and thus strengthen his influence over military affairs. Jiang repeatedly emphasized the importance of strengthening the Party's control over the military. On the other hand, in order to win over the military's political support, military modernization has been Jiang's important political agenda as symbolized by China's increasing military budget.

In effect, compromises are sometimes essential for the stability of the Jiang-centered new generation of leadership. In order to give economic development and modernization the highest priority, the new leadership had to gain the military's support on the one hand, and constrain its political influence over civilian affairs on the other. With changes in China's international environment, especially the worsening relationship between the United States and China since the 1989 Tiananmen Square Incident, the Chinese military tends to become nationalistic over the issues of China's foreign policy. The government's US policy was regarded as too weak and was criticized seriously, especially during the Taiwan Strait Crisis in 1996. However, the official campaign against "anti-China" theories remained moderate. Apparently, Jiang's compromise policy had an impact on this pursuit. Jiang Zemin and other senior leaders expressed their nationalistic voices and reminded the military that it should be on the alert against potential threats from the United States (Whiting 1995). But Jiang also emphasized the importance of the West, especially the United States, for China's further development and modernization. It seemed that a consensus was reached between Jiang and the military commanders on this point. The fact that the military played a role in fighting back the "anti-China" theories does not mean that the military was more nationalistic than the civilian government or other social and political groups. The military was assigned this task for three major reasons.

The most important factor is the leadership's consideration of socio-political stability. Nationalism without doubt is a double-edged sword. When a nationalistic movement becomes uncontrollable, socio-political stability will be endangered. This is what happened to Mao's China. After the establishment of the People's Republic, Mao preferred a mobiliza-tion strategy. In the early 1950s Mao initiated waves of nationalistic move-ments against the West's policy of containing China. During the Cultural Revolution, Mao continued to mobilize nationalistic sentiments that opposed foreign imperialism and promoted domestic development. These movements without doubt contributed to political and socio-economic chaos (Kuang-sheng Liao 1984). The Jiang-centered leader-ship realized that such a mobilization strategy could no longer be used to oppose the "anti-China" theories. Instead, popular nationalism needed to be constrained to some degree, and China's foreign policy-making could not be affected by such domestic nationalistic pressure. The issue was how the "anti-China" theories could be responded to nationalistically so that popular nationalistic sentiments could be appeased and domestic stability not affected. The campaign against the "anti-China" theories could be well controlled if the military took charge of it. Thus, instead of a nationwide political movement, the government initiated a rhetoric campaign against such theories. Jiang Zemin and other senior leaders, especially those from the military, used different occasions to speak out, nevertheless in a moderate form. While social groups expressed their strong sentiments, the leadership remained pragmatic.

A second reason is that both reformist and moderate leaders were afraid that if other government bodies, such as the Propaganda Depart-ment, took control of the campaign, conservatives within the Party and government would use this occasion to attack Deng Xiaoping's reform program since it was Deng Xiaoping who set the general guidelines of Sino–US relationship. By contrast, the military had been a reform-oriented force in the post-Mao era. It was easy for the military to control the *du* (extent) of the campaign.

The third and practical reason for the military to initiate the cam-paign was that these "anti-China" theories were based on the perception that China's rapid military modernization posed a threat to world stability and regional security.

Official Rhetoric Against anti-China Theories

To some degree, many leaders believe that containment has become a US policy against China. Although the US government has proposed an engagement policy, this trend is part of an overall strategy of contain-ment. The engagement policy aims to open and penetrate Chinese markets in order to influence China's future development while the containment policy aims to use all possible means to contain China's potential threats to US interests (Ren Weiwen 1995b). According to President Jiang Zemin (1995), major anti-China and anti-communist forces in the United States and other Western countries will not give up their efforts to westernize and fragment China and eventually contain China. These forces do not like to see a strong China with a rapid growing economy. Because they perceive China as their potential rival, they will use all possible means including the Taiwan, Tibet and human rights issues to contain China's development.

How should these anti-China forces be coped with? What Jiang did was to appeal to patriotism. After the crackdown of the 1989 pro-democracy movement, the government repeatedly emphasized the use of patriotism to oppose the West's strategy of "peaceful evolution" towards China. Earlier on, Jiang argued that patriotism is mainly manifested in devotion to building and safeguarding the course of socialist modernization and the motherland's unification. According to Jiang (1991), patriotism could be transformed into an efficient weapon against "peaceful evolution". Government propaganda initiated a campaign against peaceful evolution and showed that international bourgeois hostile forces headed by the United States had adopted an undisguised and evil strategy against China. In October 1991 Yang Shangkun, State President, spoke at the meeting commemorating the eightieth anniversary of the 1911 Revolution. He emphasized not only the importance of patriotism in promoting socialist development, but also its effectiveness in resisting any external pressure or difficulty. In September 1994 the Party's Propaganda Department issued an important document entitled, "The Outline of the Implementation of the Education of Patriotism". At the same time, the Party also published a collection of major leaders' speeches on patriotism in order to popularize the movement (*RMRB* 1994a; Liu Yunshan 1994).

Facing increasing numbers of voices with "anti-China" views in the West, Jiang repeatedly called for both Party cadres and government officials, as well as the general public, to use "political means" to resist political pressure. Jiang (1996: 1) argued that "Western hostile forces want to westernize and divide us and to impose their type of 'democracy' and 'freedom' on us. Lee Teng-hui wants to engage in Taiwan's independence. Can we not talk about 'politics'?" Jiang realized that only by promoting patriotism within could the State resist political pressure without. Also, it is important to note that patriotism could provoke and strengthen people's confidence towards the regime in dealing with the outside world.

Nonetheless, Chinese leaders also realized that even patriotism could result in excessive nationalistic sentiments over China's foreign policies and thus could have a negative impact on the regime's reform policy. Jiang thus emphasized that patriotism did not mean China had to change its established national strategy; that is, the priority of domestic development. Instead, in order to counter the West's containment strategy, China had to stick to this national strategy and maintain a fast growing economy. A major aim of the "anti-China" theories is to force China to deviate from this principle (The Editorial *RMRB* 1996).

With this perception, official discourse against the "anti-China" theories remains rational and moderate while nationalistic emotion and sentiment are also apparent. In presenting their arguments, both civilian and military officials were very cautious in order to avoid arousing and reinforcing public nationalistic sentiments.

The first argument is cultural, meaning that China is not a militaristic power. While many in the West have drawn a parallel between China today and Germany and Japan in the past, Chinese officials emphasized that Chinese culture by nature is peace-oriented. Many pointed out that the German empire after Bismarck was dominated by Prussian generals for whom war was the main function of the State. But China has no Junkers and no tradition of militarism. Major leaders often use the Confucian adage, "do not do unto others that you do not like others to do unto you" (Hsiao 1979) to stress China's pacific tradition and to argue that China will never threaten or invade others countries. Xu Xin, present Chairman of China Association of Strategic Studies and former Deputy Chief of General Staff of the PLA, argued:

> it is not difficult to understand that the Chinese nation is a nation who loves peace, and that China is a state which loves peace . . . Confucius emphasized more than 2000 years ago that "harmony should be cherished" . . . this has been incorporated into China's official philosophy and has directed Chinese international behavior (1996: 48).

Yet, many have argued that imperial China once attempted to establish its hegemony in Asia symbolized by its tributary system. However, differing from modern hegemony, whose aim is to gain political and economic interests, the main aim of China's tributary system was to spread the influence of Chinese culture. From this perspective, China had a benign track record; it had never attempted to conquer surrounding "barbarian" countries even when it was able to do so. Instead, China was conquered by these "barbarian" countries. Historically, the only real territorial expansion occurred when non-Chinese Mongols occupied China. According to Xing Sizhong, President of the National Defense University, pacifism is also the guiding line of China's international behavior today.

On the one hand, scholars in the West such as Johnston (1995; 1996) have argued that compared to other countries, China is more likely to appeal to force to solve disputes with other countries. Yet, the Chinese continue to believe in their pacific tradition and regarded their actions against other countries such as Vietnam in the late 1970s as just (Xie Yixian 1997).

Xing Sizhong contends that:

> [China's pacifism] has a close relationship with China's history and its modern misfortune. Throughout its modern history, China was bullied by the invasion of imperialism and colonialism. This bitter history has made Chinese realize the importance of independence, equality and freedom while abominating any forms of invasion and expansion. This is why anti-hegemonism has been a consistent theme of China's foreign policy (1996: 16).

Second, China's rapid economic development will not lead to military expansion. One major argument in the West is that a dramatic increase in China's economic power will lead to such a build up. But the Chinese negate this. According to them, China's pacific tradition of strategic thinking determines that it is unlikely for China to adopt an offensive strategy. This strategy has been reiterated by the Chinese government in the post-Mao era. Deng Xiaoping (1993b: 43) repeatedly emphasized that "China's strategy is always and will be defensive . . . If China is modernized in the future, its strategy will still be defensive". According to Xing, the view that China's economic development will necessarily lead to its military expansion is an anti-China prejudice or a Cold War thinking line. There is a long way to go before China becomes a developed country. China's military modernization is given the least priority in its four modernizations of industry, agriculture, national defense, and science and technology.

According to Xing, after the Cold War, economic factors came to play a growing role in international politics. A country's position of power will largely be determined by whether it is able to compete economically and technologically. In this context, China has to take every chance to develop, and the Chinese government is now determined to focus on economic building rather than military expansion. Owing to this perception, the government has made enormous efforts to convert military enterprises to civilian ones.

China's military modernization thus has to subordinate to economic modernization. From its modern history, Chinese leaders have learnt that China's military power has to be based on a solid economic foundation. In order to develop its economy, China's military spending cannot be excessive. While many in the West see a dramatic increase in China's military budget, Chinese military officials feel that they do not have enough financial resources to support the military's daily operation. Actually, if inflation is taken into account, China's military spending is in decline (Xu 1996: 49; Jing Bo 1996). Furthermore, China has also been very cautious in dealing with arms sales. Xu (1996: 49) argued that three principles have constrained China's sales: the aim of a given arms purchaser is national defense, not to undermine regional power balance, and not to interfere in other countries' domestic affairs. China adheres to these principles because they are in accordance with China's national interest.

The rise of nationalism *is* a new development in China in the 1990s. But China's new nationalism is reactive, responding to the rise of various forms of anti-China theories. Historically, Chinese nationalism has always been reactive. China is never nationalistic without any external threats. According to Chinese military analysts, China's defensive military strategy determines that China will not participate in any military alliance, establish any military bases in foreign countries, and occupy foreign land. That economic modernization will give rise to nationalism is the logic of Western imperialism. From the Sino–British War in the 1840s to the end of the Sino–Japanese War in 1945, China has been a victim of imperialism. Thousands of Chinese have lost their lives in the battle against imperialism. Now when the Chinese people, for the first time, are able to concentrate on economic modernization, the West begins to form new anti-China forces. Without doubt, this has led to the rise of Chinese nationalistic sentiment. The West should be responsible for Chinese nationalism (Xing 1996).

Another important factor also makes the "China threat" or "Chinese expansion" impossible: China is increasingly being integrated into the world system. To a great extent, Chinese officials, both military and civilian, realized that economic interdependence can promote and strengthen China's national interest. An editorial of *China National Defense* (Jing Bo 1996) argued that China's rapid economic growth will not pose a threat to the international community, but promote world peace. This is because China's economic development is not isolated. Again, China has been further integrated into the world economic system. While China has benefited from international economic activities, China's domestic development also provides a dynamism for world development. With rapid economic growth, China is increasingly eager to participate in multinational economic organizations and cooperation. There is no reason to argue that China's development is posing a major threat to world peace.

Then, why did the West, especially the United States, "produce" various anti-China theories? According to the Chinese government and military officials, by fabricating the "China threat" theory, the West aims to achieve the following goals. First, the West attempts to contain a socialist China's development. Since the collapse of the Soviet Union and the end of the Cold War, the West has begun to regard China as its potential enemy. The "China threat" theory aims to create an atmosphere for a long-term strategic goal; that is, containing China. Responding to *The Economist*'s (1995) article "Containing China", Chinese Ambassador to Britain Ma Yuzhen pointed out that, according to the logic of the "China threat" theory, only the United States has the rights to develop; China has to remain permanently poor and backward, and bow to the subjugation and exploitation of major Western powers. If economic development in the West does not pose a threat to world peace, why does China (*RMRB* 1995)? According to Xing the proponents of the "China threat" theory worry about an independent, prosperous, and strong China. This worry stems partly from their ideological anti-China prejudice and partly from their fear that the West will lose its hegemonic position in a new world order (1996: 20).

Second, United States has attempted to create a new "legitimacy" for its hegemony in the Asia–Pacific region. During the Cold War, the United States treated the Soviet Union as its enemy, deploying enormous troops in Asia and dominating international relations in the region. The "China threat" theory was "created" to justify the continuous presence of US troops, arms sales, interference in other countries' domestic affairs, and strengthening its hegemonic politics in the region.

Third, the United States also attempted to use the so-called "China threat" to undermine China's relations with its neighbors and other Asian countries, and thus to develop its containment strategy (Xu Xin 1996: 49). Although the Cold War ended, many great powers still use a Cold War line of thinking in their foreign policy-making.

According to Xing Shizhong (1996: 17), the perception of a rising power threatening the existing international order is based on the logic of Western imperialism. The West attempts to impose this logic on to China. The real cause of world instability comes from Western imperialism. For instance, the United States still maintains its overseas military bases and strengthens its military alliances, and regards foreign territories far away from its home as within the scope of its national security. Meanwhile, the United States attempts to impose its own values on other countries and interferes in their affairs. This has resulted in, and will continue to cause, international conflicts.

Conclusion

Both the "China threat" and "containing China" theories have been very controversial even in the West, let alone in Asia.[6] For instance, Malaysian Prime Minister Mahathir Mohamad repeatedly emphasized that China will not pose a threat to regional stability (Mahathir 1996). Indeed, many leaders in South-east Asia see the dangers of isolating or containing China and the importance of integrating China into multinational institutions.

Nevertheless, many Chinese believe that "containing China" is the West's strategy towards China. It is understandable that nationalistic sentiments appear among different social and political groups. Apparently, the new nationalism can be regarded as a response to the West's policy towards China. When analyzing popular Chinese nationalism against the United States, one Chinese author pointed out that "to a large extent, the United States itself sowed the seeds of discord" (Si Cheng 1996: 13). Even though nationalistic sentiments are also popular among government officials, the government is very cautious in dealing with nationalism, especially with those anti-West sentiments. One author warned that "nationalism may not succeed against the West without but may arouse national divisions within, and thus become a double-edged sword that could wound ourselves but not hurt the enemy" (Ge Jianxiong 1996: 14; cited in Wang Gungwu 1996b: 7).

The leadership realized that excessive nationalism and anti-foreignism would hurt China's open-door policy from which it had benefited for almost two decades. Although the regime needs nationalism to compensate a declining traditional Marxist and Maoist ideology, popular nationalism, especially when it becomes a social movement, will threaten China's political stability. Popular nationalism must be constrained to a certain point. Facing a rising popular nationalism, the regime initiated an official campaign against a variety of "anti-China" theories and thus appeased popular sentiment. At the same time, the government also tightened its media control. Many believe that popular nationalism has had a negative impact on China's international image and China's foreign policy-making. The Chinese leaders feel that it is hard to make rational foreign policies while dealing with intensive popular nationalism. Furthermore, popular nationalism has also had an impact on foreign countries' perceptions about China by creating an image of an irrational China. A recent example is that the government criticized the best-seller, *The China that Says No* (Song Qiang et al. 1996) because it had a negative impact on China's foreign image. However, early on, the government regarded it as a positive reaction to the United State's policy towards China (*MP* 1996).

Nonetheless, even official nationalism could become uncontrollable. The new nationalism is reactive. Whether it will become aggressive depends not only on the interaction between the State and society, but also the intensity of foreign pressure that China encounters. As one Chinese author has pointed out, the "containing China" strategy will lead to very strong nationalistic reactions from China and encourage the rise of a new authoritarian regime. In other words, the containment strategy will only make China an anti-West force and thus a real threat to the national interests of Western nations (Wu Guoguang 1995). As a New Zealand observer also pointed out, "the more talk there is of 'containing' China, the greater the danger of the Chinese becoming as paranoid as the Germans were before 1914 when they feared 'encirclement.' If China is frustrated and baited, it could become aggressive" (Marland 1996: 8).

CHAPTER 6

New Identity, National Interest, and International Behavior

I have argued that the major aim of China's new nationalism is to provide a vision of "a great future". Therefore, though new nationalists opposed China's westernization and attempted to revive traditional Confucianism-based nationalism, the new nationalism can be better regarded as a response to severe domestic issues such as the decline of central power and national identity rather than as China's intention to flex its growing muscles as a result of rapid economic growth.

Nonetheless, this does not mean in any sense that the new nationalism does not have an impact on China's international behavior. Certainly, China's "great future" is significant for the international community, especially its neighbors. Various concerns have arisen worldwide, including what are the intentions of the Chinese government and nationalist intellectuals when they make great efforts to cultivate or strengthen people's national identity? National identity is about in-group versus the out-group. An increase in the intensity of in-group identity often tends to produce or strengthen people's hatred toward out-groups. So, what does China's new national identity mean for the international community? Will China's nationalism intensify its people's hatred towards foreign countries and push the country to aggression in its foreign behavior?

Furthermore, from a materialist perspective, what does capitalistic development in China mean for the world system? Capitalism, by its nature, is expansionist. Indeed, many Marxist scholars have argued that imperialism is a natural extension of domestic nationalism (Mommsen 1977; Brewer 1980). Will capitalism lead to Chinese expansionism? China's economic reforms have already increased its capability of engaging in external economic activities. Much attention has been paid to the potential implications of growing economic interaction between different parts of China, especially between the mainland, Hong Kong, and

Taiwan. Different terms have been used to describe this phenomenon: "Greater China", the "China Economic Circle", the "China Economic Community", and the "China Economic Sphere".[1] More importantly, with the progress of the open-door policy on all fronts, Chinese economic ties go far beyond Hong Kong, Taiwan and Macau, and extend to almost all of China's neighboring countries. Though Chinese leaders have discredited such terms as "Greater China", since they remind people of Japan's efforts to build a "Greater Asian Co-Prosperity Sphere" in the 1930s, many outside China have expressed their concerns because what they have seen is exactly that. With its rapid domestic development and expanding economic connections, China is becoming more assertive regionally, if not internationally.

What is the impact of China's rapid economic development and natural economic expansion on its nationalism? It has been argued in the West that the new nationalism can be attributed to China's reform and economic growth. While some see that the new nationalism is different from China's traditional anti-imperialist nationalism and Maoist nationalism, many others believe that China is becoming increasingly aggressive in international affairs.[2]

Whiting (1983) distinguished two types of nationalism: assertive and affirmative. The former emphasizes the confrontation between "us" and "them" while compromise is possible for the latter. Oksenberg (1986–87) argued that there have been four types of nationalism in China: self-pitying, self-righteous and aggrieved nationalism; strident, xenophobic and isolationist nationalism; militant, rigid, assertive and occasionally muscular nationalism; and confident nationalism. Nationalism in post-Mao China has been identified as confident.

According to Johnston:

> China has historically exhibited a relatively consistent hard Realpolitik or *parabellum* strategic culture that has persisted across different structural contexts into the Maoist period (and beyond). Chinese decision-makers have internalized this strategic culture such that China's strategic behavior exhibits a preference for offensive uses of force (1996: 217).

Indeed, Johnston argued that the preference for offensive uses of force is still central to China's strategic culture in post-Mao China. Though China's economy has become increasingly integrated into the global economy and the country faces the most tranquil environment since 1949, hard Realpolitik decisions continue to dominate the Chinese leadership's approach to foreign policy and security affairs. The leadership's approach to international issues such as arms control, the environment, and human rights are still dominated by defection and free-riding decision rules (Johnston 1996: 257).

Under the influence of such a strategic culture, China is likely to use its economic resources to expand its political influences outward and solve its territorial disputes. Many have argued that China will eventually use whatever means to build a Sino-centric imperial power. According to two observers, because China still sticks to traditional notions of sovereignty, "China feels it is fully within its rights to change the territorial status quo, even though most other countries view such action as aggressive and dangerous" (Buzan & Segal 1994: 2). China's aggressiveness has been evident in its handling of the takeover of Hong Kong, its determination to acquire islands in the South China Sea, and its military exercises over the Taiwan Strait. One possible scenario is China's penetration through cultural, religious, and ethnic influences into South-east Asia as in the days when China's tributary system became dominant (Buzan & Segal 1994: 6).

It is not hard to argue that China's nationalism cannot be a result of its natural economic expansion. This observation has raised an important question about China's nationalism; that is: Will the Chinese government attempt to expand China's political and military influence through such means as economic expansion? A more fundamental question is: Does China still identify with its old world order that was based on the traditional tribute system (see Fairbank 1968)? Or have the Chinese changed their perceptions of national interest, national sovereignty and China's position in the world of nations?

In the discussion of the impact of Chinese nationalism on China's foreign behavior in the post-Mao era so far, an important point has been under-emphasized; that is, Chinese leaders have changed their perceptions towards the existing international system over the course of reform and open-door policy. As the external environment changes so do perceptions. The perception of China as the center of the world resulted from the external circumstances it encountered when it was a strong power prior to the arrival of Western imperialism. However, China's nationalism is not invariable. Instead, it has been repeatedly re-constructed in accordance with changing domestic priorities and international circumstances and is thus in a state of flux. Therefore, China's international intentions cannot be solely assessed by its behavior in the past. In discussing the impact of norms and identity on a given State's foreign behavior, Paul Kowert and Jeffrey Legro (1996: 454) pointed out that it is equally important is to ask, "Where do the norms themselves come from?". Without an understanding of the process of norm-building, it is still difficult to predict how a given State will conduct its foreign behavior. Similarly, a neglect of the changing aspects of China's national identity in the post-Mao era will cause a misunderstanding of the new nationalism.

I have examined China's new nationalism from various perspectives and shown the complicated nature of this new nationalism for China's domestic politics. The last chapter discusses why the Chinese leadership is constrained in allowing nationalistic voices to rise over China's foreign affairs by showing how popular nationalism and official nationalism, that is, patriotism, are contradictory to one another. This chapter further explores another important aspect of official nationalism; that is, the emergence of a new identity of national interest. Although the term "nationalism" has been used widely to indicate China's international intention, and Chinese nationalism has been compared to German and Japanese expansionism, what it means to the international community still remains unclear. As a result, this chapter will focus on China's perceptions of "comprehensive national power (CNP, *zonghe guoli*)", which has been the core of China's official discourse on nationalism, and its impact on China's strategic thinking on national interests concerning its foreign behavior and international affairs.

In post-Mao China, the concept "national interest" has replaced Maoist internationalism and become the foundation of China's official nationalism in foreign affairs. Chinese government analysts now argue that national interest should be the most important guideline in conducting China's foreign policy-making. While nationalistic sentiments over foreign affairs need to be constrained, national interest should be emphasized. Dong Zhenghua (1994: 27) claimed that, "national interest and nationalism are identical in international politics." Moreover, central to China's national interest is the notion of "comprehensive national power". Indeed, "CNP" and "national interest" are two interchangeable terms in the Chinese official discourse of nationalism. CNP links China's domestic and international polices, and is therefore significant for both China and the international community. An analysis of this concept will help explain the content of Chinese official nationalism and its impact on China's foreign policy-making.

This chapter is divided into three sections. The first explains the concept of CNP and China's strategy of raising its CNP. The second section examines whether China has changed its perception of national interests since the end of the Cold War. The third section explores how this new identity of national interest affects China's foreign behavior as shown in the cases of China's key bilateral relations with the United States, the way the Chinese government dealt with the Diaoyutai (or Senkaku) islands dispute with Japan in 1996, and the rise of multilateralism towards South-east Asia.

"Comprehensive National Power"

According to an official explanation (Zhong Cai 1995: 37), "comprehensive national power" refers to "the totality of a country's economic, military and political power in a given period. It signals the country's comprehensive development level and its position in the international system. In the content of the CNP, economic power, including labor power, material resources and financial power, is the determinant and foundation of a country's political and military power".

The concept "national power" has been used to measure a given nation–state's position concerning international power distribution for almost a century (see Cline 1994). The term "comprehensive national power" is similar to "national power". The Chinese began to use this concept in the 1980s. Senior political leaders such as Deng Xiaoping and Yang Shangkun argued that China's national power must be measured comprehensively (*RMRB* 1990: 2). It was in 1992 that CNP was introduced into official documents. The Fourteenth Party Congress of the Chinese Communist Party (CCP) convened that year, proposing a strategy called "comprehensive national power competition (*zonghe guoli jingzheng*)". Jiang Zemin, General Secretary of the CCP, emphasized that "the core of current international competition is comprehensive national power based on economic and political power".[3] Based on this perception of world affairs, Chinese strategists have developed a so-called "comprehensive national power competition strategy" since then. This strategy aims to set forth guidelines for China as a sovereign State to develop its national power to pursue national interests and strategic goals domestically and internationally. These goals include:

- To protect socialist China and its political system.
- To protect China's independence, sovereignty and security.
- To protect and facilitate China's continuous economic and technological development.
- To create a conducive and peaceful environment for China's socioeconomic and political progress.
- To respond effectively to any external threats and challenges.
- To prevent and restrain any internal and external conflicts and wars from happening.
- To maintain and raise China's international status and prestige (Huang Shuofeng 1992: 299–304).

Though this strategy was formalized recently, it has been the central guideline of China's development in the reform era. In interpreting "comprehensive national power" as a political concept, it is necessary to take a brief look at the development of China's national strategy.

China's National Strategy

China's national strategy (*guojia zhanlue*) is based largely on the perceptions of its political leaders on the international environment. According to Chinese government analysts, "international environment" (IE, *guoji huanjing*) can be defined as a framework in which power is distributed among sovereign states and where China is located. The IE affects China's national interests in three ways. First, the IE determines whether China is exposed to any external military threats. Second, it decides whether China is able to receive political support from other sovereign states. And, third, it also indicates how China could be sanctioned economically by foreign countries (Yan Xuetong 1996b; Gu Dexin & Huang Qi 1996).

The international environment that China encounters defines the significance of the CNP. A China with a stronger CNP will be in a favorable position in the hierarchy of international power distribution and will be able to gain more benefits from it. Furthermore, a strong CNP will enable China to be involved in world affairs and to be integrated into the world system. The CNP can be measured in different ways. Internationally, economic power refers to the extent that China has been integrated into the international economic system, and the amount of benefits that China will gain from the system. Military power can be measured by whether China is threatened by other countries militarily. Political power can be judged internationally by whether China is able to protect its overseas interests, and domestically by the maintenance of political stability and the achievement of national integration or unification.

Among various indices, the "level of technological development" (LTD) is especially important. It refers to China's position in the world system in terms of technological development. Whether China can pursue national interests effectively in international arenas is largely decided by China's level of technological development. The LTD also has a great impact on China's position in the international structure of power distribution (Yan Xuetong 1996b: 36–7).

Since the establishment of the PRC, China's national strategies have experienced several major changes. During the Great Leap Forward (1957–58), a "catching-up" strategy was carried out. Mao emphasized that China needed to catch up with advanced Western countries such as Great Britain and United States within fifteen years. The strategy led to an economic disaster. During the Cultural Revolution, Mao Zedong regarded class struggle rather than economic development as the nation's priority. The Maoist revolutionary movement led China to both political and economic chaos. In 1975, Zhou Enlai proposed the four modernizations of industry, agriculture, science and technology, and national defense as the national development goal. Since Chinese leaders perceived the prevention of war as China's major national interest, anti-hegemonism was given the highest priority in formulating China's foreign policy in the whole Mao era.

After Deng Xiaoping took over power at the end of the 1980s, China began to change its perception of the international environment in an attempt to promote domestic development. The historical Third Plenum of the Eleventh Congress of the Chinese Community Party (CCP) in 1978 shifted the domestic priority from class struggle to economic development. A hospitable international environment became its national strategic goal. To a great extent, this was owed to Deng Xiaoping's perception of the linkage between domestic and international politics. In 1980 Deng Xiaoping (1980, 1984) argued that the leadership had to perform three important tasks; that is, anti-hegemonism, national unification, and economic construction or modernization. Although Deng here still emphasized that China would continue to oppose hegemonism in international politics, his main goal was to create a peaceful environment for China's domestic development because he perceived that economic modernization was central to the solution of China's external and internal problems, and determined China's position in the system of nation–states. Deng acknowledged publicly that China's national power was very weak and the government had to pay full attention to domestic development, and that China's foreign policy must serve domestic economic development.[4]

In effect, it seemed to Deng that seeking a peaceful international environment should become the main goal of China's foreign policy since it was in China's national interest. According to Deng:

> For the interest of our own country, the goal of our foreign policy is a peaceful environment for achieving the four modernizations . . . This is a vital matter which conforms to the interests not only of the Chinese people but also of the people in the rest of the world (1984d: 226).

However, in order to seek a peaceful international environment, peace had to be first perceived as possible. While Mao perceived that China encountered a hostile external environment, what Deng did was to persuade other Chinese leaders to perceive a benign world.

In 1983, Deng (1983a, in 1993a: 25) again emphasized when he was talking with major Party leaders that, "there will be no large war. Don't be frightened. There is no risk. Before [we] were always afraid of war and talked about war every year. We have exaggerated the situation. I now believe that there will be no war in ten years". In 1985, Deng repeated this theme when he met a delegation from Japan. Deng argued:

> We had believed the possibility of war for many years. Recently there has been a change in our perception. We understand that although there is still a possibility of war, the forces that prevent war from occurring have been developed impressively . . . The world now faces two real problems, one is peace, another is economic development or global development (1985a, in 1993a: 104–5).

In 1987 Deng came to a conclusion that "it is possible to have long-term peace, and war is avoidable" (1987a, in 1993a: 233).

The facilitation of favorable international circumstances to serve domestic goals was the theme of China's foreign policy-making in the 1980s. The implementation of this strategy was successful. China improved bilateral relations with its neighboring countries and achieved rapid economic growth and a great success in developing foreign trade (see Robinson & Shambaugh 1995; Lardy 1994).

After the government's crackdown of the 1989 pro-democracy movement, China encountered a hostile international environment. The West imposed various sanctions on China. The collapse of the former Soviet Union and eastern European communist regimes left China as the only great power in the socialist camp. Deng's national development strategy encountered serious internal and external challenges. Nevertheless, Deng insisted that external difficulty could be overcome since peace and development were still the theme of world politics. Therefore, China should still give the highest priority to economic development. While accusing the United States of supporting the 1989 demonstration, Deng (1989b, in 1993a: 331) also expressed that China was willing to improve its relations with the United States. After the break-up of the Soviet Union, nationalist sentiments began to appear in China. But Deng remained pragmatic and realized that China's national power had to be based on its economic power. According to Deng, China had to stick to the following principles in order to concentrate on domestic priorities.

First, "China must not assume a number one position in world politics. This should be China's number one principle in dealing with foreign affairs. China should not be in such a position because it is not strong enough to be in this position. To be in the number one position will not benefit China, but make China lose many initiatives. China will forever stand on the side of Third World countries. China will never attempt to be a hegemonist, and will never attempt to be in a number one position" (Deng 1990c, in 1993a: 363).

Second, "China's foreign policy has two other principles. The first is to oppose hegemonism and power politics, and to protect world peace. The second is to establish a new international political order and economic order" (Deng 1990a, in 1993a: 353).

Third, "to facilitate rapid economic development, China needs to rely on progress in technology and education. China has to have a clear strategic goal in any major areas and once it is decided, it has to be realized. China has to occupy a position in the field of high technology" (Deng 1992, in 1993a: 377–8).

These principles were incorporated into the CPC's decision of the Fourteenth Party Congress (1992), which accommodated a capitalist economy to China's socialist system. The decision reaffirmed the policy of reform, opening to the outside, and economic development as the national priority (Jiang Zemin 1992). The strategy of "comprehensive national power competition" proposed by the Party Congress, can be regarded as a systematic expression of Deng's ideas. Even though the decision also stressed the significance of China's involvement in world affairs and military modernization, its underlying theme is that China needs to concentrate on domestic development in order to be strong in international politics.

CNP, the New Face of National Identity

According to Chinese strategists, CNP can be identified in the following terms:

- Basic power (*jichu shili*) refers to the environments against which China as a sovereign State survives and develops, including its geographic location, the quality and quantity of population, natural resources, and national spirit that binds different social groups together and strengthens their national identity.
- Economic power refers to China's capacity in industry, agriculture, commerce, finance, and technology.
- National defense power refers to China's capability to defend herself and to build deterrent forces including nuclear deterrence.
- Diplomatic power refers to China's influence in international affairs through its diplomatic activities.
- Organizational and coordination power refers to China's capacity to organize various power resources to serve its national goals.
- Rational decision-making capacity refers to China's capacity to make "right" domestic and foreign policies based on "right" knowledge about China's internal and external affairs.
- Moral and cultural power refers to the people's political attitudes, belief systems and national characters.[5]

In order to strengthen China's CNP, the regime has made and implemented a comprehensive strategy that focuses on increasing China's economic power, facilitating progress in technology, raising the educational level of population, and strengthening its military power.

Economic growth has been given the highest priority because the CCP believes that without a strong economy, the country will go nowhere. According to the Decision of the Thirteenth Party Congress in 1987, China's development goal would be achieved through three steps. The first step was to double China's gross national product (GNP) between 1980 and 1990, and to provide adequate food and clothing for the people.

The second step was to double again China's GNP by the end of this century and to achieve a relatively comfortable life or a *xiao-kang* living standard. The third step was to catch up with middle income countries by the middle of the next century (Zhao Ziyang 1987).[6] According to official interpretations, the first goal was achieved in 1988 and the second goal was realized by 1995, five years ahead of the original plan (*TKP* 1996: 8). In early 1996 the Chinese National People's Congress approved a long-term national development plan (*TKP* 1996: 8). According to this plan, China's real per capita GNP will quadruple by 2000 from the 1980 level. From 2000 to 2010, China will again double its per capita income so that in the fifteen years from 1996 China will develop into a middle-income country (this goal was already realized in 1996).

High technological development is another priority in the CCP's attempt to strengthen China's CNP. Deng emphasized that China must occupy an important position in the world of high technologies. Senior scientists such as Qian Xuesen and Zhou Guangzhao argued that the next century will be a century of high technology competition, that high technology is the key to strengthen China's CNP, and only after China has taken a leading position in high technology will it be able to meet various forms of external and internal challenges and become a world power (Zhou Guangzhao 1995).[7] In 1987 the CCP issued a plan of "Research and Development for High Technologies", which aimed to lift China's technological level in biology, space, information, energy, new materials, and so on. Later, the CCP implemented a development strategy called the "Torch Plan" to promote the development of high technologies by establishing special development zones (see Chen Liangchao 1993).

The CCP has also made various efforts to modernize China's military in order to increase its CNP, especially in the 1990s. The People's Liberation Army has attempted to shift its focus from a Maoist "people's war" strategy to a high technology-centered one and to transform itself from a land power to sea power.[8] These developments have led to various reactions from the international community. Even though there has been a controversy on the size of China's military budget, the Chinese feel that they can only provide very limited economic resources to military modernization. The military has struggled for modernization, but it has also realized that military modernization needs enormous economic resources. It seems that there is a compromise or consensus between the government and the military that China's highest priority is economic development and military modernization has to subordinate to this priority. In 1980 Deng (1980, in 1994: 285) pointed out that a large military budget was detrimental to China's economic modernization and "we should do our best to reduce the military budget to strengthen the country's economic construction". In 1985 Deng (1985b, in 1993a: 128) again agued that "the four modernizations should be taken up in order of priority. Only after a better infrastructure of national economy is laid down will the modernization of the army be possible." The military thus had to follow the government's strategy of modernization. Deng also encouraged the military to be involved in national economic construction. As a matter of fact, supporting national and local economic development has been one of the major duties of China's military, which in turn has had a negative impact on the military (Segal & Yang 1996; Richard Yang et al. 1994).

An important agenda for the CCP is how the quality of population should be increased. The Chinese government expects to implement the compulsory education system nationwide by 2000. Various policies have been carried out, including solidifying the existing compulsory system; developing occupational education, improving the existing system of high education, reforming China's educational system, and improving the quality of educators.[9]

However, it is dubious to say that the situation has improved since the reform began in the late 1970s. Owing to the decline of its financial capacity, the government is not able to provide effective financial support for basic education, especially in poor areas. The decline of state financial power also has had a very negative impact on high education, with professional educators and researchers increasingly shifting their focus to profit-making in order to improve their incomes. Commercial activities became prevalent among educators. Presently, there are about 220 million illiterate people in China, which is about a quarter of the total illiterate population of the world. Indeed, the low level of education has been a major barrier to China's economic modernization. Moreover, because of China's limited financial and personnel resources, this situation is unlikely to be improved in the short term (Huang Shuofeng 1990). China's human resource development at present is among the weakest in the Asia–Pacific region. Only 2 percent of the relevant age-group in China are receiving tertiary education, compared to 42 percent in Korea and 45 percent in Taiwan (see Wong 1996b: 14). If this situation continues, China's economic growth will slow down.

Even though the CNP strategy aims to achieve a balanced development, economic growth occupies top priority because the development of high technology, military modernization and the improvement of population quality all consume enormous economic resources. The preoccupation of the Chinese government with domestic economic growth has had a great impact on China's foreign policy, which is required to serve domestic priorities.

"Domestic priority" has been, without doubt, the principle of China's foreign policy-making in the Deng era. It can also explain the consistency of China's foreign policy in this period. However, for the international community, what is important is whether China will pursue an aggressive foreign policy following a dramatic increase in its CNP. Put it in another way: Will China change its concept of national interest with the end of the Cold War?

National Interest in the Post-Cold War Era

Three important factors have affected China's perception of national interest in the 1990s: the end of the Cold War, the political legitimacy of the new leadership, and the leadership's collective perceptions of real (not imagined) Chinese power.

During the Cold War era, the United States and Soviet Union dominated international politics. China's national interest had to be perceived within this power structure. With the end of the Cold War and the collapse of the Soviet Union, China's national interest had to be redefined. Like other major powers, the end of the Cold War brought China into an uncertain world. This dramatic change created an opportunity for China to lift its position in the international system. While many previous world powers including the United States are on the decline, China has experienced rapid economic growth for more than a decade and its comprehensive national power has increased drastically. Various studies by Chinese authors indicated that China is already one of the major world powers in terms of comprehensive national power, ranking fourth to sixth.[10]

But how should China position itself in a new international system? Chinese government analysts perceived the international system after the Cold War as possessing the following characteristics. First of all, it is more complicated than that in the Cold War era. Since all major powers have to adjust their own status in the international system, their foreign policies become uncertain. This makes it difficult for China to identify friends and foes. Second, political and military coalitions and alliances have become increasingly loose, and sovereign states tend to be more independent in their foreign policy-making than before. Third, multinational organizations and institutions are becoming an important means for increasing and strengthening the national interest of the sovereign states. Finally, international cooperation tends to be regionalized. Geographical location and culture have become more significant than ideology in promoting national interest (Yan Xuetong 1996b).

Whatever the external situation, one point is clear: China still has to focus on its domestic priorities. A collective consensus among major leaders has been formed; that is, a prerequisite for China to promote its national interest internationally is continuous economic growth and modernization. This collective consensus without doubt remains. Jiang Zemin emphasized at the Fifteenth Congress of the Chinese Communist Party (1997) that the highest priority would and should be given to economic reform. According to Jiang (Zheng Yongnian 1997), modern Chinese history shows that economic backwardness would put China in a very negative position, vulnerable to be constrained by other powers; therefore China has no way but to focus on increasing its comprehensive national power. The Ninth National People's Congress further decided to implement a large-scale government re-organization in an attempt to provide an institutional foundation for the country's economic reform (Zheng Yongnian & Li Jinshan 1998). Whatever changes have occurred to the international system, China does not need to change its domestic priority. China has benefited from the strategy of "domestic priority" for almost two decades and increased its international prestige significantly. Unless there are dramatic changes in international affairs which undermine China's domestic development, there is no need to introduce changes to the regime's current policy discourse.

The end of the Cold War coincided with the leadership succession in China. Scholars have argued that the new leadership has made great efforts to appeal to popular nationalism in an attempt to consolidate the regime. While the political legitimacy of the old generation of leaders such as Mao Zedong and Deng Xiaoping came from their revolutionary experience, the new leadership needs to establish a new base of political legitimacy. However, appealing to nationalism can become a dangerous enterprise for the Chinese leadership due to its complicated nature. Instead, the new leadership has to stick to the principle of "domestic priority" in order to strengthen its legitimacy. The regime believes that political reform can lead to political instability as occurred in other former communist countries. However, without political reform, the regime has to rely solely on economic growth to strengthen its political legitimacy. Without a continuous delivery of economic goods to the public, the regime will find it difficult to govern a vast country.

The new leadership also realized that without continuous economic growth, China's national interest cannot be served internationally. According to the government's long-term plan issued in 1996 (*TKP* 1996), Chinese GNP will continue to grow at 7.4 percent per annum in the next fifteen years. That will make China one of the economic superpowers in early 21st century. But the Chinese leaders are not as optimistic as many observers regarding China's rise. They believe that even if China does become one of the biggest economies in the world in the near future, China would still be poor. By 2010, China will have more than 1.3 billion people (*TKP* 1996), while per capita GNP will still be far below that of the developed countries. Moreover, according to the Chinese government, China will have at least 10 million people living below the poverty line by 2010.

Marxists believe that the early stages of capitalist development lead to imperialism through which domestic growth is maintained. Can China avoid this iron law? Chinese strategists now realize that it is impossible for China to support continuous economic growth by overseas military expansion. Technological progress becomes the most important means to improve China's productivity. Earlier on Deng Xiaoping identified science and technology as the sources of its productivity. According to the CCP's long-term plan mentioned above, China has to shift its focus from extensive growth to intensive growth.

The recognition of China's low level of CNP forced the leadership to continue to concentrate on domestic development. Like Deng Xiaoping, Jiang Zemin and other leaders recognized that they had to focus on lifting China's comprehensive national power and improving the people's living standards in order to increase the regime's political legitimacy. For this to happen a peaceful and hospitable international environment remains vital.

The characteristic identity of international peace and "domestic priority" therefore have not changed much after the end of the Cold War. This in turn has had an impact on the Chinese concept of national interest and thus international behavior. According to Chinese strategic analysts, in the post-Cold War era, China's national interests include national survival, political recognition, economic interest, international domination, and contribution to the international community. These types of national interest form a hierarchy with "national survival" at the top and "contribution to the international community" at the bottom (Yan Xuetong 1996c: 155). During the Cold War era, China regarded national security and political recognition or national sovereignty as the highest forms of national interest. This perception is undergoing a change with the end of the Cold War. Yan Xuetong (1996b) pointed out that "the end of the Cold War leads to a multipolar world. In terms of national power, China's gap with the major world powers has narrowed. China's security environment has improved greatly and security interest is not as important as other forms of national interest. Economic interest and technological progress have become vital to China's national interest". As a matter of fact, the most important national interest is to maintain international peace and restrain China from any form of military conflict so that China's "domestic priorities" can be implemented. According to Yan, one of China's Realpolitik thinkers, the positive correlation between peace and domestic development can be statistically proven.

In thirty years from 1949 to 1979, China was involved in military conflicts every five years. Because of frequent involvement of military conflicts, China was not able to engage in normal economic construction. By contrast, since 1980, China is no longer involved in any sort of military conflict and therefore has achieved great economic success . . . To avoid military conflicts must be China's most important national interest (1996c: 155).

On the other hand, the end of the Cold War did affect China's perception of its position in the system of nation–states. An increase in economic power seemed to have an impact on China's power ambitions. Chinese strategists argued that any country, whether it was on the decline or on the rise, had to redefine the scope and content of its national interest based on its power, and that a country whose comprehensive national power increased had to expand its national interest and participate in international affairs rather actively. As Yan (1996b: 39) pointed out, "with its increasing national power, China feels that it is necessary to take a more firm stand to protect its national interest and dignity" (see also Gu Dexin & Huang Qi 1996).

Immediately after the fall of the Soviet Union, Deng Xiaoping (1990a in 1993a: 353) argued that "changes have occurred to the international affairs that had been monopolized by the US and the USSR. The international structure will be divided into three poles, four poles, perhaps five poles in the future. In this so-called multipolar world, China must be one of the poles. China should not underestimate herself. Whatever the structure is, China is a pole". Moreover, Deng warned that "power politics is reviving and a few Western powers are attempting to monopolize world politics" (Deng 1989a, in 1993a: 329). In 1989 Deng (1989e, in 1993a: 351) contended when receiving American guests that "when the two countries (the United States and China) get along, they should respect each other and give consideration to the other part so that they can solve any conflicts between them". On other occasions, Deng emphasized that China, as an independent sovereign nation–state, has its own national dignity and self-respect. Other major powers cannot impose their own will on China without taking China's opinions into account.[11]

As a matter of fact, the new leadership has identified pursuing international respect for China as a major theme of China's foreign relations. Following Deng, China's Foreign Minister Qian Qichen also argued that while China can play a more positive role in world affairs, a strong China needs to be recognized by the outside world. According to Qian:

> More and more countries are paying attention to the rise of China . . . People are talking about the potential role that China can play in world politics . . . World peace and development need China . . . To isolate China will not go

anywhere, but hurt oneself. To respect each other and to have dialogues as equal partners are the only way to increase consensus, reduce differences and to improve inter-country relations (1993: 4).

It is important to note that there are differences between the old and new generations of leadership in the way they pursued international recognition for China. The old generation placed emphasis on China's sovereignty and strongly resisted and thus took hostile attitudes towards external pressure. By contrast, the new leadership realized that while other major powers have to respect China's national dignity, China has to "earn" international respect. Therefore, the new leaders are more likely to consider what other countries want China to do. In this sense, the impact of the new nationalism on China's foreign policy-making has been minimized rather than strengthened. In the remaining parts of this chapter, I will use three cases to show how the new concept of national interest affects China's international behavior.

New Identity and Foreign Behavior: Three Cases

Sino–US Relations: From Foe to "Strategic Partner"

After the government's crackdown of the 1989 pro-democracy movement, the West, led by the United States, imposed serious economic and political sanctions on China. Deng Xiaoping (1989b, in 1993a: 331) argued, when he met former US president Richard Nixon, that to solve the conflicts between the two countries, the United States had to take initiatives. When Deng met US National Security Advisor Brent Scrowcroft, he also expected President Bush to do something to improve Sino–US relations (Deng 1989e, in 1993a: 351). It seemed to Deng that China could not afford to take a confrontational attitude towards the United States since China really needed a peaceful international environment for domestic development. Indeed, since the Cold War ended, China's US policy has been responsive. Changes in the discourse of China's US policy depends, to a great degree, on changes in the US China policy.

When China began to carry out its reform and open-door policy in the late 1970s, optimism prevailed in the United States. It was believed that Deng had renounced Marxism–Leninism and China was becoming the first communist State to transit from a centrally planned economy and totalitarianism to a market one, and even a democratic political system (see Fukuyama 1989: 3–18). In other words, China would be "more like us (the United States)". Naturally, the government's crackdown of the 1989 pro-democracy movement shocked idealistic Americans and led to a dramatic change in the US's China policy.

However, beneath the ideological conflict between the two countries are conflicts over real interests. During the Cold War, the Sino–US relationship was based on one single common interest in international affairs; that is, a common enemy (the Soviet Union). In addition, China's reform and open-door policy were also in the US's economic interest. But over time, these real interests changed. The common strategic interest suddenly disappeared with the collapse of the Soviet Union. Dramatic changes also occurred to the Sino–US trade balance: from an American surplus in the early 1980s to a growing deficit by the late 1980s. Many Americans began to see China as another mercantilist Asian economy that was only out to hurt American economic interest.

Though the Bush Administration imposed various sanctions on China after the crackdown in Tiananmen Square, it tried to avoid a full confrontation with China. For example, it successfully resisted the revocation of China's most-favored-nation status. However, after Bill Clinton took office in 1993, dramatic changes occurred to the US's China policy. The Clinton Administration regarded human rights issues as central to its China policy by explicitly linking the renewal of China's most-favored-nation trade status with improvements in its human rights record. While the Bush Administration tried to facilitate high-level official contact with China, Clinton eschewed such dialogue for the first several months of the new administration.

Changes in the US's China policy resulted in a strong Chinese reaction. Immediately after the 1989 crackdown, the Chinese government attacked America's preoccupation with human rights as an illegitimate intervention in China's internal affairs, and as a strategy of encouraging China's "peaceful evolution" from socialism to capitalism (Whiting 1995). Deng Xiaoping (1989a, 1989c, in 1993a: 344–6; 1990b, in 1993a: 359–61) repeatedly insisted that the United States and the West did not have any legitimate rights to impose their own will on China; that China's national rights (*guoquan*) were more important than individual human rights; and that China would not bow to high external pressure. Another two events worsened the relationship between the two countries: America's opposition of China's bid to host the Olympic Games in 2000 and the Clinton Administration's order to the US Navy to search a Chinese merchant ship (*Yin He Hao*), which allegedly carried precursors for chemical weapons to the Middle East. However, in the 1980s many Chinese, especially urban intellectuals, regarded the United States as a model for China to follow. They welcomed America's outrage at the events of the 1989 crackdown. But these events, plus the rise of the "China Threat" theory in the West, changed public opinions among ordinary Chinese. As I have mentioned in previous chapters, an essential portion of the population began to regard the United States as China's foe.[12]

In late 1993, after reviewing its previous China policy, the Clinton Administration announced a policy of "engagement". The engagement strategy introduced three changes to the US's China policy. First, the Administration de-coupled the renewal of China's most-favored-nation status from the perennial human rights issue. Second, it moved its China policy beyond human rights to a broader set of issues for bilateral discussion. And third, Clinton restored higher official contact with China; that is, at the Cabinet level. Nevertheless, for the Chinese leaders and government analysts what the "engagement policy" meant was never clear. Many regarded "engagement" as an internal part of the US "containment" strategy. Practically, the Chinese did not see any major changes in the US's China policy. The United States did send a large number of American Cabinet missions to China, including the Department of Commerce, the Department of Defense, the US Trade Representative and the Human Rights Desk of the State Department, but many of them seemed to be very confrontational towards China.

Changes in the way the United States dealt with Taiwan reinforced the Chinese suspicions over the US's China policy. In 1994 the Clinton Administration reviewed its Taiwan policy. It did not clarify long-term US intentions towards Taiwan, nor did it touch the most sensitive issue of the US's outlook on the rising demands for independence on the island. Instead, it focused on the rules governing contact between US and Taiwanese officials. One of these new rules allowed Taiwanese officials to enter the United States only in transit to some other countries. But the Administration soon violated this rule when it allowed Taiwan President Lee Teng-hui to make a major speech at Cornell University in the late spring of 1995. Chinese leaders and government analysts believed that the United States was implementing its containment policy by blocking China's unification with Taiwan or even by supporting Taiwan's independence. Logically, when China fired missiles and deployed its fleet off the coast of Taiwan to demonstrate its displeasure with the advocates of Taiwanese independence, the United States expressed its willingness to protect Taiwan by sending two aircraft carriers to the Strait. Anti-America nationalistic voices reached a new peak (Ren Weiwen 1995a).

The Taiwan Strait crisis, which demonstrated China's determination to achieve the goal of national unification, had a significant impact on the US's China policy. The Clinton administration declared that its long-term goal was to integrate China into the international community with all the privileges and responsibilities of a major power. The United States would not attempt to block the rise of China. Nor did it want to contain China. "Engagement" was meant to encourage China to be a major power, a respected but responsible one. In other words, the United States would make efforts to bring China into the world power club, but China had the obligation to honor the existing international rules in its own behavior. The Clinton administration also contended that the United States did not see its core national interests as conflicting with China's. Instead, the two countries could form a cooperative relationship in the long term.

The Clinton administration expressed its willingness to resume official bilateral contact at the highest level. It dispatched Vice-President Al Gore to China in the Spring of 1997, and scheduled an exchange of visits between the presidents of the two countries with President Jiang Zemin to visit the United States in late 1997, and President Clinton to visit China in the following year. Though Jiang and Clinton met in several multilateral settings, including the United Nations and APEC, the Clinton–Jiang summit would be the first exchange of state visits since 1984 when Premier Zhao Ziyang visited the United States and since President George Bush visited China in 1989.

Chinese leaders and government analysts interpreted the new strategy of integration as that of the United States beginning to treat China as an equal partner. As a matter of fact, many Chinese had regarded the West's "integration" strategy as a way of enmeshing China in international institutions created and dominated by major Western powers and thus a way of constraining China's development (see Chapter 3). Surprisingly, once the United States expressed its willingness to acknowledge China's status as a great power, the Chinese welcomed the new concept and regarded it as a way to become a real great power. Indeed, becoming a member of the club of great powers has long been the most important theme of Chinese nationalism.

The perception of a benign United States among Chinese leaders resulted in dramatic changes in China's US policy discourse. The leadership, who had been very critical of the US's China policy, began to emphasize the importance of the Sino–US relationship. Liu Ji, Vice-President of the Chinese Academy of Social Sciences and a close advisor to President Jiang Zemin, explained this transition:

> The United States did not ever directly invade China with major force. Although there have been such unfair agreements as the Wangsha Agreement and the 1900 Indemnity, these have mainly been of interest to historians, and have not made wide and deep impression on most people . . . The frank character, pursuit of freedom, and pragmatic style of the American people have won the appreciation of the Chinese people. Therefore, although there has been hostility for nearly two generations, it is just, one could say, a single cloud in a blue sky. Now the cloud has been lifted to reveal a wide blue sky (1997: 5).

In effect, to be strong as the United States has been a dream of generations of Chinese. But for the Chinese, the real issue between the two countries is that the United States does not want to treat China as an equal partner. From this perspective, the rise of anti-US nationalistic voices is due to the Chinese perception that the United States wants to impose its own will on China, without paying any respect to it and disregarding China's national dignity.

President Jiang Zemin visited the United States in September 1997 as scheduled. Clinton and Jiang agreed to build a "strategic partnership" between the two countries though no specific meaning was given to the concept. The Clinton–Jiang summit of 1997 was regarded as symbolic, and the Chinese government viewed it as a great success. President Clinton's visit to China in June 1998 without doubt reinforced the Chinese good feeling towards the United States.

The two countries reached various agreements, including regional stability, peaceful nuclear cooperation, human rights, religious freedom, prisoner accounting, non-government organization forums, and on the United Nations' Covenant on Economic, Social, and Cultural Rights. The two sides decided to carry out political and security dialogues to contribute to a secure and stable world. The two presidents agreed to meet regularly in their respective capitals; to authorize the Secretaries of State and Defense and the National Security Advisor and their Chinese counterparts to exchange regular visits; to authorize sub-cabinet meetings on political, military, security, and arms control issues to be held on a regular basis; and to establish a direct Presidential communication link. The two sides also reached agreements on military-to-military relations, military maritime safety, armed forces exchanges, promoting rule of law, strengthening legal institutions, cooperation in law enforcement, fighting drugs and crime, science and technology cooperation, energy and the environment cooperation (see the White House 1997).

Both official and popular reactions in China to the summit were much more positive than might have been expected (Shi Lujia 1997: 43; Li Wenhao 1997: 45; Yan Xuetong 1997a: 4). When interviewed, Li Peng (*MP* 1998), China's then Premier, contended that the visit to the United States by President Jiang Zemin symbolized the end of the West's unjustified sanctions on China since 1989. More importantly, the summit resulted in "a good feeling about the United States" among people. Many Chinese began to regard President Clinton as the first American president who was willing to accommodate China's emergence as a major power, and not to make US interests the sole criteria for defining the rules of acceptable behavior for China (Interviews in Beijing, May 1998.)

Indeed, for many Chinese leaders, China does not and should not intend to challenge the dominant position of the United States in world politics. According to Li Peng, China never underestimated US power in the post-Cold War era; China has already recognized the United States as the most important power in terms of economy, science and technology, and culture. What China does not want to see is that the United States wants to impose its own will on others (*MP* 1998). Liu Ji (1997) also argued that what China needed to pursue was not confrontation, but cooperation with the United States; that while Sino–US cooperation would help the United States remain the number one superpower in the world in the next century, it also could help China achieve modernity. Even for Chinese Realpolitik thinkers, whether China can be a real power in the system of nation–states depends largely on whether it can avoid confrontations and conflicts with the United States. Yan Xuetong (1996c: 158–60) regarded "avoiding conflicts with the United States" as one of the most important "strategic interests" of China. According to Yan, a Sino–US confrontation would impose a major threat to China's strategic interests because it would lead the United States, first, to strengthen the US–Japan alliance to constrain China; second, to support Taiwan's separatist forces to block China's national unification; and third, to form various forms of military alliances with China's neighbors to contain it.

Liu Ji argued when he spoke at Harvard University that "if one is hostile to China, one will find that China is not only an unconquerable enemy, but also a most steadfast enemy; truly treat China as a friend, and you will have a real friend" (Liu Ji 1997). Liu probably has been proven right. With the new perception of a "benign US" among Chinese leaders, the Chinese fear of being contained, and thus nationalistic voices, declined. The Clinton–Jiang summit showed a willingness of the both sides to build a long-term bilateral relationship by identifying common interests, narrowing their differences on major problems and making concrete progress on critical issues. With discussions between the two countries becoming pragmatic and rational a significant stabilization of Sino–US relations and the prospect of China becoming a long-term "strategic partner", as President Jiang expected, is not impossible.

The Diaoyutai/Senkaku Dispute

The latest Diaoyutai dispute began on July 14, 1996 when some Japanese students (belonging to a rightist group) illegally built a lighthouse on the disputed Diaoyutai islands, which the Japanese call Senkaku. As usual, the Chinese government strongly condemned the Japanese action and reaffirmed the Chinese sovereignty over the islands. In Japan, the government officials expressed their regret over what had been done, but also reaffirmed their claim to the islands. But this diplomatic rhetoric worsened the situation and soon led to the rise of a popular nationalist movement in mainland China, Hong Kong, Taiwan, and among the Chinese in other parts of the world.

The Sino–Japanese dispute over the Diaoyutai islands has lasted many years. Both countries have claimed their sovereignty over the islands. In 1978 Deng Xiaoping visited Japan and proposed that the two sides shelve the dispute in order to improve the relationship between the two countries. In 1979 some Japanese attempted to build transportation facilities on the islands and a strong Chinese reaction followed. After the post-Mao reform began, pursuing a peaceful international environment for domestic modernization became a major theme of China's foreign policy. As early as 1984 Deng Xiaoping argued that when the government deals with territorial disputes including the Sino–Japanese dispute over the Diaoyutai islands, domestic economic priority must be taken into account. China's domestic development cannot be interrupted by such territorial disputes. Deng (1984c, in 1993a: 87) further proposed a principle of dealing with the territorial dispute; that is, "shelving the dispute and developing joint exploitation". It seemed to the Chinese leadership that occupying the islands would not bring China any real strategic interest, but maintaining the Sino–Japanese normal relationship could benefit China's political, economic, and strategic interests. But the Chinese proposal did not result in the expected responses from Japan.

At the beginning of the 1996 event, it was widely expected, especially in Hong Kong, that the Chinese government would be likely to stand by the movement against Japan. Such an expectation was without any sound reasons. Since the reform began, both government officials and ordinary people had maintained their sensitivity over the Sino–Japanese relationship. After the reform began, Japanese investment flowed into China, which welcomed growing connections with Japan. But soon troubles developed between the two countries. In the mid-1980s anti-Japan nationalistic sentiments formed among students in Beijing. By 1985 China's foreign trade with Japan reached $10.8 billion, but China had a $5.2 billion trade deficit. The Japanese also exported a large amount of outdated industrial equipment to China. Moreover, the Japanese leaders refused to apologize for Japan's aggressive behavior during the Second World War. Many Chinese believed that China's Japan policy was too soft. In the mid-1980s, when Hu Yaobang, then General Secretary of the CCP, showed his friendliness towards Japan by having Japanese guests at home, Chinese intellectuals and students expressed their deep disappointment with him (Chuan Fu 1989: 89). Since then, no leader has attempted to soften their attitudes towards Japan.

More importantly, in recent years Japanese political influence in the Asia–Pacific region has risen. Japan signed a new security treaty with the

United States in 1996, and attempted to extend the treaty to the Taiwan Strait. Domestically, many Japanese government officials visited the Yasukuni Jinja Shrine, which holds the memorial tablets of many war criminals, and even tried to deny Japanese aggression against China during the Second World War. Indeed, the Chinese have responded to these new developments strongly. Government analysts contended that the new US–Japanese security treaty was aimed at containing China's rise. The attempt to deny the aggression of the Second World War was widely seen as a growth of Japanese militarism (Wei Yang 1996: 44).

For the Chinese nationalists, the hard posture of the Chinese government towards Japan could be beneficial. First, the government could utilize popular nationalism to show the Japanese China's determination in recovering sovereignty over the Diaoyutai islands. Second, anti-Japan sentiment could be used to increase and strengthen the political legitimacy of the new leadership. Patriotism without doubt was the theme of growing anti-Japan nationalistic voices. Indeed, it was reported that when Jiang Zemin reviewed students' anti-Japan demonstrations in Shanghai, he regarded them as patriotic. Beijing officials, for the first time in years, accepted students' petitions with alacrity (Nu Chao 1996).

Third, growing anti-Japanese patriotism in Hong Kong, Taiwan, and among the Chinese in different parts of the world could become a powerful force for unifying different parts of China. On the mainland, the government expressed its willingness to cooperate with Taiwan in defending Chinese sovereignty over the islands. In Taiwan, some senior government officials not only expressed their support for anti-Japan demonstrations, but also called for "defending the sovereignty" collectively by the mainland and Taiwan. In Hong Kong, the drama began with some 12 000 people on the streets protesting against the Japanese assertion of sovereignty over the Diaoyutai islands. Many public organizations led the demonstrations, including six universities and several other tertiary institutions. More importantly, among the most vocal of the demonstrations were the leaders of the democratic groups who had been strongly critical of the mainland government since the government's crackdown of the 1989 pro-democracy movement. These included elected legislators who had consistently opposed the policy of the mainland government to hold back the development of democracy in Hong Kong (see *YZZK* 1996a, 1996b, 1996c, 1996d). Actually, it was a rare opportunity for the mainland government to unify so many diverse political forces and form a national solidarity among different parts of China.

However, for Chinese patriots things turned out quite badly. Initially, the mainland government did react strongly to the Japanese assertion of sovereignty over the Diaoyutai islands. Nevertheless, with the development of anti-Japan demonstrations in Hong Kong, Taiwan, Macau, and different cities in the mainland, the government clearly expressed its unwillingness to support these demonstrations by adopting hard measures to control rising anti-Japanese voices on the mainland. However, it did not mean that the Chinese government made any compromise on the matter of sovereignty. The government made great efforts to impose "official" pressure on the Japanese government. What the government did was to ensure that popular nationalism would not affect domestic stability and foreign policy-making.

The efforts of the government were not without sound reasons. Various factors led the government officials to change their initial ideas of supporting popular nationalism. First, the complicated nature of popular nationalism made it difficult for the government to predict potential consequences. Though different political forces, especially the democratic forces in Hong Kong, aired their patriotic voices, the government was uncertain as to whether it would link the event to domestic political issues such as democracy. Second, demonstrations were not in accordance with the government's priority of political stability. The rise of student movements could become uncontrollable and thus undermine China's stability and endanger modernization. Third, and more importantly, like Deng Xiaoping, the new leadership realized the importance of a stable Sino–Japanese relationship to China's domestic development. The government did not want China's domestic development to be interrupted by any external conflicts. It is from Japan that the Chinese learned that if China remained backward, it was destined to be bullied. Therefore China does not have much choice but to focus on domestic development even though the government's benign behavior towards Japan often resulted in popular disappointment.

Japan remains the most critical zone in all aspects of China's foreign relations. The Chinese not only pay attention to changes in Japan's China policy, but also watch closely on what happens inside Japan to examine the implications on Sino–Japanese relations. The reason seems simple. According to Wang Gungwu:

> Nationalist history is more sharply black and white here. Memories are longer, the hurt is deeper. The Japanese were the last invaders of China, and thus the most recent, and they not only held large chunks of Chinese territory but also sought to rule China through their puppets. What was worse, many Chinese leaders succumbed to their power-shaping blandishments and collaborated with them. Furthermore, Japanese leaders have appeared unrepentant, almost amnesiac, about the atrocities conducted by their soldiers in China (1996a: 4).

Indeed, as Liu Ji (1997) pointed out in his speech, "in Chinese minds, memories of Japanese invasions in recent times have been slow to fade."

Modern Chinese history is closely associated with Japanese aggression in China. For many Chinese, Japan's modern success was based on China's humiliation. So, once Japan does "bad" things to China, they immediately remind the Chinese of countless Japanese atrocities in the past: the Sino–Japanese naval battle of 1894–95, the "Shimonoseki Treaty", the support of the puppet Manchurian government, the "Jiuyiba (September 18) Incident, the autonomy of the five provinces in north China, the Lugouqiao Incident, and the Nanjing Massacre. According to a survey held by the China Youth Development Fund and the *China Youth* among 100 000 youths in China and other overseas areas in early 1997, 99.4 percent said that they would remember the history of Japan's invasion of China; and that 76.4 percent of the respondents said that the sight of the Japanese flag reminded them of the viciousness of the Japanese invaders. The average age of those surveyed was about 25 (The Xinhua News Agency 1997). Another survey, carried out in early 1997 at the Beijing Aerospace University, also showed that more than 90 percent of the students were clearly aware of what had happened in the past between China and Japan; 82.7 percent of students surveyed believed that Chinese young people should always remember that Japan had invaded China in the past (Wang Yi 1997: 44).

According to the Chinese, Japan still lacks respect for China and ignores the awareness of the Chinese nation of past atrocities. While Germany has repeatedly recognized that its atrocities during the Second World War had hurt people in Europe and elsewhere, Japan continuously denies its war crimes. This led the young Japanese to learn little about the dark side of their country's history. According to the Chinese, only by admitting to historical facts will it be possible for the Japanese to face history correctly. Japanese denial of war crimes sent a signal of the rise of Japanese militarism. In the past twenty-five years, Japanese politicians have frequently issued statements to deny the history of Japanese aggression against China. In the primary and middle-school textbooks, this period of history is only vaguely mentioned.

The China Youth Development Fund and *China Youth* survey found that 96.8 percent of the respondents said that they felt great indignation about Japanese denial of war crimes, and 93.3 percent of them believed that Japan's attitude towards its history of invasion in China is one of the major factors affecting relations between the two countries (The Xinhua News Agency 1997). In effect, many believed that Japan's denial of war crimes will continuously threaten China, as exemplified by the fact that Japan had actively taken part in implementing the strategy of containment launched by the Western world against China. This obviously affects China's view of Japan. For example, only 3 percent of the respondents believed that Japanese investment in China was aimed at helping China, while as many as 83.3 percent believed that it was aimed at seizing the market and making profits, and still 45.6 percent argued that Japan was seeking to control China economically (The Xinhua News Agency 1997).

Chinese government analysts realized that popular nationalism could not be the way to solve the disputes between the two countries. They also have emphasized that if the two countries want to establish a long-term stable and peaceful relationship, both need to resolve the burden of history. Like Germany recognizing its own war guilt, Japan should be aware of the Chinese national "feeling" of being humiliated (Shen Jiru 1998: 146–54). Certainly, whether the Chinese can forgive for the past very much depends on the attitude of the Japanese towards their war crimes.

From Bilateralism to Multilateralism

The new identity of national interest has also promoted the transformation of China's strategic thinking from bilateralism to multilateralism. The importance of multinational political cooperation and collective security are appreciated among Chinese government analysts. During the Cold War, China's regional policy was overwhelmingly characterized by bilateralism because bilateralism strengthened China's hand and over the long term could help China position itself for a dominant role in Asia (Levine 1984: 118). Chinese strategists now realized that bilateralism was no longer the most effective means of pursuing China's national interest, especially security interest. According to Yan Xuetong:

> After the Cold War, peace as the foundation of national interest has become a consensus among major powers. A given country will not be able to protect its security by relying solely on its military power. Collective security has to be established in order to protect individual countries' national interest and security (1996b: 40).

According to Chinese strategists, collective security is a much more secure system for China than individual security. This is because in a system of collective security, China can rely on not only its own strength, but also on the collective security treaty with other countries. Moreover, since a system of collective security plays a role of deterrence, no single country will dare to take the risk of initiating aggression (Yan 1996c: 161).

This perception of collective security was reflected in China's policy towards South-east Asian countries. During the Cold War, China strongly opposed collective security among South-east Asian countries. For example, China regarded the formation of the Association of South-east Asian Nations (ASEAN) in 1967 as a threat to China's security and ASEAN as an anti-China military alliance led by the United States.[13] But the perception has changed. Chinese strategists realized that "establishing a system of collective security in the Asia–Pacific region is in accordance with China's macro-strategic security interest" (Yan Xuetong 1996c: 161).

China's main conflict with South-east Asian nations concerns territorial disputes over islands in the South China Sea, mainly the Spratlys (Catley & Keliat 1997; Dzurek 1996; Greenfield 1992). In 1984 Deng Xiaoping (1984a, in 1993a: 49) argued, when he met American guests, that "in dealing with some international territorial disputes, the issue of sovereignty can be avoided and joint exploitation can be developed; that a new way must be found in accordance with reality to solve such issues (territorial disputes)". In the same year, Deng (1984c, in 1993a: 83–93) proposed, when talking at the Advisory Committee of the Central Party Committee of the CCP, that "shelving territorial disputes and developing joint exploitation" be China's official guideline in handling the conflicts over the islands in the South China Sea.

On the other hand, South-east Asian nations persuaded China to be involved in multinational security dialogues with ASEAN. In 1994 China officially proposed some basic principles on collective security in Asia (*RMRB* 1994b). Its proposal to shelve the sovereignty disputes with other Asian nations aims "to promote the formation of collective security among Asian nations" (Yan Xuetong 1996b: 40). Although no major progress has been made, this perception no doubt helps China to readjust its relations with its neighbors. China has participated in various forms of dialogues; for example, on Asia–Pacific Economic Cooperation (APEC), the ASEAN Regional Forum (ARF), and it has expressed its willingness to discuss ways to solve territorial issues by different means with those nations with whom it has such disputes.

Participation in a multinational security system has become a major goal of China in the Asia–Pacific region. Such an arrangement can avoid an arms race in the region, and is conducive to China's peaceful peripheral environment. But the real issue is, according to Yan Xuetong (1996c: 162–3), that if other nations use forces to occupy disputed islands without discussion with China, China has to appeal to forces to "defend its territories and its sovereignty".

Conclusion

The perception of national interest affects both domestic and international policy-making, since leaders base their policies on such perceptions. Comprehensive national power (CNP) means that China's national power will not be measured by any one single dimension of power, such as military power, economic power, and so forth. Therefore, different aspects of national development should be balanced. By using economic interests as the core of CNP, the Chinese believe that the national interest can be measured quantitatively.

This logic makes the Chinese leadership more pragmatic in its foreign policy-making. Ideological factors no longer play a major impact on China's foreign behavior. The Chinese analysts recognized that "with the end of the Cold War, ideologies are no longer the key to political competition in international arenas" (Yan Xuetong 1996c: 43). In principle, China has abandoned ideology as its guideline in foreign policy-making since the late 1970s. Chinese leaders repeatedly emphasize that ideological factors cannot be used in dealing with international relations. No doubt, pragmatism has increasingly dominated China's foreign policy-making, especially as shown in Sino–US relations. Even on territory-related issues, the regime is likely to make compromises if non-compromise will cost China economically.

Post-Mao reforms have resulted in drastic domestic changes in China, especially rapid economic growth. The Chinese feel that with this increasing economic wealth, their country is for the first time in modern history capable of pursuing power in the international system. Understandably, China tends to be more assertive in its foreign affairs. This, however, does not necessarily mean that China will become aggressive in its relations with other countries. Due to a changing domestic and international environment, China's view concerning its national interests has also changed. The Chinese have encountered enormous difficulties over their identity, particularly in the transition from the old world order to the modern system of nation–states.

After centuries of humiliation, the Chinese have desperately longed for international respect. Outsiders might regard this as obsessive, but the Chinese believe that they deserve it. With rapid economic growth and increasing national wealth, many even believe that they have the right to demand such respect. Nationalism arises when other great powers ignore China's national dignity in their dealings with it. The impact of China's nationalism on its international behavior therefore depends, to a great degree, on the ways other major powers deal with China.

CHAPTER 7

Identity Transition and Chinese Power: To What End China's New Nationalism?

China's new nationalism is a response not only to domestic modernization, but also to the inflow of Western influences into China, and the China policies of other major powers. The previous chapters have discussed how different social groups and government officials have responded to China's changing internal and external environments, and how the new nationalism has presented itself through various outlets. This chapter summarizes the major findings of the earlier chapters and draws conclusions on where China's new nationalism is heading. It is divided into three parts. The first discusses why "voice" has been the theme of China's new nationalism. The second analyzes the Chinese realists' perceptions and their rational choice of China's international strategy. The third section shows the rise of liberalism or globalism, and its impact on China's domestic development and international affairs.

"Voice": China's Strategic Choice in the Post-Cold War Era

Will China's new nationalism become aggressive and aim to compete for military and political power with other major powers, especially Western powers? Many Western scholars have argued that a major power's rapid economic growth will change the existing power distribution among nation–states and challenge the status of the existing hegemony. Power competition among major states will eventually lead to war. Due to this view, many in the West have argued that the rise of China will challenge the existing world order and pose a threat to world peace and security (see Chapter 1). This study shows a complex picture about Chinese thoughts on China's role in the international system. With changes in perceptions of their national identities, the rise of Chinese economic power will not necessarily follow the direction these scholars have predicted. Using Albert Hirschman's (1970) analogy of "exit, voice, and loyalty" (see explanations below), China is most likely to choose "voice" rather than "exit" and "loyalty" as its international strategy.

China is unlikely to adhere to "loyalty" in the existing international system without any conditions for two reasons. On one hand, as discussed earlier, with the rise of the new nationalism, more and more Chinese began to believe that the existing international system was not necessarily in accordance with China's national interests. Owing to weaknesses in national power throughout its modern history, China was not able to participate in the establishment of the existing international system, whose rules and norms were set up by the West. Though China can benefit from these rules and norms, its development will eventually be constrained by them. This is the rationale behind Chinese leaders' talk about establishing a new international economic and political order. On the other hand, many Chinese also perceive that the existing international system is unwilling to accept China's rise because the West believes that the rise of China will challenge the existing power distribution among nations and thus pose a threat to international stability.

China is also unlikely to "exit" the existing international system. First, major Western powers will not allow China to do so. It is dangerous to allow a communist power with nuclear weapons to "live" outside the international system. Indeed, as discussed in Chapter 1, except for some "hard realists", preventing China's isolation has been a consensus among major Western powers (see Vogel 1997; Brown, Lynn-Jones & Miller 1997; Curtis 1994).

Second, the economic integration and interdependence between China and the outside world also make "exit" unlikely to occur. Major Western powers have developed extensive economic ties with China and this provides an internal part of China's domestic development. More importantly, after two decades of reform and opening to the outside, China's economy has been greatly integrated into the world system (see Lardy 1992, 1994). At the early stages of the economic reform, China attracted enormous foreign capital from overseas Chinese. But the government was unable to absorb Western high technologies. The Chinese leadership has realized the vital importance of Western capital and technology for China's further development and for China to be a real world power. Without doubt, the most effective way for China to acquire high technologies from the West is to integrate itself into the international system. Therefore, one major task Jiang Zemin performed when he met President Bill Clinton in Washington in September 1997 was to persuade the United States to lift its sanctions on the exports of high technologies to China, sanctions imposed after the government's crackdown of the 1989 pro-democracy movement. Similarly, Zhu Rongji has proposed a strategy of reviving the nation through sciences and education and promised that his government would make great efforts on this regard. During his trip to Europe in March 1998, immediately after he took over the position of Premier, Zhu called for Sino–European cooperation in science and technology (Han Hua & Fan Qiang 1998).

Third, even if the West does not want to accept China's rise, China is unlikely to establish a China-centered world system. During the Cold War, Mao Zedong once attempted to build a China-centered international order. But eventually it turned out to be a disaster for China's domestic development. Since the reform began, China has achieved rapid economic growth and is likely to become a super economic power early next century. Rapid modernization, however, also created enormous domestic problems and a crisis of state power (see Chapter 2). Without a solid institutional foundation, it is hard for China to build a self-centered international order. Also, Chinese communist ideology has long lost its attractiveness to its own people and outsiders as well: the Chinese believe that the old ideology has been a major barrier for China to establish its international prestige, which is vital for a world power. Although many Chinese intellectuals have begun to make efforts to revive Confucian civilization (see Chapter 4), it is doubtful whether Confucianism can help China establish a new international order. For instance, Lucian Pye (1996: 86–7) argued that "in spite of the greatness of Chinese history . . . the historical pattern of China's modernization has left China with a relatively inchoate and incoherent form of nationalism." (see also Wang Gungwu 1995: 59–68).

China is likely to choose "voice" as its strategy to be a world power in the post-Cold War era. As a matter of fact, China has voiced its complaints about the West-dominated international system and has called for the establishment of a new international order. This does not mean, however, that China attempts to "exit" the existing system. Nor does it mean that China wants to establish a self-centered new order. What China is attempting to do is to "reform" the existing system and to make it more accommodating to China's rise and its national interests.

Will the rise of the new nationalism change China's "voice" strategy? The following sections aim to show why the Chinese perceive this strategy as China's only path to becoming a great power. Nationalistic voices have been strong among China's government analysts and hard realists. Will they be able to make a rational national choice under the influence of nationalism? With changes in their concept of national interest, such analysts will remain rational in policy-making though they still use nationalistic language. More importantly, the new nationalism does not rise without any challenges domestically. Nationalism has been one, not *the*, major political force in the 1990s. Given the fact that China's reform and open-door policy have been implemented for two decades, rapid economic development has generated enormous social and political forces other than nationalism. During the 1980s political liberalism was prevalent among different social groups even though it was resisted by the State. The rise of nationalism in the 1990s does not mean in any sense the end of liberalism. Embedded in liberalism is an identity towards globalism. Indeed, liberalism or globalism has imposed serious challenges to nationalism. It is difficult to understand the future of the new nationalism without an understanding of the challenges it encounters.

Realists: Perception and National Choice

I have argued in the previous chapters that the rise of China's new nationalism is a response not only to domestic modernization, but also to changes in China's international environment. The rise of various forms of anti-China theories in the West has resulted in an enormous nationalistic reaction from different social and political groups in China. Many Chinese now believe that the West does not want to see China develop and will use all possible means to contain it. Nationalism needs to be promoted so that national resources can be mobilized to resist and counter the West's containment policy. Nevertheless, the impact of this perception on China's policy-making is complicated.

Internationally, the aim of the new nationalism is to establish a new international economic and political order. As discussed before, the proponents of the new nationalism believe that the existing international power distribution is not in accordance with China's national interests. Therefore, changes have to be introduced. From this perspective, China's nationalism tends to be aggressive. Nevertheless, it is unlikely for China to choose the "exit" strategy. Which strategy China will choose depends not only on various domestic and international constraints, but also on China's perceptions of whether China can be actually contained by the West and how China can rise. The government analysts and strategists believe that the "voice" or "participation" strategy is the only strategy for China to be a great power, even though they are also nationalistic.

However, can China be contained? Chinese realistic analysts saw the nature of anti-China theories and the impossibility of a containment strategy. According to them, the rise of the "containing China" theory is a natural result of the end of the Cold War. Since then, the US's China policy has been in a state of flux. With the collapse of the Soviet Union, China and the United States lost their old common enemy – that is, the Soviet Union – and China lost its strategic importance in the US global strategy. China's rapid development has naturally led many Americans to wonder whether China will challenge US interests in the global setting. The rise of the "containing China" theory occurred only because its proponents have over-emphasized the conflicting aspects of US–China interests while under-emphasizing the cooperative aspects. As long as the two countries have their common interests either in the global or regional setting, it is not necessary for the United States to implement its so-called containment strategy and for China to mobilize nationalistic sentiments to counter the United States.

Though the West, led by the United States, is developing a containment strategy, it will be constrained by various factors (Jiang Lingfei 1996; Chu Shulong 1996; Wu Jiong 1996). A Cold War between the West and China seems unlikely. This is because China differs from the former Soviet Union. China does not want to isolate itself and form a bloc of its own. Central to China's national strategy is the open-door policy. Both China and the West want to take part in each other's development. Two decades of the open-door policy has resulted in the interdependence between China and the West. As long as China is able to maintain the dynamism of domestic development, and as long as the West can benefit from China's development, it is unlikely for the West to isolate and contain China.

Furthermore, it is almost impossible for the United States to succeed in containing China. After the Cold War, world power has become multipolar; that is, the United States is not without its challengers. The so-called common interests between the United States and other major world powers cannot be overestimated and potential conflicts among them cannot be underestimated. In Europe, it is still possible for a unified Germany to become a first-rank power again. In Asia, Japan tends to turn its priority to ASEAN (Association of South-east Asian Nations) and struggles to be a major political leader in the region. The rise of Japan is not only a challenge to China, but also to US interests in Asia. The rise of regional identity has resulted in the formation of various regional economic, military, and political blocs. The United States could be the first among these powers, but it is hard for it to maintain its hegemonic position in the world system.

From a perspective of geopolitics, the United States is also unlikely to pursue an aggressive China policy. The United States does not want to see China become another Soviet Union that will form a new threat to its national interests on one hand, and attempts to prevent Russia from becoming a major power again on the other. This is the rationale behind the US's attempts to expand NATO eastward, and its involvement in the Taiwan Strait crisis. The US's action on both sides cannot be too aggressive, however. An aggressive US policy towards China and Russia will likely result in the formation of another Sino–Russia alliance. The formation of such an alliance will become a vital threat to US interests in the global setting.

The rise of the Asia–Pacific region as a center of world economic development also constrains the US's China policy. If the United States wants to maintain its hegemonic position in world affairs, it has to control further development in the Asia–Pacific region. That means, first, the United States will not allow any other nation to lead the region, and second, it needs to maintain economic dynamism in the Asia–Pacific. Challenges to the US's leading position in the region could come from either China or Japan. Though Japan and the United States have formed a new alliance, it is different from the old one formed during the Cold War. The United States has to use Japan to constrain China while using China to constrain Japan. For Japan, the new US–Japan alliance can be used to constrain both China and the United States in order to create more political space in the region because, to some extent, the new alliance means a confrontation between the United States and China. In order to constrain Japan's role in the region, the United States has to be very cautious in designing its policy of containment of China. Moreover, in order to maintain the region's development dynamism, the United States is unlikely to implement a "containing China" policy simply because it will be counter-productive. Without China's participation, continuous development in the region will be less likely. If the United States carries out such a policy, other major powers will take over China's markets (Jiang Lingfei 1996: 48).

The most important reason that the United States is unlikely to contain China is that the two countries have common interests. First, Sino–US economic relations are interdependent. Since the Cold War era ended, central to the great powers' strategic interests is economic interest. It is increasingly difficult to separate economic from strategic interests. If the United States does not want to give up its economic interest in China, a "containing China" policy is unlikely. Second, the United States needs China to play an important role in achieving a power balance in the global setting. Third, China has played a vital role in promoting rapid regional economic development. Fourth, China can also play an important role in coping with international and regional problems. If China becomes uncooperative or irresponsible in policies concerning the proliferation of weapons of mass destruction, Korea, Taiwan, the South China Seas, or global issues, US interests will be seriously challenged (Jiang Lingfei 1996: 48; Zhou Qi 1995; Wang Jisi 1996).

The United States is unlikely to implement a strategy of containment. But this does not mean that China can go ahead with its own will to seek power and wealth in the system of nation–states. Instead, whether China can become a great power depends on the type of international environment China encounters. According to Yan Xuetong (1997b), the international environment can be judged from three perspectives: the risk associated with the involvement in international and regional wars and conflicts, the extent to which the existing major powers are willing to accept China's rise, and the extent of China's economic involvement in the international system.

Whether China can become a real great power depends on its avoiding wars and international conflicts because large military activities consume a great deal of economic and other resources, and thus weaken the foundation for further development. Moreover, China's rise also depends on the major powers' China policy. China's rapid development has made many countries nervous about its ambitions internationally. If China cannot improve its relations with other major powers, China's development will be slowed down, or even contained. Nevertheless, whether major powers will contain China or not depends on the extent to which China's interests are in conflict with theirs. Also, China's rise depends on its involvement in international economic activities; for example, exports, technological introduction, and overseas investment. International economic involvement means not only that China can benefit from such involvement, but also that other countries are able to benefit from their involvement in China's domestic development. Without mutual beneficial relations, China's international economic environment cannot be improved (Yan Xuetong 1997b).

Therefore, if China wants to become a great power, nationalism has to be contained. The meaning of this containment is multi-fold. First, China does need a strategy against the West's attempt to isolate China. China's rapid development has led to the rise of various "anti-China" theories, and the West has attempted to align itself to China's neighbors to contain China. If the West succeeds, it will be impossible for China to rise. But China's counter-strategy should be participation rather than nationalistic reaction; that is, China needs to participate in the existing international system even though it is dominated by the West. If China is isolated from this system, it will be easily contained by the United States and other major powers. Second, in order to participate in the existing international system, China has to take active part in various forms of multinational organizations and security arrangements, especially in east Asia. China may not be able to change the existing system, but participation will reduce the constraints that the West will impose on China on one hand, and it will benefit from international involvement on the other. Third, the aim of China's participation is not to "buy" time for further domestic development, but to integrate China into the world system and make it a constructive force in this system (Yan Xuetong 1995: 13–14).

Chinese realists see the West's attempt to contain China, but they argue that nationalism cannot become an effective counter-strategy. China is not able to and should not challenge the existing system. The reason is simple. Though China has achieved rapid development for decades, it still cannot afford to be a leading world power. China's rise only means that it is possible to become a great regional power. Whether China can be a great world power is not only dependent on "hard power" such as military and economic power, but also on "soft power" such as culture and values. Western civilization has dominated the world system for centuries, and the West is dominant in almost all aspects of "soft power". It is doubtful whether the Chinese civilization will be able to achieve such a status. Also, it is impossible for China to be a "free rider". Whatever China's international strategy is, its rise will have a major impact on the international system. So, China cannot choose to be either a challenger or a follower, but something in-between (Li Jianyong 1995).

While many new nationalists have argued against the existing international system, others have called for giving priority to internal reform so that China can be integrated into the world system, even though it is dominated by the West (Rong Jingben 1994; He Fang 1995). First, a free market system needs to be promoted. Without such a system, the Chinese economy cannot be fully integrated into the world system. The existing international rules and norms should be respected and followed even though they are not necessarily in accordance with China's national interests. Second, China needs to abandon traditional mercantilism. State power is important for China's sovereignty, social order, and market development. State power, however, should not be used excessively to gain wealth from international economic activities. China has been receiving benefits from a free international market while insisting on establishing a new international political and economic order. The aim of China's efforts should be a free international market system. Only by promoting this can China's rise contribute to the world system. Third, some changes have to be introduced into China's perception of national sovereignty. Without doubt, to protect national sovereignty is the responsibility of state power. However, according to Rong Jingben (1994: 6), "in the process of establishing a new international order, national sovereignty has to be respected. If [we] put too much emphasis on history, international conflicts will occur among nations". Any international conflict will have a major impact on China's domestic development and stability. Therefore, when considering national sovereignty and national interests, China's economic interests also need to be taken into account.

Nationalism does stir the emotions and it can impede rational decision-making. Many outsiders are worried that with rising nationalism, the Chinese might make an irrational national choice in foreign policy-making. Nonetheless, nationalism and rational choices are not necessarily contradictory to each other when Chinese leaders deal with international affairs. The aim of China's nationalism is to pursue national power and wealth through domestic development. As long as the leadership pursues its "interest", its nationalistic "passion" can be constrained and remain rational.[1]

Liberalism, Globalism, and Nationalism

Chapters 2, 3, and 4 have discussed different aspects of the new nationalism. The proponents of the new nationalism argued that a strong Chinese identity can be established by "anti-westernization" and "anti-western civilization", that China should not be integrated into the existing international system established by the West, and that recentralization of state power is a precondition of Chinese development. However, these arguments have encountered serious challenges from the proponents of liberalism and globalism.

Globalism and International Integration

Liberals argue that liberalism is a super-national (*chao minzu*) or a super-civilizational (*chao wenming*) value system. Nationalists regard China's post-Mao reform as a process of westernization because they perceive both marketization and liberalization as belonging to the Western civilization. On the contrary, liberals argue that liberalism belongs to human civilization as a whole rather than to any particular civilization. So, if China wants to be modernized, it cannot and should not reject liberalism. As one author pointed out:

> "Natural" institutes are superior to "artificial" ones, [the] market economy is superior to a command one, democracy is superior to dictatorship, the separation of church from the state is superior to the combination of the two, religious freedom is superior to religious trial, etc. (Qin Hui 1996b: 45).

Individual freedom resulting from economic reforms cannot be regarded as a process of "westernization". Individual freedom and liberalization as universal values should become the aim of nationalism. If nationalism is used to constrain individual civil rights it will become irrational. In terms of individual freedom there is no conflict between civilizations. Human dignity and freedom are the ultimate goals of all civilizations. If China wants to be "civilized" it has to accept liberalism.

> A precondition of rational nationalism is the realization of civil rights . . . National interests that nationalism wants to protect is only an aggregate of individual interests of a society. So, the representatives of national interests can only be generated by democratic procedures. No one has the right to

claim to be the representative of national interests without following this pro-
cedure and ask others to subordinate their interests to national ones. In other
words, rational nationalism is based on democracy (Qin Hui 1996b: 45).

Liu Xinwu, Chairman of the China Writers Association, argues that
all nations have to appreciate a "shared civilization" regardless of its origin, and China, as a member of the human civilization, needs to recognize its value. According to Liu Xinwu:

> This shared civilization may be developed by a given nation, or by several
> nations. As long as it can promote other nations' productivity and improve
> their living standards, it is a shared civilization . . . We have to recognize that
> in the past few centuries, peoples in western Europe and North America have
> contributed to this shared civilization more than any other peoples. We do
> not need to ask its origins. We have the rights to enjoy it (1996: 25).

While nationalists expressed their strong resistance to the Western civilization as exemplified by the best-seller *The China that Says No*,
liberals argued that saying "No" to the West will only delay China's
progress towards becoming a strong nation–state. According to Xu Jilin,
the popular anti-West sentiment such as that expressed in *The China that
Says No* has been one major factor leading to China's backwardness
throughout modern history. When Japan faced severe external threats,
the Japanese were willing to learn from the advanced West to make their
nation strong. By contrast, after China encountered the West, Chinese
nationalists often appealed to race-based national sentiment to resist the
West as exemplified by the Yi Ho Tuan movement (the Boxers). True,
China needs to oppose US hegemonism because it is detrimental to
China's national interest. Nevertheless, hegemonism cannot represent
the Western civilization as a whole. China wants to learn from the West.
What China needs is a rational nationalism or liberal nationalism, but not
anti-foreignism. Behind the strengths of the Western powers are the market economy, freedom, democracy, rule of law, and other forms of "soft
power". If Chinese nationalists want China to be strong, nationalism needs
to incorporate all these elements of "soft power". Otherwise, anti-West
nationalism will again weaken Chinese power (Xu Jilin 1997: 290–97).

The proponents of the new nationalism identified nationalism as a
pre-condition for China's modernization and argued that without
nationalism, modernization would not lead to a strong China. By contrast, liberals identified globalism as a goal of China's modernization.
According to the liberals, excessive nationalism will slow China's integration into the world system. As Sun Liping points out:

> The rise of nationalistic sentiment and its impact on social life raise a serious
> question, that is, "Does China still want to be integrated into the world

system?" . . . After World War Two, in many countries, nationalism became a rationale for self-closing and a major barrier to economic development. If we look at the world today, we will find that countries where radical nationalism continues often refuse the mainstream modernization and become the most backward countries (1996a: 18–19).

According to Sun, nationalism can be used to strengthen national integration and cohesiveness. However, nationalism cannot be a goal; nationalists often exaggerate a given national culture's advantages and refuse to see those of other national cultures. Nationalism as a means can promote China's modernization while nationalism as a goal will mislead and thus become a barrier to China's modernization. Whether China will be able to modernize itself and cope with challenges from the outside world depend on whether it can integrate itself into the mainstream world civilization. Nationalism often prevents China from learning from other nations and thus will slow China's modernization (Sun Liping 1996a: 19).

The proponents of the new nationalism believe that the existing rules and norms are established by the West and are not in accordance with China's national interests. They argue that China needs to reform the existing power distribution of the international system and at least modify international rules and norms in order to promote its national interests. By contrast, liberals argue that it is in China's interests to accept the existing international rules and norms. Li Shenzhi (1994a), one major proponent of liberalism, argued that internationally China has to abandon the old concept of geopolitics and to accept the fact that every nation can benefit from globalism and interdependence among nations. Since China has been humiliated by the West throughout its modern history, it is easy for nationalism to develop into Chinese chauvinism, which in effect will constrain China from becoming a great power. So, the only way for China to become a strong nation–state, and an important force to promote international peace and security, is to accept the existing international rules and norms. As Li argued:

> Because globalism has become an irreversible trend, the way in which China can be modernized is not to establish different rules and norms, but to understand and actively participate in the process of globalization. By doing so, China can promote globalization to a higher degree (1994b: 6; see also Li 1994c).

Without doubt, the existing rules and norms of international politics, economics, and diplomacy have been established under the influence of the major Western powers, and can be regarded as a product of the Western civilization. But this does not mean that China cannot benefit from accepting these rules and norms.

Chen Shaoming (1996: 75) argued that China cannot reject international rules and norms by claiming that it is still a developing country, and these rules and norms are not applicable to China's domestic situation. This is because China can change its domestic situations by accepting these rules and norms as exemplified by other east Asian countries (Chen Shaoming 1996: 75).

While *The China that Says No* has been widely circulated among different social and political groups, a more recent book, *China Does not Want to Be "Mr. No"* by Shen Jiru (1998), Research Fellow in the Institute of World Economics and Politics at the Chinese Academy of Social Sciences, has become equally popular among the Chinese. In his work, Shen presented a set of arguments against "saying No". According to Shen, globalism should become the identity of the Chinese nation–state. China cannot afford to say "No" to the West and to reject its integration with the existing international community, let alone pursue a policy of isolation and hegemonism. Indeed, it was the "say No" strategy that led to the breakdown of the old Soviet Union.

The Soviet Union attempted to be a hegemonic world power. It took a confrontational, non-cooperative approach to international relations, refused to join the IMF and World Bank, and did not cooperate with the United Nations. This strategy posed a serious threat to the United States and enabled the latter to build an alliance against the Soviet Union. Soviet expansion in the Western sphere of influence strengthened opposition to the USSR, and the Soviet insistence on matching the US's weaponry exhausted its economy. Failed economic reforms worsened the plight of the Soviet Union, and the worsening of the economy accentuated conflicts among the nationalities Shen Jiru (1998: 14–22).

According to Shen, since the Cold War, four great powers have emerged: the United States, the European Union, Russia, and China. China needs to play a role as a fully fledged cooperative partner in international affairs working towards a multipolar world rather than the one dominated by the United States. Nevertheless, China also needs to work with the United States to assure that US security interests are satisfied so that it will not feel the rise of China as a threat to its global interests. Although China must stand firm against US hegemonism, it needs to recognize the role that the United States plays in world politics Shen Jiru (1998: 99–112).

Furthermore, Shen argued that China needs to consider the West's economic interests in international economic negotiations. International cooperation can become a win–win game. By making reasonable compromises in international negotiations, China's national honor is not insulted and China is not forced to accept a dishonorable result. China has benefited and can continue to benefit from international economic cooperation, but it also needs to accept the constraints imposed by the international trade regime (Shen Jiru 1998: 344–50). More importantly, it is important for China to take the initiative to integrate itself, rather than to be integrated, into the international system. China's involvement in international organizations such as Asia-Pacific Economic Cooperation (APEC) has shown this tendency. Without doubt, China needs to continue to make efforts on this regard (Shen Jiru 1998: 254).

Democracy versus Nationalism

On the domestic side, liberals pose an even more serious challenge to the new nationalism. The proponents of the new nationalism called for statism and argued that only through recentralization could China become a strong nation–state, both in domestic and international affairs. By contrast, liberals argue that statism and recentralization would only weaken state power and thus called for democratization through political reforms.

Towards the end of the 1980s a debate concerning neo-authoritarianism occurred between Chinese intellectuals and government officials. The proponents of neo-authoritarianism saw the vital importance of central authority in promoting China's economic reform and proposed to establish a neo-authoritarian regime. On the other hand, liberals tended to support China's democratization (see Liu Jun & Li Lin 1989). The debate was interrupted by the 1989 Tiananmen Incident. After the collapse of the former Soviet Union and the east European communist regimes in the early 1990s, Chinese intellectuals preferred socio-political stability rather than radical reforms and democratization. But with the rise of the new nationalism, the old debate revived to some extent.

Liberals also see the importance of strong central power, but doubt whether the foundation of a strong State needs to be based on nationalism. Instead, they argue that a prerequisite for China to be strong is democracy. According to such liberals, throughout China's modern history, a major theme of Chinese nationalism was independence and national survival. But once national liberation was achieved and national rights were realized, it became imperative to prioritize democracy to promote individual rights or civil rights (Luo Rongqu 1996). Li Zehou and Wang Desheng argued:

> [In terms of] social order, I stand for centralization. The central government must be strong and have great authority. If power is too decentralized and local governments do not follow the mandate from the center, then a civil war will be inevitable. Without a strong central government to co-ordinate, regulate and control diverse local interests, there will be a disaster . . . Neo-authoritarianism aims to institutionalize centralized power. But China needs to transit to democracy and the rule of law (1994: 69–70).

Chen Shaoming, one major opponent of the new nationalism, argued that nationalism can be used to promote so-called "national interests", but not every type of "national interest" is in accordance with the people's interests:

> For instance, during World War Two, both fascist states and anti-fascist states claimed that their national interests were above individual interests. But in reality, in some countries, national and individual interests were identical while in others, the two were in conflict. In fascist Germany, the state promoted its alleged "national interests" at the expense of individual interests . . . It is easy for nationalism to become statism. In peace time, if we overemphasize statism, we will return to the old system, i.e. the planned economy (1996: 75).

The proponents of statism called for recentralizing central fiscal power. Although liberals also argued for strong central fiscal power, they contended that without any constraint on central power, there was no guarantee that the central state would not abuse its power. Institutional constraints on central power is a pre-condition for recentralization (Zhang Shuguang 1995).

Leaders cannot use nationalism to consolidate power or for national integration if it means resisting international and universal rules and norms. Without a strong internal competitive system [democracy], any political system will eventually fail. According to Zhang Shuguang (1995: 9), "The former Soviet Union did not lack advanced weapons, and its people did not lose their national confidence, but the political system collapsed eventually." Apparently, Zhang here pointed out the danger of the new nationalism. If China wants to be strong, its political system needs to be open to its people. Chen Shaoming also contended:

> Nationalism can be used for social mobilization under certain conditions. In times of national crisis, nationalism could become attractive to the people. But once the crisis disappears, society will become less integrated . . . If individuals cannot relate their individual interests to national interests, they will naturally be indifferent to any political mobilization . . . [Great internal dynamism] depends on whether individuals can participate in [the] political process and have more opportunities to express their opinions (1996: 75).

According to Shen Jiru, not only China's economic system needs to be integrated with the world system; it is also important for China to learn from the United States with regards to constructing political and social systems. When looking at the United States as a world power, its political and social institutions have to be taken into account. The United States has maintained its status as a world power not only because of its wealth, but also because its liberal environment and tolerant society have successfully absorbed top talent from all over the world

(Shen Jiru 1998: 351). Shen (1998: 36–42) also argued that with changes in capitalist societies, capitalism and the Chinese style of socialism are increasingly convergent. Therefore China should welcome "peaceful evolution" (*heping yanbian*) since it is the natural and positive way for social progress, even though China has opposed such a strategy before (Shen Jiru 1998: 36–42).

In effect, various surveys have confirmed Shen's argument. For example, according to a survey among Beijing youth, when asked for their opinions on socialism and capitalism, the distribution of responses is as follows: China has achieved great success, but the people increasingly cast doubts on socialism (Yes: 35 percent, No: 31 percent); with the development of science and technology, international trade, global communication, and transportation the world is getting smaller, and the difference between socialism and capitalism has also reduced greatly (Yes: 34 percent, No: 36 percent); although China's development is heading in right direction, its political and social system needs to be reformed (Yes: 77 percent) (The Lingdian Survey Company, et al. 1997: 777).

As I discussed in Chapter 2, throughout China's modern history, Chinese nationalism has developed around three types of sovereignties: national, State, and popular. Both the proponents of state sovereignty and popular sovereignty stood for a strong State, but disagreed with each other on how such a strong State could be built. These differences still remain in the post-Mao era. Both have attracted their own audience and created their own social and political forces. Without doubt, the development of the new nationalism has been constrained by China's liberal forces. Similarly, the transition of the concept of national interest from confrontation to cooperation with the West has been promoted by the forces of globalism within Chinese society.

"Voice", Discontent, and Cooperation

In the early 1990s, after reviewing the development of China's nationalism, Lucian Pye argued that most Chinese intellectuals and political leaders had vacillated between the two extremes of either nihilistically denouncing Chinese civilization and romanticizing it in contrast to their counterparts in the rest of the developing world. These counterparts were making great efforts to create a new sense of nationalism that would combine elements of traditions with the appropriate features of the modern world culture (Pye 1996: 92.)

Pye would agree that this is no longer the case now. After the two decades of reform and open-door policy, China has become increasingly integrated into the system of nation–states. It is also the first time since 1949 that China's external environment is the most peaceful. Increasing

integration with the outside world and a peaceful external environment
have had a major impact on the attitude of the Chinese towards other
powers. No doubt, when ordinary people can access to the information
on what happens outside, they tend to be able to make rational
judgments about China and other nation–states. According to a survey
in five major Chinese cities (Beijing, Shanghai, Guangzhou, Wuhan, and
Ha'erbin) conducted by the *China Youth* in 1996, nearly 57 percent of
the respondents said that they paid close attention to world affairs, and
only 5 percent said "no interest in that" (The Lingdian Survey Company
et al. 1997: 32).

The effects of the transition from a closed society to an open one are
twofold. First, the Chinese's perceptions of world order have been under
change and become more diversified. When respondents were asked
about China's position in the world system, the distribution of responses
was as follows: China occupies a unique position in the world (33
percent); China's world position is uncertain because of its continuous
dramatic changes (30 percent); China can be a great economic power
(17 percent); China can be a great political, economic and cultural
power (13 percent); and China is still a backward country (3 percent)
(The Lingdian Survey Company et al. 1997: 32–3). Most appreciated the
impact of China's integration into the world system on its domestic
progress, and believed that the country needed to make great efforts to
learn from the West. Second, the Chinese have become more rational
in their learning from the West. In other words, they are no longer
fetishistic towards the West and are reluctant to accept what the outsiders tell them to do. They attempt to build a Chinese way of national
building by "selecting" different elements from various countries.

In effect, the interaction between the new nationalism and liberalism
(globalism) is better understood in this context. Obviously, "voice" implies
something between "loyalty" and "exit". China will not totally accept the
existing international system. Nor will it reject the world system.

A "voice" strategy is in accordance with the theme of Chinese nationalism; that is, national sovereignty and independence. Throughout China's
modern history, Chinese nationalism was a reaction to the humiliation
that China suffered at the hands of Western imperialism, and Chinese
leaders aimed to achieve an independent national sovereignty, to protect
national self-respect, and enhance China's international position.
Nationalism meant that China deserved an equal position in the international system as other major powers did. This is the theme of Chinese
nationalism from Sun Yat-sen (see Chapter 2) to the new nationalists. For
Sun and other nationalists, China's equal position in the international
system could be achieved by expressing China's discontent, rather than
establishing a China-centered new international system. In other words, a

"cooperative approach" could better serve China's national interest than a "confrontational" one. After the establishment of People's Republic in 1949, China became a close ally of the Soviet Union. With the worsening of Sino–Soviet relations in the late 1950s, China attempted to establish a self-centered international order based on Mao's self-sufficient policy. But with the normalization of Sino–US relations in 1972, Mao changed China's foreign policy drastically and allied the country with the United States against the Soviet Union. Since then, China has made various efforts to integrate itself with a West-established international system. In the post-Mao era, even with the rise of the new nationalism, this stand has not changed at least in terms of foreign behavior.

With the end of the Cold War, Chinese leaders have repeatedly emphasized that a new international order needs to be established so that China's national interests can be better served. It is worthwhile to note that a major aspect of this "new international order" is to enhance China's independence and sovereign status. Chinese leaders rarely use the term "new world order" (*xin shijie zhixu*) to express their normative vision of world politics. Rather, they prefer the term "new international order" (*xin guoji zhixu*). According to the Chinese, the term "world order" is associated with a system in which a hegemonic power (that is, the United States) is the primary impetus behind this order and similarly, a "new world order" connotes a system of inter-state norms that will undermine state sovereignty ostensibly in the search for cooperative solutions to world problems. On the other hand, a "new international order" means that the sovereign state remains the unit of this order and the primary objective of this is to preserve the sovereignty and independence of states (Li Shisheng 1992).

To establish such a new international order, China does not need to initiate a revolution to the existing system. What China wants is to air its discontent towards it in the hope of reform. Chinese leaders and international analysts realized the importance of the West, especially the United States, in world affairs. The Chinese believed that the collapse of the Soviet Union constituted the end of bipolarity and the international system was in a transitionary stage from unipolarity to multipolarity. Although China could become a "pole", the United States's leading position is without doubt. As one senior foreign policy expert commented, "it must be acknowledged that the US really does possess an all-round superiority in political, economic and military affairs, and in science and technology" (He Fang 1991). More importantly, Chinese analysts contended that in all these perspectives, the United States is the standard that China's modernization should aim for. This is the psychological basis for which the Chinese leadership repeatedly emphasizes the importance of Sino–US cooperation in international affairs.

With the rise of various anti-China theories in the West, many Chinese now perceive newer threats from Western powers. According to a Hong Kong report of a PLA conference held in late 1993, about 60 percent of attendees believed that China's primary threat in the next century will be Japan, 30 percent believed the United States, and 10 percent thought it would be a resurgent Russia (Zong Lanhai 1994). As discussed earlier, many Chinese thought that the new military alliance between Japan and the United States was aimed at containing China. But with the rise of Japan's ambition to be a major political and military power in east Asia, the Chinese realized that US involvement in east Asian affairs could balance Japanese power. According to Wang Jianwei (1994: 268–9), Chinese leaders and analysts have seen the United States as a world leader, and about 40 percent of the respondents expressed varying degrees of "appreciation of or support for American leadership in world affairs" because, first, the international system needed a leader, and second, the United States was less overbearing and dangerous than other contenders. Taiwan's Lee Teng-hui's visit to the United States in 1995 led to strong nationalistic reactions in China. But the leadership was very cautious in dealing with the event and was keen to avoid causing any irreparable damage to Sino–US relations. In different areas, China has voiced its discontent with the West, but its leadership has also made enormous efforts to avoid any direct confrontation with the West, especially the United States.

It is important to note that when the West, especially the United States, shows its respect to China, nationalistic voices decline. As discussed in Chapter 6, the Chinese want their country to be increasingly integrated into the world system. China also shows its willingness to cooperate with other major powers as exemplified by changes in Sino–US relations and its relations with its neighboring countries. The Chinese government tends to behave as a fully pledged partner in world affairs. During his summit with President Bill Clinton, Jiang Zemin confirmed that China would accede to the 1966 United Nations International Covenant on Economic, Social, and Cultural Rights (ICESCR) (*South China Morning Post* 1997: 1). Though the original date the media speculated on was sometime in April 1998, it was announced in Beijing on March 13, 1998 that the Chinese government had in fact signed the ICESCR convention back in October 1997. Meanwhile, the Chinese government also announced that China would sign the International Covenant on Civil and Political Rights (ICCPR), a multilateral convention in force since 1976 (*South China Morning Post* 1998: 1). Given the fact that China had strongly resisted these two international conventions, China's behavior came as a surprise to the outside world. Nonetheless, considering that "to be a member of the system of great powers" has been the dream of the Chinese for centuries, the government's behavior is expectable.

Equally important is its integration into the world system, China has taken on the responsibility of a great power in managing regional, if not international, world order as exemplified by its performance in the 1997 Asian financial crisis. China contributed $100 million as a part of the IMF's efforts to bail out Thailand's financial crisis. The government also repeatedly insisted that China's *yuan* would not be devalued despite high pressure for devaluation, as a devaluation would ignite a further wave of crises. One major reason, as Premier Zhu Rongji indicated, was that it was China's responsibility to maintain economic stability in the region (Zhu Rongji 1998).

With the sudden collapse of the Soviet Union and the end of the Cold War, both China and the West lost their old foundation of national strategies and encountered enormous difficulties in adjusting their international behavior to the new circumstances. After the disappearance of their common enemy, China and the West have not found a new solid foundation for cooperation. Their interests, ranging from material interests to cultural values, tend to be in serious conflict.

China is growing economically. The collapse of the Soviet Union suddenly pushed it to a unique position. For the first time in its modern history, China faced an opportunity to be a great power and to exonerate the humiliation caused by the intrusion of Western powers. With its rapid economic growth, China's position in the international hierarchy has risen. Moreover, it also became a major actor in international affairs. For Chinese nationalists, changes have to be made to the existing international system, or even a new international order is necessary because current international rules were set up by the West and are not necessarily in accordance with China's interest. Chinese strategists also saw that to be in a dominant power position in the international system can bring the country enormous benefits (Yan Xuetong 1996b: 33–4). Domestically, nationalists saw the impact of decentralization-oriented modernization on the Chinese nation–state and believed that nationalism needed to be promoted in order to establish a new type of national identity. Anti-westernization became a major theme of the new nationalism (see Chapter 3). Also, with the rapid economic development, the Chinese have revived their confidence in their traditional civilization. Confucianism is no longer regarded as a barrier to China's modernization. Westernization-oriented modernization has brought in numerous "diseases" to the Chinese nation–state, and it is Confucianism that can be used to cure these diseases. In order to revive Confucianism, an anti-Western civilization movement seemed important (see Chapter 4). From these perspectives, China tends to be nationalistic.

This, however, does not mean that China's foreign policy will be nationalistic. China's new nationalism is primarily reactive. Its leaders have realized that Chinese international domination is only a dream, owing to China's backwardness and limited resources. The regime has to give the highest priority to the growth of China's comprehensive national power. Chinese leaders are afraid that China will again be a target of foreign imperialism if it cannot raise its comprehensive national power, the foundation of China's international status. The most important task for China is therefore to focus on domestic development. As long as China can benefit from current international rules, it is willing to accept them. China is also willing to compromise on various matters of international affairs because the major goal of its foreign policy is to create a hospitable international circumstance for domestic development. The Chinese have insisted that a new international economic and political order needs to be established to reflect the changing power distribution among the major powers. But this does not mean that China will mobilize its resources to overthrow the existing system. Instead, many Chinese want China to be integrated into the existing system through participation. The Chinese have also debated China's role in the east Asian region and in the global setting as well. But they also talked about China's "responsibility" in promoting regional and global peace and security (Zhao Gancheng 1996). "Voice" is China's strategic choice. What China cannot accept is that the West uses these rules to constrain China's development. As Wang Jisi (1997: 7) noted: "The United States attempts to force China's gear to revolve around its own gear . . . When the United States attempts to impose its own will on China, friction will arise".

What does the concept of a strong China mean to China itself and the international community? For the United States, with the collapse of the Soviet Union, China has lost its strategic weight and is no longer its strategic partner. The United States became the only superpower, and from the old perspective of geopolitics, it had no reason to maintain a good relationship with China. Once the strategic partnership dissolved, the Sino–US relationship was doomed to be chaotic. Without a grand strategy, the United States and China were in serious conflict in a number of areas: security, trade, human rights, Taiwan, Hong Kong, and Tibet. Furthermore, during the 1980s, many Westerners believed that China's reform would lead to economic liberalization and political democratization, and that Western values would prevail in China. But it did not turn out that way. Shortly after the end of the Cold War, there were predictions in the West that China would experience chaos as in the Soviet Union and its political system would change. But again, this prediction turned out to be false. Consequently, many in the West believe that a strong China could be a major threat. With its continuous rapid economic growth, China will inevitably become a regional, or even a world hegemonic power. What the West can do is to constrain China's development. This perception has led to the rise of the "China threat" theory in the early 1990s. How this threat can be reduced or even eliminated became a major issue for the West. Various theories including "containing China" and "fragmenting China" came into being.

However, it is hard for the West to contain China's rise. If the West seeks to block its development, China's emergence as a major global player in the next two or three decades can be slowed down somewhat, but it cannot be stopped. This is due to China's great internal dynamism. As Singapore's Prime Minister Goh Chok Tong (1995: 7) argued, "I do not believe that China's growth can be stifled. The genie is already out of the bottle and cannot be put back. There is sufficient internal dynamism for China to grow robustly even without outside help".

More importantly, the West's reaction to China's domestic development, in turn, led to strong nationalistic responses from China. In this sense, the rise of China's nationalism is not because of China's rapid development, but due to external stimulation. In other words, China's new nationalism is a reaction to a changing international environment. Despite the rise of popular nationalism, the Chinese leadership remains rational. The government does not want China's modernization to be interrupted by any external developments. Certainly, the regime also faces increasing domestic pressure from popular nationalism. Whether or not China's nationalism will be benign depends on the interplay between China and the West. Put another way, to what end China's new nationalism depends on whether the West can gradually accommodate and accept China as a major power. History will prove that continuous engagement (not containment) with China is likely not only to ease China's nationalism, but also to bring China into the world system.

Notes

1 Discovering Chinese Nationalism in China

1 This can be exemplified by Chinese responses to Bernstein's & Munro's work, *The Coming Conflict with China* (1997). See, the interviews with Wang Jisi, Shi Yihong & Zhang Baijia (1997).

2 *The Economist* (1997b: 22) (October 25). See also *The Economist* March 29, (1997a: 29–30).

3 Song Qiang, Zhang Zangzang & Qiao Bian (1996); Li Xiguang, Liu Kang et al. (1997). See also He Xin (1996); Chen Feng et al. (1996).

4 Yan Xuetong (1994). Yan is a University of California/Berkeley-trained political scientist and is now a Research Fellow at the Institute of Contemporary International Relations in Beijing.

5 Most contributors to *Behind a Demonized China* are Chinese scholars in the United States. See also Tian Yuan (ed.) (1997).

6 The two classic works on this subject are Morgenthau (1973); Waltz (1979). See also Mearsheimer (1990; 1994–95).

7 See also Oxnam (1993); Crowe, Jr. & Romberg (1991); Bosworth (1993); Roy (1995). It is also worth noting that many doubt that there is or will be a power vacuum in East Asia and South-east Asia. For example, see Mack (1993: 147–59); and Singh (1993: 263–77). Mack argued that it is false to believe that a US departure would create a power vacuum in the Asia-Pacific. Indeed, the risk of military conflict in the region has declined for military conquest has become less attractive than international trade as a means of pursuing national interests (ibid. pp. 154–6). According to Singh, there is no single power, including China, that can replace the former position of the United States; constructive engagements under the auspices of ASEAN have restrained any bids for regional dominance; and ASEAN member-states themselves have tried to fill the emerging power void through increasing military spending (ibid. 268).

8 "Local governmental State" refers to development-oriented local governments at the provincial level and below (see Wu Guoguang & Zheng Yongnian 1995). The concept is similar to Walder's "local governments as industrial firms" (1995: 263–301); and Oi's "local state corporatism" (1993).

2   Nationalism and Statism

1 For a discussion of modernization and nation-destroying, see Connor (1972); for the "de-construction" argument, see Goodman & Segal (1994).
2 For an examination of the development of modern European national states, see Tilly (1975).
3 Frank J. Goodnow (1859–1939) was one of the principal founders of the American Political Science Association and became its first president in 1903. From 1914 to his retirement in 1929, he was the president of Johns Hopkins University. He also served on President Taft's commission on economy and efficiency from 1911–12. In 1913, Goodnow was invited by Yuan Shikai to be his legal adviser.
4 In addition, for a case study on Guangdong, see Vogel (1989).
5 See *The China Quarterly*, special issue, *China's Military in Transition* 146 (June 1996).

3   Identity Crisis, the "New Left" and Anti-Westernization

1 It is important to point out that the term "the New Left" is a direct translation of a Western terminology, but it is different from the New Left in the West. The term was given by many Chinese commentators both home and abroad and referred to different schools of thoughts in post-Mao China such as new conservatism and new authoritarianism. The New Left can be distinguished from Mao's Left in the pre-reform period. See *YZZK* (September 18, 1994: 26–27); *DDYK* (November 15, 1994: 26–30). This book uses this "term" and only attempts to describe the link between the New Left and nationalism. See also Wei Suwu (1996); Bian Wu (1996).
2 For a discussion of how Chinese leaders, including Hu Yaobang and Zhao Ziyang, were interested in Western ideas, see Hamrin (1990).
3 For a discussion of Chinese intellectuals' identity crisis, see Goldman, Link & Su (1993: 125–53). On the relations between the State and intellectuals in the 1980s, see Goldman (1994).
4 After the 1989 Tiananmen Incident, the Chinese government almost initiated a campaign against *Heshang*. But early on, many intellectuals disagreed with the arguments presented in *Heshang*. For various official and unofficial comments on *Heshang*, see Zhong Huamin et al. 1989; Hua Yan et al. 1989; and The Propaganda Department of the Central Committee of the Chinese Communist Party (1990). For an interpretation of "River Elegy" as cultural nationalism, see Waldron (1993).
5 Many people, including reformist leaders, argued that if China was not able to reform its economic and political system, China's survival as a nation–state would be problematic.
6 According to a case study of Nanjie Village, Maoist ideology and its collective institutions played an important role in leading the village's successful economic growth. See Deng Yingtao, Miao Zhuang & Cui Zhiyuan (1996).

4   The Clash of Civilizations?

1 For a discussion of the relationship between culturalism and nationalism, see Duara (1996). For a discussion of racial discourse in modern China, see Dikotter (1992).
2 For discussions of policy changes of the Chinese Communist Party toward minorities, see Teufel Dreyer (1976); Mackerras (1994).

3 For the translation of the text, see *Chinese Economic Studies* 28: 2 (March–April 1995: 15–31). The cited text is on p. 15.
4 For Yan Fu's theory of nationalism, see Benjamin Schwartz (1964).
5 For a more detailed discussion, see Huntington (1996).
6 See Wang Jisi (1995). The book is a collection of articles written by Chinese scholars on Huntington's theme of "The Clash of Civilizations".
7 For comments on Sheng's articles, see Sun Liping (1996b); Xu Youyu (1996); Shi Zhong (1996); Pang Pu (1996); Qin Hui (1996a, 1996b).
8 For a detailed discussion of the link between China's nuclear weapons strategy and its cultural tradition, see Lin (1988).

5   The Official Discourse of Nationalism

1 According to Christensen, the view of the world of Chinese intellectuals is important because they influence the thinking of government decision-makers. See Christensen (1996).
2 In the Chinese context, see Lieberthal (1984); Lieberthal (1997).
3 See a summary in *SJJJDB*, February 15, 1988. The newspaper was closed down by the authorities owing to its allegedly involvement in the 1989 pro-democracy movement.
4 See also Shi (1995, 1996b).
5 For a discussion of the fall of Hu Yaobang, see Whiting (1989).
6 For a brief review of arguments for and against viewing China as a threat, see Roy (1996).

6   New Identity, National Interest, and International Behavior

1 See "Greater China", *China Quarterly*, special issue, 136 (1993).
2 For example, Whiting (1995); Christensen (1996). Whiting changed his early view of Chinese nationalism and argued that it now tends to be characterized by aggressiveness in terms of China's foreign policy-making.
3 The Political Department of the China News Agency (1992: 15). For a relevant study of international competition power, see Di Angzhao et al. (1992).
4 Deng made this point when he talked about Sino–American relations. He argued that China was still very poor and its infrastructure backward. China's policy toward the United States must be made in this context. See Deng (1987b: 265).
5 The Research Group of China's Comprehensive National Power (1995); Li Tianran (1990); Zhang Boli (1989); Dong Xiuling (1991); Huang Shoufeng (1992).
6 For an interpretation of *xiao-kang*, see Wong (1996a).
7 For state policy on science and technology, see The State Commission of Science and Technology (1986, 1992).
8 On the PLA's strategic shifts, see Shen Mingshi (1995).
9 For an introduction to the educational system in post-Mao China, see Bih-jaw Lin & Li-min Fan (1990).
10 The Research Group of China's Comprehensive National Power (1995); The Group of Comprehensive National Power Comparison among Five Countries (USA, Japan, Germany, China and India) (1995).

11 Deng met former US president Nixon on October 31, 1989, and a Japanese delegation on December 1, 1989. See Deng (1989b), and Deng (1989d), in Deng (1993a: 330–3 and 347–9), respectively.

12 The media in mainland China and Hong Kong watched the event of Yin He Hao very closely. Most opinions regarded the United States as hegemonic power, disregarding China's national dignity. For example, see Bao Xin (1993); Chen Wenru (1993), both in *LW* (overseas edition) 37 (September 13, 1993): 2 and 4–5, respectively.

13 For a discussion of China's policy towards the South-east Asian nations, see Zheng Yongnian (1996: 48–62).

7 Identity Transition and Chinese Power

1 For a discussion of this point in the case of the Diaoyutai dispute 1996, see Wang Gungwu (1996a).

Bibliography

Anderson, Benedict, *Imagined Communities: Reflections on the Origins and Spread of Nationalism*, London, Verso, 1991.

Averill, Stephen C., "The New Life in Action: The Nationalist Government in South Jiangxi", *China Quarterly*, 88 (December 1981): 594–628.

Bao Xin, "Meiguo baquan zhuyi zuilian de dabaolu" ("A Total Disclosure of US Hegemonism"), *LW*, 37 (September 13, 1993): 2.

Barme, Geremie R., "To Screw Foreigners Is Patriotic: China's Avant-Garde Nationalists", in Jonathan Unger (ed.), *China's Nationalism*, Armond, NY, M. E. Sharpe, 1996: 183–208.

Bernstein, Richard & Ross H. Munro, *The Coming Conflict with China*, NY, Knopf, 1997.

Bian Wu, "Huai ju wei zhi, chu ju zhe mi" ("The Amazing Metamorphosis of Neo-Leftism in China"), *ESYSJ*, 33 (1996): 4–17.

Bosworth, Stephen W., "The United States and Asia", *Foreign Affairs*, 72, 5 (November/December 1993): 59–85.

Breuilly, J., *Nationalism and the State*, Manchester University Press, 1982.

Brewer, Anthony, *Marxist Theories of Imperialism: A Critical Survey*, London, Routledge, 1980.

Brown, Michael E., Sean M. Lynn-Jones & Steven E. Miller (eds), *East Asian Security*, Cambridge, MA, MIT Press, 1997.

Buzan, Barry & Gerald Segal, "Rethinking East Asian Security", *Survival*, 36, 2 (Summer 1994): 3–21.

Catley, Bob & Makmur Keliat, *Spratlys: The Dispute in the South China Sea*, Aldershot, Ashgate Publishing Limited, 1997.

Chen Feng et al. *Zhongmei da jiaoliang* (*A Depiction of Trials of Strength between China and the US*), 2 vols, Beijing, Zhongguo renshi chubanshe, 1996.

Chen Fengjun, "Lun dongya chenggong de zonghe yaosu: dongya jingji minzu zhuyi" ("A Comprehensive Factor of the East Asian Miracle: East Asian Economic Nationalism"), *ZGSHKXJK*, 15 (Summer 1996): 88–99.

Chen Liangchao, *Dalu keji fazhan yanjiu* (*A Study of the Development of Science and Technology in Mainland China*), Taipei, 1993.

Chen Runyun, *Xiandai Zhongguo zhengfu* (*Modern Chinese Government*), Jilin wenshi chubanshe, 1988.

Chen Shaoming, "Minzu zhuyi: fuxing zhidao?" ("Nationalism: A Way for Revival?"), *DF*, 2 (1996): 74–6.

Chen Wenru, "Yin He Hao diaocha jishi" ("A Chronicle of the Investigation of the Yin He Hao"), *LW*, 37 (September 13, 1993): 4–5.

Chen Yizi, *Zhongguo: shinian gaige yu bajiu minyun (China: Ten Years of Reform and the 1989 People's Movement)*, Taipei, Lianjing chuban gongsi, 1990.

Chen Yuan, "Woguo jingji de shenceng wenti he xuanze" ("Deep Problems in the Economy and Our Choice"), internal circulation (March 1991).

Cheng Ming, "Dongya moshi de meili" ("The Glamour of the East Asian Model"), *ZLGL*, 2 (1994): 18–27.

The China Quarterly, "Greater China", special issue 136 (1993).

The China Quarterly, "China's Military in Transition", special issue 146 (June 1996).

Chou, Yu-sun, "Nationalism and Patriotism in China", *Issues and Studies*, 32, 11 (November 1996): 67–86.

Christensen, Thomas F., "Chinese Realpolitik", *Foreign Affairs*, 75, 5 (September/ October 1996): 37–52.

Chu Shulong, "Zhongmei guanxi mianlin zhanlue xuanze" ("Sino–US Relationship Encounters: A Strategic Choice"), *XDGJGX*, 11 (1996): 2–7.

Chuan Fu, *Shinian xuechao jishi, 1979–1989 (Ten Years of Student Movement)*, Beijing, Beijing renmin chubanshe, 1989.

Cline, Ray S., *The Power of Nations in the 1990s: A Strategic Assessment*, Lanham, Maryland, University of American Press, 1994.

Clinton, Bill, "Advance the Common Interest in a More Open China", *International Herald Tribune* (June 1, 1994): 8.

Cohen, Paul A., *Between Tradition and Modernity: Wang T'ao and Reform in Late Ch'ing China*, Cambridge, MA, Harvard University Press, 1974.

Cohen, Paul A., *Discovering History in China: American historical Writing on the Recent Chinese Past*, NY, Columbia University Press, 1984.

Cohen, Paul A., "Post-Mao Reform in Historical Perspective", *The Journal of Asian Studies*, 47, 3 (1988): 519–41.

Connor, Walker, "Nation-Building or Nation-Destroying?", *World Politics*, 24 (April 1972): 319–55.

Crowe, William J. Jr. & Alan D. Romberg, "Rethinking Security in the Pacific", *Foreign Affairs*, 70: 2 (Spring 1991): 123–40.

Cui Zhiyuan, "Zhidu chuangxin yu dierci sixiang jiefang" ("Institutional Innovation and A Second Liberation of Thoughts"), *ESYSJ*, 24 (1994): 5–15.

Cui Zhiyuan, "Zhongguo shijian dui xinggudian zhuyi jingjixue de tiaozhan" ("China's Practice and Its Challenges to Neo-Classical Economics"), *XGSHKXXB*, Special issue (July 1995): 1–33.

Cui Zhiyuan, "Angang xianfa yu hou fute zhuyi" ("The Angang Constitution and Post-Fordism"), *DS*, 3 (1996a): 11–21.

Cui Zhiyuan, "Mao Zedong 'wenge' lilun de deshi yu 'xiandaixing' de chongjian" ("Mao Zedong's Idea of Cultural Revolution and the Restructuring of Chinese Modernity"), *XGSHKXXB*, 7 (Spring 1996b): 49–74.

Cumings, Bruce, "The World Shakes China", *The National Interest*, 43 (Spring 1996): 20–7.

Curtis, Gerald L. (ed.), *The United States, Japan, and Asia: Challenge for U.S. Policy*, NY, W. W. Norton & Company, Inc., 1994.

DDYK, November 15, 1994.

Deng Xiaoping, "Jingjian jundui, tigao zhangdouli" ("Streamline the Military and Raise its Combat Effectiveness", March 20, 1980), in Deng, *Deng Xiaoping wenxuan* (*Selected Works of Deng Xiaoping*), vol. 2, Beijing: Renmin chuban-she, 1994: 284–290.

Deng Xiaoping, "Shicha Jiangsu dengdi hui Beijing hou de tanhua" ("A Talk after Coming back to Beijing from a Tour in Jiangsu and Other Places", March 2, 1983a), in Deng, *Deng Xiaoping wenxuan*, vol. 3, 1993a: 24–6.

Deng Xiaoping, *Deng Xiaoping wenxuan* (*Selected Works of Deng Xiaoping*), Beijing: Renmin chubanshe, 1983b.

Deng Xiaoping, "Wending shijie jushi de xinbanfa" ("A New Way to Stabilize the World Situation", February 22, 1984a), in Deng, *Deng Xiaoping wenxuan*, vol. 3, Beijing: Renmin chubanshe, 1993a: 49–50.

Deng Xiaoping, "Yige guojia, liangzhong zhidu" ("One Country and Two Systems", June 22 and 23, 1984b), in Deng, *Deng Xiaoping wenxuan*, vol. 3, 1993a: 58–61.

Deng Xiaoping, "Zai zhongyang guwen weiyuanhui disanci quanti huiyi shang de jianghua" ("Talk in the Third Plenum of the Advisory Committee of the Central Party Committee", October 22, 1984c), in Deng, *Deng Xiaoping wenxuan*, vol. 3, 1993a: 83–93.

Deng Xiaoping, "The Present Situation and the Tasks before Us", in *Deng, Selected Works of Deng Xiaoping 1975–1982*, Beijing, Foreign Languages Press, 1984d: 224–58.

Deng Xiaoping, "Heping he fazhan shi dangdai shijie de liangda wenti" ("Peace and Development Are the Two Problems that the World Faces Today", March 4, 1985a), in Deng, *Deng Xiaoping wenxuan*, vol. 3, 1993a: 104–6.

Deng Xiaoping, "Zai junwei kuoda huiyi shang de jianghua" ("Talk in an Enlarged Session of the Central Military Committee", June 4, 1985b), in Deng, *Deng Xiaoping wenxuan*, vol. 3, 1993a: 126–9.

Deng Xiaoping, "Gaige kaifang shi Zhongguo zhenzheng huoyue qilai", ("Reforms and Opening Animates China in Real Term", May 20, 1987a), in Deng, *Deng Xiaoping wenxuan*, vol. 3, 1993a: 232–5.

Deng Xiaoping, "Fazhan zhongmei guanxi de yuanze lichang" ("Principles in Developing Sino-American Relations"), in *Shiyijie sanzhong quanhui yilai zhongyao wenxian xuandu*, The Document Research Office of the Central Committee of the CCP (ed.), Selected Important Documents since the Third Plenum of the Eleventh Party Congress, vol. 1, Beijing, Renmin chubanshe, 1987b: 264–8.

Deng Xiaoping, *Deng Xiaoping tongzhi zhongyao jianghua* (*Important Talks of Comrade Deng Xiaoping*), Beijing, Renmin chubanshe, 1988.

Deng Xiaoping, "Shehui zhuyi Zhongguo shuiye dongyao buliao" ("No One Can Shake a Socialist China", October 26, 1989a), in Deng, *Deng Xiaoping wenxuan*, vol. 3, 1993a: 328–9.

Deng Xiaoping, "Jieshu yanjun de zhongmei guanxi, yaoyou Meiguo caiqu zhudong" ("To End A Grim Sino–US Relationship, the US Needs to Take Initiatives", October 31, 1989b), in Deng, *Deng Xiaoping wenxuan*, vol. 3, 1993a: 330–3.

Deng Xiaoping, "Jianchi shehui zhuyi, fangzhi heping yanbian" ("Adhering to Socialism and Guarding against Peaceful Evolution", November 23, 1989c), in Deng, *Deng Xiaoping wenxuan*, vol. 3, 1993a: 344–6.

Deng Xiaoping, "Guojia de zhuquan he anquan yao shizhong fangzai diyiwei" ("Nation's Sovereignty and Security Must Be of the First Importance", December 1, 1989d), in Deng, *Deng Xiaoping wenxuan*, vol. 3, 1993a: 347–9.

Deng Xiaoping, "Zhongmei guanxi zhonggui yao haoqilai cai xing" ("The

Sino–US Relationship Needs to Be Improved", December 10, 1989e, in Deng, *Deng Xiaoping wenxuan*, vol. 3, 1993a: 350–1.

Deng Xiaoping, "Guoji xingshi he jingji wenti" ("International Situation and Economic Issues", March 3, 1990a), in Deng, *Deng Xiaoping wenxuan*, vol. 3, 1993a: 353–6.

Deng Xiaoping, "Zhongguo yongyuan bu yunxu bieguo ganshe neizheng" ("China Always Does Not Allow Other Powers to Interfere in Domestic Affairs", July 11, 1990b), in Deng, *Deng Xiaoping wenxuan*, vol. 3, 1993a: 359–61.

Deng Xiaoping, "Shanyu liyong shiji jiejue fazhan wenti" ("To Catch the Opportunity to Resolve Development Problems", December 24, 1990c), in Deng, *Deng Xiaoping wenxuan*, vol. 3, 1993a: 363–5.

Deng Xiaoping, "Zai Wuchang, Shenzhen, Shanghai dengdi de tanhua yaodian" ("Main Points in the Speeches Made in Wuchang, Shenzhen, and Shanghai", January 18–February 21, 1992), in Deng, *Deng Xiaoping wenxuan*, vol. 3, 1993a: 370–83.

Deng Xiaoping, *Deng Xiaoping guanyu xinshiqi jundui jianshe lunshu xuanbian* (Selected Works of Deng Xiaoping of Military Building in a New Era), Beijing, Bayi chubanshe, 1993b.

Deng Xiaoping, "Opening Speech at the Twelfth National Congress of the CPC", in Deng, *Selected Works of Deng Xiaoping 1975-1982*, 1993a: 394–7.

Deng Yingtao, Miao Zhuang & Cui Zhiyuan, "Nanjie cun jingyan de sikao" ("Reflection on the Experience of Nanjie Village"), *ZLGL*, 3 (1996): 14–24.

The Department of Thought and Theory of China's Youth, "Sulian jubian zhihou Zhongguo de xianshi yingdui yu zhanlue xuanze" ("China's Feasible Countermeasures and Strategic Choice after Dramatic Changes in the Soviet Union"), internal circulation, September 9, 1991.

Deutsch, Karl W. et al., *Political Community in the North Atlantic Area: International Organization in the Light of Historical Experience*, Princeton, NJ, Princeton University Press, 1957.

Di Angzhao et al., *Guoji jingzheng li* (International Competition Power), Beijing, Gaige chubanshe, 1992.

Diao Dingtian, et al., *Zhongguo difang guojia jigou gaiyao* (*An Introduction to Chinese Local State Organizations*), Beijing, Falu chubanshe, 1989.

Dikotter, Frank, *The Discourse of Race in Modern China*, Stanford, CA, Stanford University Press, 1992.

Ding Jinhong & Luo Zude, "Lun woguo quyu jingji fazhan yu xingzheng quhua tizhi gaige" ("On Regional Economic Development and the Reform of Regional Administrative Systems in China"), The Development Research Center, the State Council, internal circulation, 1993.

Dittmer, Lowell & Samuel S. Kim, "Whither China's Quest for National Identity?", in *China's Quest for National Identity*, Ithaca, NY, Cornell University Press, 1993: 237–90.

Dogan, M. & D. Pelassy, *How to Compare Nations: Strategies in Comparative Politics*, Catham, NJ, Chatham House, 1984.

Dong Liwen, "Zhonggong de quanqiu zhanlue yu Zhongguo weixie lun" ("The Chinese Communist Party's Global Strategy and the Theory of 'China Threat'"), *ZGDLYJ*, 39, 9 (September 1996): 27–46.

Dong Xiuling, "Zonghe guoli lilun yanjiu zongshu" ("A Review of the Studies of Comprehensive National Power"), *XSYJDT*, 9 (1991): 2–5.

Dong Zhenghua, "Minzu zhuyi yu guojia liyi" ("Nationalism and National Interest"), *ZLGL*, 4 (1994): 26–7.

Doyle, Michael, "Kant, Liberal Legacies, and Foreign Affairs", Part I and II, *Philosophy and Public Affairs*, 12, 3–4 (1983): 205–35, 323–53.

Doyle, Michael, "Liberalism and World Politics", *American Political Science Review*, 80, 4 (1986): 1151–61.

Dreyer, June Teufel, *China's Forty Millions: Minority Nationalities and National Integration in the People's Republic of China*, Cambridge, MA, Harvard University Press, 1976.

Dreyer, June Teufel, "The PLA and Regionalism in Xinjiang", *The Pacific Review*, 7, 1 (1994): 41–56.

Duara, Prasenjit, "De-Constructing the Chinese Nation", in Jonathan Unger (ed.), *Chinese Nationalism*, Armonk, NY, M. E. Sharpe, 1996: 31–55.

Dzurek, Daniel J., *The Spratly Islands Dispute: Who's On First?*, Maritime Briefing, vol. 2, no. 2, International Boundaries Research Unit, University of Durham, UK, 1996.

The Economist, "A Survey of China" (November 28, 1992): 1–18.

The Economist, "Containing China" (July 31, 1995): 11–12.

The Economist, November 23, 1996.

The Economist, "American's Dose of Sinophobia" (March 29, 1997a): 29–30.

The Economist, "How American See China" (October 25, 1997b): 22.

The Editorial, "Jinfang lengzhan siwei taitou—bo 'e' zhi Zhongguo' lun" ("Beware of the Revival of a Cold-War Thinking Line—Critique on 'Containing China' Theory"), *RMRB*, January 26, 1996.

Evans, Peter B., Harold K. Jacobson & Robert D. Putnam (eds.), *Double-Edged Diplomacy: International Bargaining and Domestic Politics*, Berkeley, CA, University of California Press, 1993.

Fairbank, John King (ed.), *The Chinese World Order: Traditional China's Foreign Relations*, Cambridge MA, Harvard University Press, 1968.

Fan Shen, "Duiwai kaifang yu liyong zibenzhuyi" ("Opening Door and Making Use of Capitalism"), *RMRB* (overseas edition), February 24, 1992.

Fitzgerald, John, "The Nationless State: The Search for a Nation in Modern Chinese Nationalism", in Jonathan Unger (ed.), *Chinese Nationalism*, NY, M. E. Sharpe, 1996: 56–85.

Friedberg, Aaron L., "Ripe for Rivalry: Prospects for Peace in a Multipolar Asia", *International Security*, 18, 3 (Winter 1993/1994): 5–33.

Friedman, Edward, *National Identity and Democratic Prospects in Socialist China*, Armond, NY, M. E. Sharpe, 1995.

Friedman, Edward, "Chinese Nationalism, Taiwan Autonomy and the Prospects of a Larger War," *Journal of Contemporary China*, 6, 14 (1997): 5–32.

Friedman, Milton, *Friedman in China* (in Chinese), Hong Kong, The Chinese University of Hong Kong Press, 1991.

Friend, Theodore, *The Blue-Eyed Enemy: Japan Against the West in Java and Luzon, 1942–1945*, Princeton, NJ, Princeton University Press, 1988.

Fukuyama, Francis, "The End of History?", *The National Interest*, 16 (Summer 1989): 3–18.

Gallagher, Michael G., "China's Illusory Threat to the South China Sea", *International Security*, 19, 1 (Summer 1994): 169–94.

Gan Yang, "'Jiangcun jingji' zai renshi" ("A Re-Evaluation of 'The Jiang Village Economy'"), *DS*, 10 (1994): 50–7.

Garnaut, Ross & Guonan Ma, "How Rich Is China?", *Australian Journal of Chinese Affairs*, 30 (1993): 121–47.

Ge Jianxiong, "Minzu zhuyi shi jiuguo lingdan?" ("Is Nationalism a Panacea to Save the Nation?"), *YZZK*, (April 21, 1996): 14.

Gellner, Ernest, *Nations and Nationalism*, Ithaca, NY, Cornell University Press, 1983.

Gilpin, Robert, *War and Change in World Politics*, NY, Cambridge University Press, 1981.

Gladney, Dru C., *Muslim Chinese: Ethnic Nationalism in the People's Republic*, Cambridge, MA, Harvard University Press, 1991.

Gladney, Dru C., "China's Ethnic Reawakening," *Asia Pacific Issues*, Analysis from the East-West Center, 18 (January 1995).

Goh Chok Tong, "Global Economic Trends and Development: The China Factor in the World Economy", keynote address at the Asia Society International Corporate Conference in Beijing on May 13, 1995, press release by Singapore's Ministry of Information and the Arts, Release no. 14, May 1995.

Goldman, Merle, *Sowing the Seeds of Democracy in China: Political Reform in the Deng Xiaoping Era*, Cambridge, MA, Harvard University Press, 1994.

Goldman, Merle, Perry Link & Su Wei, "China's Intellectuals in the Deng Era: Loss of Identity with the State", in Lowell Dittmer & Samuel Kim (eds), *China's Quest for National Identity*, Ithaca, NY, Cornell University Press, 1993: 125–53.

Goodman, David, "The PLA and Regionalism in Guangdong", *The Pacific Review*, 7, 1 (1994): 29–40.

Goodman, David & Gerald Segal (eds.), *China Deconstructs*, London, Routledge, 1994.

Gourevitch, Peter, *Politics in Hard Time: Comparative Responses to International Economic Crisis*, Ithaca, NY, Cornell University Press, 1986.

Greenfield, Jeanette, *China's Practice in the Law of the Sea*, Oxford, Clarendon Press, 1992.

The Group of Comprehensive National Power Comparison among Five Countries (USA, Japan, Germany, China, and India), "Wuguo zonghe guoli bijiao yu yuce" ("A Comparison and Forecast of Comprehensive National Power"), *ZGGQGL*, 3 (1995): 43–4.

Gu Dexin & Huang Qi, "Guojia shili de texing, pinggu yu yunyong" ("National Power: Characteristics, Judgment, and Application") *ZLGL*, 5 (1996): 57–65.

Guilbernau, Montserrat, *Nationalism: The Nation–State and Nationalism in the Twentieth Century*, Cambridge, Polity Press, 1996.

Haas, Ernest B., *The Uniting of Europe: Political, Social, and Economic Forces, 1950–1957*, Stanford, CA, Stanford University Press, 1958.

Hamrin, Lee Carol, *China and the Challenge of the Future: Changing Political Patterns*, Boulder, CO, Westview Press, 1990.

Han Hua & Fan Qiang, "Zhongying zhong'ou guanxi de xin jieduan" ("A New Era in Sino–British Relationships and Sino–European Relationships"), *WHP*, April 5, 1998.

Harding, Harry, *China's Second Revolution: Reform after Mao*, Washington, DC, Brookings Institution, 1987.

Harrison, James, *Modern Chinese Nationalism*, NY, Research Institute on Modern Asia, Hunter College of the City of New York, no date.

Harrison, Selig S., *The Widening Gulf: Asian Nationalism and American Policy*, NY, The Free Press, 1978.

He Fang, "Shijie geju yu guoji xingshi" ("The World System and the International Situation"), *SJJJZZ*, 11 (1991): 6–14.

He Fang, "Xiashiji chu Zhongguo guoji huanjing de ruogan sikao" ("Some Thoughts on China's International Environment in the Early 21st Century"), *ZLGL*, 3 (1995): 86–93.

He Gaochao & Luo Jinyi, "Zhishi de benzhi shi kaifang de" ("The Nature of Knowledge Is Its Openness"), *XGSHKXXB*, Special issue (July 1995): vii–x.

The Heritage Foundation, "China Should Adhere to Rules of the Road", *Backgrounder*, 243 (March 29 1995).

He Xin, *He Xin zhengzhi jingji lunwenji* (*Essays on Politics and Economy of He Xin*), Ha'erbin, Heilongjiang jiaoyu chubanshe, 1993.

He Xin, *Zhonghua fuxing yu shijie weilai* (*The Revival of China and the Future of the World*), 2 vols, Chengdu, Sichuan renmin chubanshe, 1996.

Hinsley, F. H., *Nationalism and the International System*, London, 1973.

Hirschman, Albert O., *Exit, Voice, and Loyalty: Responses to Decline in Firms, Organizations, and States*, Cambridge, MA, Harvard University Press, 1970.

Hobsbawn, Eric & Terrance Ranger, *The Invention of Tradition*, Cambridge, Cambridge University Press, 1983.

Hsiao, Kung-chuan, *A History of Chinese Political Thought*, translated by F. W. Mote, vol. 1, Princeton, NJ, Princeton University Press, 1979.

Hsu, Immanuel C. Y., *China's Entrances into the Family of Nations: The Diplomatic Phase, 1858–1880*, Cambridge, MA, Harvard University Press, 1960.

Hu Angang, "Shengdiji ganbu yanzhong de dongxibu chaju" ("Income Disparities between Eastern and Western China in the Eye of Leading Cadres of the Provincial and Prefect Levels"), *ZLGL*, (1994): 88–90.

Hu Angang, "Fenshuizhi: pingjia yu jianyi" ("On Tax-Division System: Assessment and Suggestion"), *ZLGL*, 5 (1996): 1–9.

Hu Wei, "Zhongguo fazhan de 'bijiao youshi' hezai?—chaoyue chun jingji guandian de fenxi" ("Where Does China's Comparative Advantage Locate for Its Development?—An Analysis beyond a Pure Economic Point of View"), *ZLGL*, 5 (1995): 69–78.

Hua Yan, et al., *Heshang pipan* (*Critiques on the "River Elegy"*), Beijing, Wenhua yishu chubanshe, 1989.

Huang Shuofeng, "Manian xinchun hua guoli" ("Talking about National Power in the Spring of the Year of the Horse"), *RMRB*, February 26, 1990.

Huang Shuofeng, *Zonghe guoli lun* (*A Study on Comprehensive National Power*), Beijing, Zhongguo shehui kexue chubanshe, 1992.

Huang Yasheng, "Why China Will Not Collapse", *Foreign Policy*, 99 (Summer 1995): 54–68.

Huang Yasheng, *Inflation and Investment Control in China: The Political Economy of Central-Local Relations During the Reform Era*, NY, Cambridge University Press, 1996.

Hunt, Michael H., "Chinese National Identity and the Strong State: The Late Qing-Republican Crisis", in Lowell Dittmer & Samuel S. Kim (eds), *China Quest for National Identity*, Ithaca, NY, Cornell University Press, 1993: 62–79.

Huntington, Samuel P., "The Clash of Civilizations?", *Foreign Affairs*, 72, 3 (Summer 1993): 22–49.

Huntington, Samuel P., "Political Conflict after the Cold War," in Arthur Melzer (ed.), *History and the Idea of Progress*, Ithaca, NY, Cornell University Press, 1995: 137–54.

Huntington, Samuel P., *The Clash of Civilizations and the Remaking of World Order*, NY, Simon & Schuster, 1996.

Iriye, Akira, *China and Japan in Global Setting*, Cambridge, MA, Harvard University Press, 1992.

Jansen, Marius B., *Japan and China: From War to Peace, 1894–1972*, Chicago, Rand McNally Publishing Company, 1975.

Jiang Lingfei, "Meiguo duihua e'zhi zhanlue de zhiyue yinsu he keneng de zoux-iang" ("The Factors that Constrain the US's 'Containing China' Policy and their Possible Trends"), *ZLGL*. 5 (1996): 46–50.

Jiang Shixue, "Lamei, dongya fazhan moshi de bijiao yu qishi" ("A Comparison of the Development Models in Latin America and East Asia and Its Impli-cations"), *ZLGL*, 5 (1995): 58–68.

Jiang Zemin, "Aiguo zhuyi he woguo zhishi fenzi de shiming" ("Patriotism and the Mission of Chinese Intellectuals"), *RMRB*, May 4, 1990: 1, 3.

Jiang Zemin, "Zai qingzhu Zhongguo gongchandang chengli qishi zhounian shangde jianghua" ("Speech at the Meeting Commemorating the Seventi-eth Anniversary of the CCP's Founding"), *RMRB*, July 2, 1991: 1–3.

Jiang Zemin, "Jiakuai gaige kaifang he xiandaihua jianshe bufa, duoqu you Zhongguo tese shehui zhuyi shiye de gengda shengli" ("Speeding up the Implementation of Reform and Opening, and the Construction of a Socialist Economy: Striving for the Great Victory of Our Enterprise of Socialist Modernization"), *RMRB*, October 21, 1992.

Jiang Zemin, "Lingdao ganbu yiding yao jiang zhengzhi" ("Leading Cadres have to Talk about Politics", September 27, 1995), *RMRB*, January 17, 1996: 1–2.

Jing Bo, "Bo 'Zhongguo weixie lun'" ("Refuting the 'Theory of China Threat'"), *ZGGFB*, January 5, 1996.

Joffe, Ellis, "The PLA and the Chinese Economy: the Impact on Involvement", *Survival*, 37, 2 (Summer 1995): 24–43.

Joffe, Ellis, "Regionalism in China: the Role of the PLA", *The Pacific Review*, 7, 1 (1994): 17–28.

Johnson, Chalmers A., *Peasant Nationalism and Communist Power: The Emergence of Revolutionary China, 1937–1945*, Stanford, CA, Stanford University Press, 1962.

Johnston, Alastair Iain, *Cultural Realism: Strategic Culture and Grand Strategy in Chi-nese History*, Princeton, NJ, Princeton University Press, 1995.

Johnston, Alastair Iain, "Cultural Realism and Strategy in Maoist China", in Peter J. Katzenstein (ed.), *The Culture of National Security: Norms and Identity in World Politics*, NY, Columbia University Press, 1996: 216–68.

Kang Xiaoguang, "Zhongguo xiandaihua de mailuo yu chulu" ("The Course and Outlet of China's Modernization"), *ZLGL*, 1 (1994): 10–12.

Karmel, Solomon M., "Ethnic Tension and the Struggle for Order: China's Poli-cies in Tibet", *Pacific Affairs*, 68, 4 (Winter 1995–96): 485–508.

Katzenstein, Peter J., "International Relations and Domestic Structures: Foreign Economic Policies of Advanced Industrial States", *International Organiza-tion*, 30 (Winter 1976): 1–45.

Katzenstein, Peter J., *Small States in World Politics: Industrial Policy in Europe*, Ithaca, NY, Cornell University Press, 1985.

Katzenstein, Peter J. (ed.), *The Culture of National Security*, NY, Columbia Univer-sity Press, 1996a.

Katzenstein, Peter J., *Cultural Norms and National Security: Police and Military in Post War Japan*, Ithaca, NY, Cornell University Press, 1996b.

Kellas, James, *The Politics of Nationalism and Ethnicity*, London, Macmilan, 1991.

Kennedy, Paul, *The Rise and Fall of the Great Powers: Economic Change and Military Conflict from 1500 to 2000*, NY, Random House, 1987.

Keohane, Robert O. & Joseph S. Nye, *Power and Interdependence*, Boston, Little & Brown, 1977.

Kim, Samuel S., "China and the World in Theory and Practice", in Kim (ed.), *China and the World: Chinese Foreign Relations in the Post-Cold War Era*, 3rd edition, Boulder, CO, Westview Press, 1994: 3–41.

Kissinger, Henry, "Four Proposals to Get the United States and China off their Collision Course", *International Herald Tribune* (July 24, 1995): 9.

Klotz, Audie, *Norms in International Relations: The Struggle against Apartheid*, Ithaca, NY, Cornell University Press, 1995.

Kornberg, Judith F., "Comprehensive Engagement: New Framework for Sino–American Relations", *The Journal of East Asian Affairs*, 4, 1 (Winter/ Spring 1996): 18–23.

Kowert, Paul & Jeffrey Legro, "Norms, Identity, and Their Limits: A Theoretical Reprise", in Peter J. Katzenstein (ed.), *The Culture of National Security: Norms and Identity in World Politics*, NY, Columbia University Press, 1996: 451–97.

Krasner, Stephen D., *Defending the National Interest: Raw Material Investment and U.S. Foreign Policy*, Princeton, NJ, Princeton University Press, 1978.

Krauthmmer, Charles, "Why We Must Contain China", *Time*, 146, 5 (July 31, 1995): 72.

Kristof, Nicholas D., "The Rise of China", *Foreign Affairs*, 72, 5 (November/ December 1993): 59–73.

Kuhn, Philip A., "Local Self-Government under the Republic: Problems of Control, Autonomy, and Modernization", in Frederic Wakeman, Jr. & Carolyn Grant (eds), *Conflict and Control in Late Imperial China*, Berkeley, CA, University of California Press, 1975: 257–98.

Kumar, Anjali, "China's Reform, Internal Trade and Marketing", *The Pacific Review*, 7, 3 (1994): 323–40.

Kurth, James, "America's Grand Strategy: A Pattern of History", *The National Interest*, 43 (Spring 1996): 3–19.

Lardy, Nicholas R., *Foreign Trade and Economic Reform in China, 1978–1990*, Cambridge, Cambridge University Press, 1992.

Lardy, Nicholas R., *China in the World Economy*, Washington, DC, Institute for International Economy, 1994.

Layne, Christopher, "The Unipolar Illusion: Why New Great Powers Will Rise", *International Security*, 17, 4 (Spring 1993): 5–51.

Lee, Peter, N. S., *Industrial Management and Economic Reform in China, 1949–1984*, Hong Kong, Oxford University Press, 1987.

Lee Siew Hua, "China Will Be 'More Democratic over Time'", *The Straits Times*, Singapore (January 30, 1997): 1.

Lei Yi, "Sanshi niandai 'xinshi ducai' yu 'minzhu' de lunzhan" ("The Debates between the Proponents of 'New Dictatorship' and 'Democratic Regime' in the 1930s"), *DF*, 3 (1995): 26–30.

Levenson, Joseph L., *Modern China and Its Confucian Past: The Problem of Intellectual Continuity*, NY, Anchor Books, 1964.

Levenson, Joseph L., *Liang Ch'i Ch'ao and the Mind of Modern China*, Berkeley, CA, University of California Press, 1970.

Levine, Steven I., "China in Asia: The PRC as a Regional Power", in Harry Harding (ed.), *China's Foreign Relations in the 1980s*, New Haven, Yale University Press, 1984: 107–45.

Li Jianyong, "Tiaozhan yu jiyu" ("Challenges and Opportunities: A Conspicuous Topic—A Summary of the "Forum on the Concept of International Strategy at the Turn of the Century"), *ZLGL*, 6 (1995): 23–5.

Li Shenzhi, "Quanqiuhua shidai zhongguoren de shiming" ("Chinese Mission in an Age of Globalization"), *DF*, 5 (1994a): 13–18.

Li Shenzhi, "Cong quanqiuhua shidai kan Zhongguo de xiandaihua wenti" ("Understanding the Problems of China's Modernization From a Perspective of Globalization"), *ZLGL*, 1 (1994b): 5–6.

Li Shenzhi, "Quanqiuhua yu Zhongguo wenhua" ("Globalizaiton and Chinese Culture"), *TPYXB*, 2 (1994c): 3–11.

Li Shisheng, "Guanyu guoji xin zhixu jige wenti de tantao" ("Discussion of Several Questions Relating to the New International Order"), *SJJJZZ*, 10 (1992): 43–4.

Li Tianran, "Guanyu zonghe guoli wenti" ("About Comprehensive National Power"), *GJWTYJ*, 2 (1990): 52–8.

Li Wenhao, "Zhongmei shounao huiyi jiang dui shijie weilai chansheng zhongda yingxiang" ("The Sino–US Summit Will Have a Major Impact on the World's Future"), *LW*, 43 (1997): 45.

Li Xiguang, Liu Kang et al., *Yaomohua Zhongguo de beihou* (*Behind a Demonized China*), Beijing, Zhongguo shehui kexue chubanshe, 1997.

Li Zehou & Wang Desheng, "Guanyu wenhua xianzhuang daode chongjian de duihua" ("A Dialogue Regarding Cultural Development and Moral Reconstruction"), Parts I and II, *DF*, 5, 6 (1994): 69–73, 85–7.

Liao, Kuang-sheng, *Anti-foreignism and Modernization in China*, 1860–1980, Hong Kong, The Chinese University Press, 1984.

Lieberthal, Kenneth, "Domestic Politics and Foreign Policy", in Harry Harding (ed.), *China's Foreign Relations in the 1980s*, New Haven, Yale University Press, 1984: 43–70.

Lieberthal, Kenneth, "Domestic Forces and Sino–U.S. Relations", in Ezra F. Vogel (ed.), *Living With China: U. S.–China Relations in the Twenty-First Century*, NY, W. W. Norton & Company, 1997: 254–76.

Lin Bih-jaw & Li-min Fan (eds.), *Education in Mainland China: Review and Evaluation*, Taipei, Institute of International Relations, 1990.

Lin, Chong-Pin, *China's Nuclear Weapons Strategy: Transition within Evolution*, Lexington, MA, Lexington Books, 1988.

Lin, Chong-Pin, The Role of the PLA in China's Center-Regional Interactions, paper presented at the Conference on "Regulating Decentralization and System Alternation in China", sponsored by the Center for Contemporary China Studies, Princeton University, October 22, 1994.

Lin Yifu, Cai Fang & Li Zhou, *Zhongguo de qiji: fazhan zhanlue he jingji gaige* (China's Miracle: Development Strategy and Economic Reform), Shanghai, Sanlian shudian, 1994a.

Lin Yifu, Cai Fang & Li Zhou, "Dui ganchao zhanlue de fansi" ("Reflections on the Catching-up and Surpassing Strategy"), *ZLGL*, 6 (1994b): 1–12.

Lin Yifu, Cai Fang & Li Zhou, "Ganchao zhanlue de zai fansi ji kegong tidai de bijiao youshi zhanlue" ("On the Catching-up and Surpassing Strategy and the Alternative of the Strategy to Comparative Advantage"), *ZLGL*, 5 (1995): 1–10.

Lin Yifu, Cai Fang & Li Zhou, "Ziyuan jiegou shengji: ganchao zhanlue de wuqu—dui 'bijiao youshi zhanlue' piping de jidian huiying" ("The Upgrading of the Resource Structure: Misunderstanding the Catching-up and Surpassing Strategy—Some Responses to Criticism on the 'Comparative Advantage Strategy'"), *ZLGL*, 1 (1996): 35–45.

Lin, Yu-sheng, *The Crisis of Chinese Consciousness*, Madison, The University of Wisconsin Press, 1979.

The Lingdian Survey Company et al., *Guancha Zhongguo* (Surveying China), Beijing, Gongshang chubanshe, 1997.

Liu, Alan P. L., *How China Is Ruled*, Englewood Cliffs, NJ, Prentice-Hall, Inc., 1986.

Liu, Ji, "Making the Right Choices in Twenty-First Century Sino–American Relations", speech delivered at the Fairbank Center for East Asian Research, Harvard University, May 27, 1997.

Liu Jinghua, "Ershiyi shiji 20–30 niandai Zhongguo jueqi yiji waijiao zhanlue xuanze" ("The Rise of China in the 20s–30s of the 21st century, and Alternatives for Diplomatic Strategy"), *ZLGL*, 3 (1994): 119–20.

Liu Jun & Li Lin (eds.), *Xin quanwei zhuyi* (*New Authoritarianism*), Beijing, Jingji xueyuan chubanshe, 1989.

Liu Liqun, "Chukou daoxiang xing jingji fazhan moshi bu shihe Zhongguo guoqing" ("An Export-Led Model of Economic Development Does not Fit China's National Conditions"), *ZLGL*, 2 (1994): 43–6.

Liu Xinwu, "Queli renlei gongxiang wenmin guannian" ("To Establish the Concept of Shared Human Civilization"), *DF*, 6 (1996): 21–5.

Liu Yunshan, "Ba 'Aiguo zhuyi jiaoyu shishi gangyao' luodao shichu" ("Practising the Policy of 'The Outline of Patriotic Education'"), *RMRB*, September 7, 1994: 3.

Lo, Chi-kin, *China's Policy Towards Territorial Disputes: The Case of the South China Sea Islands*, London: Routledge, 1989.

Luo Rongqu, "Zouxiang xiandaihua de Zhongguo daolu: youguan jinbainian Zhongguo da biange de yixie lilun wenti" ("The Chinese Way to Modernization: Certain Theoretical Issues on China's Great Transition in the Last Century"), *ZGSHKXJK*, 17 (Winter 1996): 43–53.

Mack, Andrew, "Key Issues in the Asia–Pacific", in Richard Leaver & James L. Richardson (eds.), *The Post-Cold War Order: Diagnoses and Prognoses*, Allen & Unwin, 1993: 147–59.

Mackerras, Colin, *China's Minorities: Integration and Modernization in the Twentieth Century*, Hong Kong, Oxford University Press, 1994.

Mahathir Mohamed, "Dongya guojia bing nu renwei Zhongguo dui anquan goucheng weixi" ("East Asian Nations Do Not Think that China Poses a Threat to Security"), *LHZB*, December 5, 1996.

Mancall, Mark, *China at the Center: 300 Years of Foreign Policy*, NY, Free Press, 1984.

Mao Zedong, *Lun shida guanxi* (*On the Ten Great Relationships, 1956*), Beijing, Renmin chubanshe, 1976.

Mao Zedong, "The Role of the Chinese Communist Party in the National War", in Mao, *Selected Works of Mao Tse-Tung*, vol. II, Beijing, Foreign Languages Press, 1975: 195–211.

Marland, Bryce, "China Isn't a Military Power", *International Herald Tribune*, November 15, 1996: 8.

Mayall, James, *Nationalism and International Society*, Cambridge, Cambridge University Press, 1991.

Mccord Edward Allen, *The Power of Gun*, Berkeley, CA, University of California Press, 1993.

Mcmillen, Donald H., "The PLA and Regionalism in Hong Kong", *The Pacific Review*, 7, 1 (1994): 57–66.

Mearsheimer, John J., "Back to the Future: Instability in Europe After the Cold War", *International Security*, 15, 1 (Summer 1990): 5–56.

Mearsheimer, John J., "The False Promise of International Institutions", *International Security*, 19: 3 (Winter 1994–95): 5–49.

Mercer, Jonathan, "Anarchy and Identity", *International Security*, 49, 2 (Spring 1995): 229–52.

Metzger, Thomas A. & Ramon H. Myers (eds), *Greater China and U.S. Foreign Policy*, Stanford, CA, Hoover Institution Press, 1996.

Min Qi, *Zhongguo zhengzhi wenhua* (*Political Culture in China*), Kunming, Yunnan renmin chubanshe, 1989.

Mommsen, Wolfgang J., *Theories of Imperialism*, translated by P. S. Falla, Chicago, The University of Chicago Press, 1977.

Mongenthau, Hans J., "The Paradoxes of Nationalism", *Yale Review*, xlvi, 4 (June 1957): 481.

Morgenthau, Hans J., *Politics among Nations: The Struggle for Power and Peace*, 5th edition, NY, Knopf, 1973.

MP, December 10, 1996.

MP, "Li Peng: chengren Meiguo shili, fandui zhudao shijie" ("Li Peng: Recognizing US Power and Oppose US Hegemony"), February 5, 1998.

Munck, Ronaldo, *The Difficult Dialogue: Marxism and Nationalism*, London, Zed Books Ltd, 1986.

Munro, Ross H., "Awakening Dragon: The Real Danger in Asia Is from China", *Policy Review*, 62 (Fall 1992): 10–16.

Nathan, Andrew, *Chinese Democracy*, NY, Alfred A. Knopf, 1985.

Nu Chao, "Minqing junxin tuidong, Beijing baodiao shengwen" ("Beijing's Determination to Protect the Diaoyutai Islands Is Strengthened by People's Sentiments and the Army's Morale"), *YZZK*, September 16–22, 1996: 24–8.

Nye, Joseph S. Jr., "The Case for Deep Engagement", *Foreign Affairs*, 74, 4 (1995): 90–102.

Oi, Jean C., "Fiscal Reform and the Economic Foundation of Local State Corporatism in China", *World Politics*, 45 (October 1993): 99–126.

Oi, Jean C., *Rural China Takes Off: Incentives for Industrialization*, Berkeley, CA, University of California Press, 1996.

Ojha, Ishwer C., *Chinese Foreign Policy in an Age of Transition: The Diplomacy of Cultural Despair*, Boston, Beacon Press, 1971.

Oksenberg, Michel, "China's Confident Nationalism", *Foreign Affairs*, 65, 3 (1986–87): 501–23.

Overholt, William H., "Asia and America in Clinton's Second Term: A New Cold War?", *Bankers Trust Research*, Hong Kong, April 21, 1997.

Owen, John M., "How Liberalism Produces Democratic Peace", *International Security*, 19, 2 (1994): 87–125.

Oxnam, Robert B., "Asia–Pacific Challenges", *Foreign Affairs*, 72, 1 (1993): 58–73.

Pan Xiao, "What Is the Meaning of Life?", *JSND*, 1 (1981): 82–5.

Pang Pu, "'Wenming' jieshuo" ("The Definition of 'Civilization'"), *ZLGL*, 4 (1996): 92–5.

Petracca, Mark P. & Mong Xiong, "The Concept of Chinese Neo-Authoritarianism: An Exploration and Democratic Critique", *Asian Survey*, xxx, 11 (November 1990): 1099–117.

Pi Mingyong, "Minzu zhuyi yu rujia wenhua" ("Nationalism and the Confucian Culture—Liang Qichao's theory on Nationalism and its Predicament"), *ZLGL*, 2 (1996): 51–7.

The Political Department of the China News Agency, *Shisida neiwai* (Inside and Outside of the Fourteenth Party Congress), Beijing, Hualing chubanshe, 1992.

The Propaganda Department of the Central Committee of the Chinese Communist Party (ed.), *Heshang de wuqu—cong Heshang dao wusi* (The Mistakes in River Elegy: From the "River Elegy" to the May-Fourth Movement), Nanchang, Jiangxi renmin chubanshe, 1990.

Putnam, Robert D., "Diplomacy and Domestic Politics: the Logic of Two-Level Games", *International Organization*, 42, 3 (Summer 1988): 427–60.

Pye, Lucian, "China: Erratic State, Frustrated Society", *Foreign Affairs*, 69, 4 (Fall 1990): 56–74.

Pye, Lucian, "How China's Nationalism Was Shanghaied?", in Jonathan Unger (ed.), *Chinese Nationalism*, Armonk, NY, M. E. Sharpe, 1996: 86–112.

Qian Qichen, "1993: shijie kaishi chongxin renshi Zhongguo" ("1993: The World Begins to Recognize China), *RMRB*, December 15, 1993.

Qin Hui, "Guanyu 'xin yeman zhengfu lun' yu wenming zhengjiu zhilu—yu Sheng Hong xiansheng shangqu" ("On the Theory of 'New Barbarians Conquest' and the Way to Save Civilizations—A Discussion with Mr Sheng Hong"), *ZLGL*, 4 (1996a): 96–101.

Qin Hui, "Ziyou zhuyi yu minzu zhuyi de jihedian zai nali?" ("Where Is the Junction between Liberalism and Nationalism?"), *DF*, 3 (1996b): 45–8.

Rankin, Mary, *Early Chinese Revolutionaries: Radical Intellectuals in Shanghai and Chekiang, 1902–1911*, Cambridge, MA, Harvard University Press, 1971.

Ren Weiwen, "Deng Xiaoping pingjia Yangjiajiang" ("Deng Xiaoping's Comments on the Yang Brothers"), *XB*, November 18, 1992.

Ren Weiwen, "Beijing yi daodan yanxi jinggao Li Denghui" ("Beijing Uses Missile Test to Warn Lee Teng-hui"), *XB*, July 19, 1995a.

Ren Weiwen, "Beijing chongxin renshi meiguo he Li Deng-hui" ("Beijing's Rethinking of the US and Lee Teng-hui"), *XB*, June 14, 1995b.

The Research Group of China's Comprehensive National Power, "Dui Zhongguo zonghe guoli de cedu he yiban fenxi" ("The Measurement and Analysis of China's Comprehensive National Power"), *ZGSHKX*, 5 (1995): 4–19.

Rielly, John E., *American Public Opinion and U.S. Foreign Policy, 1995*, Chicago, Chicago Council on Foreign Relations, 1995.

RMRB, May 18, 1979.

RMRB, June 10, 1980.

RMRB, January 30, 1988.

RMRB, 26 February 1990: 2.

RMRB, July 2, 1991: 1–3.

RMRB, "Aiguo zhuyi jiaoyu shishi gangyao" ("The Outline of Patriotic Education"), September 6, 1994a: 3.

RMRB, "Pibo 'Zhongguo weixie lun'" ("Refuting the Theory of 'China Threat'"), August 19, 1995.

Qian Qichen's talk in the first conference of the ASEAN Forum, *RMRB* (overseas edition), 26 July 1994b.

Robinson, Thomas W. & David Shambaugh (eds.), *Chinese Foreign Policy: Theory and Practice*, Oxford University Press, 1995.

Rong Jingben, "Jianli guoji zhengzhi jingji xin zhixu shi jiejue minzu wenti de genben tujing" ("To Establish a New International Economic and Political Order is a Fundamental Approach to the Resolution of National Problems"), *ZLGL*, 3 (1994): 2–6.

Rosen, Stanley & Gary Zou (eds), "The Chinese Debate on the New Authoritarianism, I, II, III, and IV", in *Chinese Sociology and Anthropology*, Winter 1990–91, Spring, Summer, and Fall, 1991.

Rosenau, James, *Linkage Politics: Essays on the Convergence of National and International Systems*, NY, Free Press, 1969.

Ross, Robert S., "Beijing as a Conservative Power", *Foreign Affairs*, 76, 2 (March/ April 1997a): 35–44.

Ross, Robert S., "Why Our Hardliners Are Wrong", *The National Interest*, 49 (Fall 1997b): 42–51.

Rousseau, Jean-Jacques, *Rousseau: Political Writings*, Frederick Watkins (editor/translator), Edinburg, Nelson, 1953.

Roy, Denny, "Hegemon on the Horizon? China's Threat to East Asian Security", *International Security*, 19, 1 (Summer 1994): 149–68.

Roy, Denny, "Assessing the Asian-Pacific 'Power Vacuum'", *Survival*, 37, 3 (Autumn 1995): 45–60.

Roy, Denny, "'The 'China Threat' Issue: Major Arguments", *Asian Survey*, xxxvi, 8 (August 1996): 758–71.

Rozman, Gilbert, *The Chinese Debate about Soviet Socialism, 1978–1985*, Princeton, NJ, Princeton University Press, 1984.

Russett, Bruce, *Grasping the Democratic Peace: Principles for a Post-Cold War World*, Princeton, NJ, Princeton University Press, 1993.

Said, Edward W., *Orientalism*, NY, Vintage Book, 1979.

Schrecker, John E., *Imperialism and Chinese Nationalism: Germany in Shantung*, Cambridge, MA, Harvard University Press, 1971.

Schurmann, Franz, *Ideologies and Organization in Communist China*, Berkeley, CA, University of California Press, 1968.

Schwartz, Benjamin, *In Search of Wealth and Power*, NY, Harper Torchbook, 1964.

Segal, Gerald, *China Changes Shape: Regionalism and Foreign Policy*, Adephi Paper 287, London, Brassey's For IISS, March 1994.

Segal, Gerald, "Tying China into the International System", *Survival*, 37, 2 (Summer 1995a): 6–73.

Segal, Gerald, "Rising Nationalism in China Worries the Japanese", *International Herald Tribune*, 28 (September 1995b): 10.

Segal, Gerald, "East Asia and the 'Containment' of China", *International Security*, 20, 4 (Spring 1996): 107–35.

Segal, Gerald & Richard Yang (eds), *Chinese Economic Reform: the Impact on Security*, London, Routledge, 1996.

Shambaugh, David, *Beautiful Imperialism: China Perceives America, 1972–1990*, Princeton, NJ, Princeton University Press, 1991.

Shambaugh, David, "Growing Strong: China's Challenge to Asian Security", *Survival*, 36, 2 (Summer 1994): 43–59

Shee, Poon Kim, "Is China a Threat to the Asia–Pacific Region?", in Wang Gungwu and John Wong (eds.), *China's Political Economy*, World Scientific and Singapore University Press, 1998: 339–58.

Shen Jiru, *Zhongguo bu dang "bu xiansheng"* (*China Does not Want to Be "Mr No"*), Beijing, Jinri Zhongguo chubanshe, 1998.

Shen Liren & Dai Yuanchen, "Woguo 'zhuhou jingji' de xingcheng jiqi biduan he genyuan" ("The Formation, Defects, and Origins of the Economy of 'Dukedoms' in China"), *JJYJ*, 3 (1992): 10–20.

Shen Mingshi, *Gaige kaifang hou de jiefangjun* (*The People's Liberation Army since the Reform and Opening*), Taipei, Huizong wenhua chubanshe, 1995.

Sheng Hong, "Shenmo shi wenming?" ("What Are Civilizations?"), *ZLGL*, 5 (1995): 88–98.

Sheng Hong, "Cong minzu zhuyi dao tianxia zhuyi?" ("From Nationalism to Cosmopolitanism") *ZLGL*, 1 (1996a): 14–19.

Sheng Hong, "Jingjixue zenyang tiaozhan lishi" ("How Does Economics Challenge History?"), *DF*, 1 (1996b): 49–55.

Shi Lujia, "Gongpu zhongmei guanxi de xin pianzhang" ("To Write a New Chapter on Sino–US Relations"), *LW*, 45 (1997): 43.

Shi Yinhong, "Guoji zhengzhi de shijixing guilu yiji dui Zhongguo de qishi" ("The Law of Centurial Significance in International Politics and its Revelation to China"), *ZLGL*, 5 (1995): 1–3.

Shi Yinhong, "Why Against China?" *BR*, (October 21–27, 1996a): 11.

Shi Yinhong, "Xifang dui feixifang: dangjin meiguo duihua taidu de genben yuanyin" ("The West vs the Non-West: the Fundamental Reasons of America's Current Attitude Towards China"), *ZLGL*, 3 (1996b): 8–9.

Shi Zhong, "Zhongguo xiandaihua mianlin de tiaozhan" ("The Challenges that China's Modernization Encounters"), *ZLGL*, 1 (1994): 7–9.

Shi Zhong, "Bu ying ba bijiao youshi de luoji tuixiang jiduan" ("The Logic of Comparative Advantage Should not be Pushed to an Extreme"), *ZLGL*, 3 (1995): 11–15.

Shi Zhong, "Wenming de bijiao zhishi yizhong cankao" ("Civilizations Can Be Compared Only for Reference"), *ZLGL*, 2 (1996): 98–100.

Shinn, James (ed.), *Weaving the Net: Conditional Engagement with China*, NY, Council on Foreign Relations Press, 1996.

Shirk, Susan, *The Political Logic of Economic Reform in China*, Berkeley, CA, University of California Press, 1993.

Shue, Vivienne, *The Reach of the State: Sketches of the Chinese Body Politic*, Stanford, CA, Stanford University Press, 1988.

Si Cheng, "Chinese Say 'No' to the United States", *BR* (October 21–27, 1996): 13.

Singh, Bilveer, "The Challenge of the Security Environment in South-east Asia in the Post-Cold War Era", *Australian Journal of International Affairs*, 47, 2 (October 1993): 263–77.

SJJJDB, February 15, 1988.

Song Qiang, Zhang Zangzang & Qiao Bian, *Zhongguo keyi shuo bu* (The China that Says No), Beijing, Zhongguo gongshang chubanshe, 1996.

South China Morning Post, October 26, 1997.

South China Morning Post, March 13, 1998.

The State Commission of Science and Technology, *Zhongguo kexue jishu zhengce zhinan* (Directory of China's State Policy of Science and Technology), vols. 1–5, Beijing, Kexue jishu wenxian chubanshe, 1986, 1992.

Strand, David, "Political Participation and Political Reform in Post-Mao China (1985)", *Copenhagen Discussion Papers No. 6*, Center for East and Southeast Asian Studies, University of Copenhagen, 1989.

Su Xiaokang, et al., *Heshang* (River Elegy), Beijing, Xiandai chubanshe, 1988.

Sullivan, Roger W., "Discarding the China Card", *Foreign Policy*, (Spring 1992): 3–23.

Sun Liping, "Huiru shijie zhuliu wenming—minzu zhuyi santi" ("Flowing Together with the World's Mainstream Civilization"), *DF*, 1 (1996a): 15–19.

Sun Liping, "'Shenmo shi wenming' de yanyi luoji yu taolun yujing" ("The Logic and Language Environment of Discourse on 'What Are Civilizations'"), *ZLGL*, 2 (1996b): 87–93.

Sun Wen (Sun Yat-sen), *Sanmin Chu I: The Three Principles of the People*, F. W. Price (translator), Shanghai, China Committee, Institute of Pacific Relations, 1927.

Sun Yat-sen, *Sun Zhongshan quanji* (*Collected Works of Sun Yat-sen*), vol. 9, Beijing, Zhonghua shuju, 1986.

Swaine, Michael, "Don't Demonize China; Rhetoric about its Military Might Doesn't Reflect Reality", *Washington Post* (May 18, 1997), C1 and C4.

Swidler, Ann, "Culture in Action: Symbols and Strategies", *American Sociological Review*, 51, 2 (1986): 273–86.

Szporluk, Roman, *Communism and Nationalism: Karl Marx versus Friedich List*, NY, Oxford University Press, 1988.

Talbot, Strobe, "Democracy and the National Interest", *Foreign Affairs*, 75, 6 (1996): 47–63.

Tang Tianri, "Zhongmeiri sanjiao bixu pingheng" ("Power Must Be Balanced among China, the USA, and Japan"), *LW*, 23 (1996): 44.

Taylor, Bruce, "Regional Planning for Reciprocal Benefit in South China", in Kwan-yiu Wong et al. (eds), *Perspectives on China's Modernization*, Hong Kong, The Chinese University of Hong Kong Press, 1990: 18–27.

Teng, Ssu-yu & John King Fairbank, *China's Response to the West: A Documentary Survey, 1839–1923*, Cambridge, MA, Harvard University Press, 1979.

Tian Yuan (ed.), *Riben xin yinmou* (Japan's New Conspiracy), Hong Kong, Mirror Books Ltd, 1997.

Tilly, Charles (ed.), *The Formation of National States in Western Europe*, Princeton, NJ, Princeton University Press, 1975.

TKP, "Zhonghua renmin gongheguo guomin jingji he shehui fazhan "jiuwu" jihua he 2010nian yuanjing mubiao de gangyao" ("The Outline of the Ninth Five-Year Plan of the National Economy, and Social Development and Long-Term Goals by 2010 of the People's Republic of China"), March 20, 1996.

Vogel, Ezra F., *One Step Ahead in China: Guangdong under Reform*, Cambridge, MA, Harvard University Press, 1989.

Vogel, Ezra F. (ed.), *Living with China: U.S.–China Relations in the Twenty-First Century*, NY, W. W. Norton & Company, 1997.

Walder, Andrew G. "Local Governments as Industrial Firms: An Organizational Analysis of China's Transitional Economy", *American Journal of Sociology*, 101, 2 (September 1995): 263–301.

Waldron, Authur N., "Representing China: The Great Wall and Cultural Nationalism in the Twentieth Century", in Harumi Befu (ed.), *Cultural Nationalism in East Asia: Representation and Identity*, Berkeley, Institute of East Asian Studies, University of California, 1993: 36–60.

Waldron, Arthur N., "Theories of Nationalism and Historical Explanation", *World Politics*, xxxvii, 3 (April 1985): 416–31.

Waltz, Kenneth, *Theory of International Politics*, Reading, MA, Addison-Wesley, 1979.

Wang, David, "The East Turkestan Movement in Xinjiang: A Chinese Potential Source of Instability?", *EAI background Brief No. 7*, East Asian Institute, National University of Singapore, January 31, 1998.

Wang Gungwu, *The Chinese Way: China's Position in International Relations*, Oslo, Scandinavian University Press, 1995.

Wang Gungwu, "National Choice", *Pacific Economic Paper No. 260*, Australia–Japan Research Center, Research School of Pacific and Asian Studies, The Australian National University, October 1996a.

Wang Gungwu, *The Revival of Chinese Nationalism*, Leiden, International Institute for Asian Studies, 1996b.

Wang Gungwu, *Nationalism and Confucianism*, Wu Teh Yao Memorial Lectures 1996, Singapore, National University of Singapore, UniPress, 1996c.

Wang Hui, "Wenhua pipan lilun yu dangdai Zhongguo minzu zhuyi wenti" ("Cultural Critical Theories and the Problems of Contemporary Chinese Nationalism"), *ZLGL*, 4 (1994): 17–20.

Wang Huning, "Zhongguo gaige nanti de fei jingji sikao" ("Non-Economic Causes of Difficulties in China's Reform"), *QS*, 7 (1988): 35–6.

Wang Jian & Pei Xiaolin, "Woguo de chanye jiegou waimao fazhan zhanlue" ("China's Industrial Structure and the Strategy of Foreign Trade Development"), *DWJMYJ*, 1 (1988): 20–8.

Wang Jisi (ed.), *Wenming yu guoji zhengzhi: Zhongguo xuezhe ping Heng Ting Dun de wenming chongtu lun* (*Civilizations and International Politics: Chinese Scholars' Comment on Huntington's Theory of the Clash of Civilizations*), Shanghai, Shanghai renmin chubanshe, 1995.

Wang Jisi, "US China Policy: Containment or Engagement?", *BR* (October 21–27, 1997): 6–8.

Wang Jisi, Shi Yihong & Zhang Baijia, "Scholars Refute Book's Views on US–China Relations", *BR* (June 2–8, 1997): 8–12.

Wang Jianwei, *United States–China Mutual Images in the Post-Tiananmen Era: A Regression or Sophistication?* Ann Arbor, University of Michigan, Political Science Department, doctoral dissertation, 1994.

Wang Mingming, "Wenhua xiangxiang de liliang—du Sa Yi De zhu dong-fangxue" ("The Power of Cultural Imagination: Readings on Edward Said's *Orientalism*"), *ZGSP*, 6 (July 1995): 5–18.

Wang Shaoguang, "Jianli yige qiangyouli de minzhu guojia" ("Building a Strong Democratic State"), *Paper of the Center for Modern China*, 4 (1991).

Wang Shaoguang, "Fenquan de dixian" ("The Limits of Decentralization"), *ZLGL*, 2 (1995): 37–56.

Wang Shaoguang & Hu Angang, *Zhongguo guojia nengli baogao* (*A Report of State Capacity in China*), Shenyang, Liaoning renmin chubanshe, 1993.

Wang Yi, "Young Chinese Are Closely Watching Japan," *Da xue sheng* (University Students), 7 (July 10, 1997), FBIS-CHI-97-287, October 14, 1997.

Wang Ying, "Xin jiti zhuyi yu Zhongguo tese de shichang jingji" ("New Collectivism and A Market Economy with Chinese Characteristics"), *ESYSJ*, 25 (1994): 11–14.

Wei Dekuang & Dao Liang, "Touzi haiwai, daidong chukou—dui 'guoji daxunhuan' jingji zhanlue gouxiang de buchong" ("Investing Abroad and Leading Exports—Some Supplements to the Economic Strategy of 'International Circulation'"), *JJSB*, January 19, 1988.

Wei Suwu, "Dalu xinzuopai sichao jiqi xingqi" ("New Leftism and its Rise in Mainland China"), *LHB* (Taiwan), September 8, 1996: 9.

Wei Yang, "Riben xiang hechuqu" ("Where Is Japan Going?"), *LW*, 45 (1996): 45.

White, Gordon, "Developmental States and Socialist Industrialization in the Third World", *Journal of Development Studies*, 21, 1 (1984): 97–120.

The White House, *Fact Sheet: Accomplishments of the U.S.–China Summit*, October 29, 1997.

Whiting, Allen S., "Assertive Nationalism in Chinese Foreign Policy", *Asian Survey*, 23, 8 (1983): 913–33.

Whiting, Allen S., *China Eyes Japan*, Berkeley, CA, University of California Press, 1989.

Whiting, Allen S., "Chinese Nationalism and Foreign Policy After Deng", *China Quarterly*, 142 (1995): 295–316.

Whitney, Joseph B. R., *China: Area, Administration, and Nation Building*, Chicago, Department of Geography, The University of Chicago, 1970.

Wong, John, "*Xiao-Kang:* China's Concepts of Socio-Economic Development", *IEAPE Background Brief No. 101*, Singapore, September 14, 1996a.

Wong, John, "China's Economy in the 21st Century: An Asian Perspective", *JETRO China Newsletter*, 120 (Jan.–Feb. 1996b): 12–19.

Wu Guoguang, "Leadership, Power Structure, and Possible Policy Conflicts of the CCP after its 14th Congress", *Paper of the Center for Modern China*, 4, 27 (1993).

Wu Guoguang, "Weidu Denghuo Zhongguo" ("Containing Post-Deng China"), *ZGSBZK*, 193 (1995): 8–9.

Wu Guoguang & Zheng Yongnian, *Lun zhongyang difang guanxi* (*On the Central–Local Relationship: the Key to China's Institutional Transformation*), Hong Kong, Oxford University Press, 1995.

Wu Jiaxiang & Zhang Bingjiu, "Jijin minzhu haishi wenjian minzhu?" ("Radical or Moderate Democracy?"), in Liu Jun & Li Lin (eds), *Xin quanwei zhuyi* (Neo-Authoritarianism), Beijing, Jingji xueyuan chubanshe, 1989: 27–33.

Wu Jiong, "Ping meiguo 'quanmin e' zhi Zhongguo' lun" ("A Critique on the US's Theory of 'All-out Containment of China'"), *XDGJGX*, 11 (1996): 8–11.

Wu Yuetao & Zhang Haitao, *Waizi nengfou tunbing Zhongguo—Zhongguo minzu chanye xiang hechuqu* (*Can Foreign Capital Swallow up China: Where to China's National Industries?*), Beijing, Qiye guanli chubanshe, 1997.

Xi Laiwang, "Meiguo dui ri anquan de zhongda tiaozheng" ("Major Adjustment in the US's Security Strategy towards Japan"), *XDGJGX*, 6 (1996): 7–9.

Xiao Gongqin, "Lun dangdai Zhongguo langman gaige guan: dui 'zhidu jueding lun' de piping" ("On Romanticism of Contemporary China's Reform: A Critique on 'Institutional Determinism'"), *ZSFZ*, (1989): 69–72.

Xiao Gongqin, "Zouxiang chengshu: dui dangdai Zhongguo zhengzhi gaige de fanxing yu zhanwang" ("To Be Mature: The Reflection and Perspective of Contemporary Chinese Political Reform"), *BJQNB*, May 13, 1993: 3.

Xiao Gongqin, "Dongya quanwei zhengzhi yu xiandaihua" ("East Asian Authoritarian Politics and Modernization"), *ZLGL*, 2 (1994a): 28–34.

Xiao Gongqin, "Minzu zhuyi yu Zhongguo zhuanxing shiqi de yishi xingtai" ("Nationalism and the Ideology in China's Transitional Period"), *ZLGL*, 4 (1994b): 21–5. For the translation of the text, see *Chinese Economic Studies*, 28: 2 (March–April 1995: 15–31).

Xiao Gongqin, "Zhongguo minzu zhuyi de lishi yu qianjing" ("The History of Chinese Nationalism and Its Prospects"), *ZLGL*, 2 (1996a): 58–62.

Xiao Gongqin, "Sikao Zhongguo biange zhong de jijin zhuyi" ("A Reflection on Radicalism in China's Transition"), *MP* (December 9, 1996b): E2.

Xiao Gongqin & Zhu Wei, "Tongku de liangnan xuanze: Guanyu 'xin quanwei zhuyi' lilun dawenlu" ("A Painful Dilemma: A Dialogue on the Theory of 'New Authoritarianism'"), *WHB*, January 17, 1989.

Xie Yixian (ed.), *Dangdai Zhongguo waijiao shi* (*Contemporary History of China's Foreign Affairs 1949–1995*), Beijing, Zhongguo qingnian chubanshe, 1997.

Xing Shizhong, "'Zhongguo weixie lun' keyi xiuyi" ("The 'China Threat' Theory Can Come to an End"), *QS*, 3 (1996): 16–20.

Xinhua English Newswire, "Policy on the Dalai Lama Remains Unchanged", September 5, 1997.

The Xinhua News Agency, "Youth Polled on Japan's Invasion of China", FBIS-CHI-97-032, February 16, 1997.

Xu Jilin, "Fan xifang zhuyi yu minzu zhuyi" ("Anti-Foreignism and Nationalism"), in Xu, *Xunqiu yiyi: xiandaihua bianqian yu wenhua pipan* (Seeking Means, Modernization and Cultural Critique), Shanghai, Sanlian shudian, 1997: 290–97.

Xu Xin, "Daodi shui weixie shui" ("Who Threatens Who?"), *LW*, nos. 8–9 (1996): 48–9.

Xu Yimin et al., "The United States Must Correct Its Stance on Taiwan," *CD*, January 6, 1996: 4.

Xu Youyu, "Shi jingjixue tiaozhan lishi, haishi yi luoji daiti jingyan shishi?" ("Which Is It, Challenges of Economics to History or a Substitution of Logic for Empirical Facts?"), *ZLGL* (1996): 94–7.

Yan Changjiang, *Guangdong da liebian* (*Great Transformation in Guangdong*), Guangzhou, Jinan daxue chubanshe, 1993.

Yan Xuetong, "Containment Policy Harms all Interests", *CD*, June 9, 1994: 4.

Yan Xuetong, "Zhongguo jueqi de keneng xuanze" ("Possible Alternatives for China's Rise"), *ZLGL*, 6 (1995): 11–14.

Yan Xuetong, "Zhongguo anquan zhanlue de fazhan qushi" ("The Trend in China's Security Strategy"), *LW*, 8–9 (1996a): 51–2.

Yan Xuetong, "Guojia liyi de panduan" ("The Measurement of National Interests"), *ZLGL*, 3 (1996b): 35–44.

Yan Xuetong, *Zhongguo guojia liyi fenxi* (*An Analysis of China's National Interest*), Tianjin, Tianjin renmin chubanshe, 1996c.

Yan Xuetong, "Sino–US Dialogue Cuts Misunderstanding", *CD* (November 8, 1997a): 4.

Yan Xuetong, "Zhongguo jueqi de guoji huanjing pinggu" ("An Evaluation of the International Environment Facing China's Rise"), *ZLGL*, 1 (1997b): 17–25.

Yang Bojiang, "'Rimei anquan baozhang lianhe xuanyan' yiwei zhe shenmo" ("What Does the 'United States–Japan Mutual Security Treaty" Mean:"), *XDGJGX*, 6 (1996): 2–6.

Yang, Richard et al. (eds), *Chinese Regionalism: the Security Dimension*, Boulder, CO, Westview Press, 1994.

Yin Baoyun, "Jiquan guanliaozhi de xiandaihua daolu: hanguo fazhan jingyan tansuo" ("The Central-Bureaucratic Model of Modernization: An Exploration of the Experiences of Development in South Korea"), *ZLGL*, 2 (1994): 35–42.

Young, Crawford, *The Politics of Cultural Pluralism*, Madison, University of Wisconsin Press, 1976.

Young, Ernest P., *The Presidency of Yuan Shih-K'ai: Liberalism and Dictatorship in Early Republic China*, Ann Arbor, University of Michigan Press, 1977.

Yu, Bin, "The Study of Chinese Foreign Policy: Problems and Prospect", *World Politics*, 46 (January 1994): 235–61.

Yuan Wenqi, *Zhongguo duiwai maoyi fazhan moshi yanjiu* (*A Study of Foreign Trade Development Models in China*), Beijing, Zhongguo duiwai maoyi chubanshe, 1990.

YZZK, September 18, 1994.

YZZK, August 4, 1996a.

YZZK, September 16–September 22, 1996b.

YZZK, September 30–October 6, 1996c

YZZK, October 7–October 13, 1996d.

YZZK, October 14–October 20, 1996e.

Zang, Xiaowei, "The Fourteenth Central Committee of the CCP", *Asian Survey*, xxxiii, 8 (August 1993): 787–803.

Zhang Boli, "Lun zonghe guoli yaosu" ("On the Elements of Comprehensive National Power"), *SJJJZZ*, 12 (1989): 7–15.

Zhang Guocheng, "Riben xianfa mianlin kaoyan" ("Japan's Constitution Is Facing a Test"), *RMRB*, (April 23, 1996): 6.

Zhang Kuan, "Oumei ren yanzhong de 'fei wo zu lei," ("'No Western Races' in the Eyes of Westerners"), *DS*, 9 (1993): 3–9.

Zhang Kuan, "Zai tan Sayide" ("Talking About Edward Said Once Again"), *DS*, 10 (1994): 8–14.

Zhang Shuguang, "Guojia nengli yu zhidu biange he shehui zhuanxing" ("State Capacity, Institutional Change, and Social Transformation"), *ZGSP*, 3 (1995): 5–22.

Zhang Yajun, "Zhongguo dui meiguo de zhanlue siwei yu xingdong: weidu yu fanweidu" ("Mainland China's Strategic Thinking and Action Towards the US: Containment and Counter-Containment"), *ZGDLYJ*, 40, 5 (May 1997): 19–35.

Zhao Gancheng, "Yatai diqu xin zhixu yu Zhongguo de zeren" ("New Order in the Asia–Pacific Region and China's Responsibility"), *GJWTLT*, 3 (1996): 49–59.

Zhao Jun, "'Tianxia weigong' yu shiji zhijiao de Zhongguo minzu zhuyi" ("'The Whole World as One Community' and Chinese Nationalism at the Turn of the Century"), *ZLGL*, 1 (1996): 1–3.

Zhao, Shusheng, "Chinese Intellectuals' Quest for National Greatness and Nationalistic Writing in the 1990s", *China Quarterly*, 152 (9 December 1997): 725–45.

Zhao Ziyang, "Yanzhe you Zhongguo tese de shehui zhuyi daolu qianjin" ("Take the Chinese Socialist Road"), *RMRB*, November 4, 1987: 1–4.

Zheng, Yongnian, "Development and Democracy: Are They Compatible in China?", *Political Science Quarterly*, 109: 2 (Summer 1994a): 35–59.

Zheng, Yongnian, "Perforated Sovereignty: Provincial Dynamism and China's Foreign Trade", *The Pacific Review*, 7, 3 (1994b): 309–21.

Zheng Yongnian, "Hou lengzhan shiqi dongnanya quanli geju yu Zhongguo juese" ("Power Distribution in South-east Asia and the Role of China After the Cold War"), *DDZGYJ*, 2 (1996): 48–62.

Zheng, Yongnian, "Power and Agenda: Jiang Zemin's New Political Initiatives at the CCP's Fifteenth Congress", *Issues and Studies*, 33, 11 (November 1997): 35–57.

Zheng, Yongnian & Li Jinshan, "China's Politics after the Ninth National People's Congress: Power Realignment", *EAI Background Brief 11*, The East Asian Institute, National University of Singapore, March 1998.

Zhong Cai (ed.), *Zhonggong zhongyang guanyu zhiding guomin jingji he shehui fazhan "jiuwu" jihua he 2010nian yuanjing mubiao de jianyi (mingci shuyu jieshi (The Proposal of the Central Committee of the Chinese Communist Party on the Ninth Five-Year Plan of the National Economy, and Social Development and Long-Term Goals by 2010)*, Beijing: Renmin chubanshe, 1995.

Zhong Huamin, et al., *Chongping Heshang (A Re-Evaluation of the "River Elegy")*, Hangzhou, Hangzhou daxue chubanshe, 1989.

Zhou Guangzhao, "Lun chixu fazhan zhanlue" ("On the Strategy of Continuous Development"), *QS*, 12 (1995): 7–11.

Zhou Qi, "Lengzhanhou zhongmei guanxi xianzhuang-gongtong liyi yu zhengzhi" ("Sino–US Relations after the Cold War: Common Interests and Conflicts"), *DF*, 6 (1995): 73–7.

Zhou Xiaochuan, *Waimao tizhi gaige de tantao (A Study of the Reform of the Foreign Trade System)*, Beijing, Zhongguo zhanwang chubanshe, 1990.

Zhu Rongji, "Zhongguo wei huanjie yazhou jingji weiji zuochu 'xisheng'" ("China Makes 'Sacrifice' in Order to Alleviate Asian Economic Crisis"), *LHZB*, April 7, 1998.

Zong Lanhai, "Zhonggong yiding guoji touhao diren" ("The Chinese Communists Identify Their Main International Adversary"), *CM*, 185 (1994): 16–18.

Zwick, Peter, *National Communism*, Boulder, CO, Westview Press, 1983.

Index